Flexibility, Foresight, and *Fortuna* in Taiwan's Development:
Navigating between Scylla and Charybdis

Flexibility, Foresight, and *Fortuna* in Taiwan's Development:
Navigating between Scylla and Charybdis

STEVE CHAN

University of Colorado (Boulder)

CAL CLARK

University of Wyoming (Laramie)

London and New York

First published 1992
by Routledge
11 New Fetter Lane, London EC4P 4EE

Simultaneously published in the USA and Canada
by Routledge
a division of Routledge, Chapman and Hall, Inc.
29 West 35th Street, New York, NY 10001

Typeset in Times by Columns Design and Production Services Ltd
Printed and bound in Great Britain
by Richard Clay Ltd, Bungay, Suffolk

British Library Cataloguing in Publication Data
A catalogue record for this book is available from the British Library.

Library of Congress Cataloging in Publication Data is available.

ISBN 0–415–07596–3

To our families

Jennifer and Andrew Chan
Janet, Emily, Ellen, and Evelyn Clark

Contents

List of figures

List of tables

List of tables in the appendix

About the authors

Steve Chan is Professor of Political Science at the University of Colorado (Boulder) and was a former Fulbright Exchange Professor at Tamkang University (Taipei) during 1984–5. He is the author of *East Asian dynamism* (Westview, 1990) and *International relations in perspective* (Macmillan, 1984), coauthor of *Understanding foreign policy decisions* (Free Press, 1979), and coeditor of *Foreign policy decision making* (Praeger, 1984). He has published widely on international relations and political economy in such journals as the *American Political Science Review*, *Comparative Political Studies*, *International Interactions*, *International Studies Quarterly*, *Journal of Conflict Resolution*, *Journal of Peace Research*, *Orbis*, *Western Political Quarterly*, and *World Politics*. He received his Ph.D. in political science from the University of Minnesota in 1976.

Cal Clark is Professor of Political Science at the University of Wyoming (Laramie) and a former Visiting Professor of Business Administration at Chung Yuan Christian University in Taiwan. He is author of *The Taiwan exception* (Greenwood, 1989), coauthor of *Women in Taiwan politics* (Rienner, 1990), and coeditor of *State and development* (Brill, 1988) and *North/South relations: studies in dependency reversal* (Praeger, 1983). His primary field of teaching and research is political economy. He has published in such journals as the *American Political Science Review*, *Comparative Political Studies*, *International Studies Quarterly*, and *Journal of Conflict Resolution*. He received his Ph.D. in political science from the University of Illinois in 1973.

Preface

Since the late 1960s, the study of the political economy of development has been dominated by two conflicting theoretical schools. On the one hand, the developmentalist model views development as a "virtuous cycle" in which different dimensions of capitalist economics, cultural modernization, and political change produce a self-reinforcing developmental syndrome. On the other, dependency theory contends that the global capitalist system precludes meaningful economic, social, and political change in the Third World, thereby perpetuating a "vicious cycle" of underdevelopment. The assumptions of these two scholarly paradigms are so different that attempted debates between them usually resemble a "dialogue of the deaf." More recently, two nascent theoretical approaches have appeared that offer some promise of bridging the gap between developmentalism and *dependencia*. One argues that development almost inevitably involves tradeoffs among its several supposed goals (that is, that neither a completely virtuous nor vicious cycle exists); and the other emphasizes the role of the state in directing a country's developmental project. Neither of us have been intellectually comfortable with the stark contrasts suggested by the developmental and dependency approaches, so that the more variegated visions of the two new approaches are quite appealing. Yet, they do not represent a theoretical panacea since neither claims to provide a full-blown model of development.

In this book, we examine the developmental history of Taiwan and compare it with the predictions of these four scholarly traditions. We believe that Taiwan's history can yield theoretical insights for several reasons. First, it has had one of the highest sustained economic growth rates in the world during the postwar period, so that it might offer lessons in successful development. Second, it represents a very dynamic region (East Asia) which is quite different in many regards from the geographical foci of both developmentalism (Western Europe and North America) and *dependencia* (Latin America and Africa), so that its developmental dynamics might well be significantly different. Third, most of the key variables in the competing perspectives have had a significant impact upon Taiwan, so that an analysis of this country should yield theoretically informed conclusions.

We find that each approach possesses both insights and oversights for explaining the evolution of Taiwan's political economy during the postwar era. Thus, there appears to be a clear need to combine existing paradigms of development in a more contingent and sophisticated fashion. We hope that this analysis will be of interest to two very distinct audiences. First, for those interested in Taiwan, we try to show that more general social science theory can illuminate the nature of that island's political economy. Second, for those interested in broader theory, we try to draw implications that challenge existing orthodoxies and point the way toward theoretical development from a case study of rapid socioeconomic change.

Our biggest debt of gratitude is owed to our many colleagues and friends in Taiwan who have shared many insights with us and who have been extremely hospitable during our visits to the island. They will remain anonymous here, both because there are too many to list and because many would disagree with at least some of our major arguments. More specifically, James Hsiung and two other (anonymous) readers for Unwin Hyman contributed many felicitous comments. We would especially like to thank Lauren M. Osborne and Sarah Dann of Unwin Hyman (now HarperCollins) for their respective guidance at the beginning and conclusion of our project. The institutional support which we received from the Universities of Colorado at Boulder and Wyoming at Laramie proved invaluable to the completion of our research. In addition, Linda Marston of the University of Wyoming did an excellent job of preparing the map used in Chapter 5. Finally, we owe a tremendous debt to our families for all their patience and support. To Jennifer and Andrew and to Janet, Emily, Ellen, and Evelyn, all we can say is—to you with love.

Chapter 1

The Problematique

We assume that the principal purpose of government is to secure the conditions for public well-being. This public well-being includes the paramount values of prosperity, welfare, equality, freedom, stability, and security. How these values can best be attained has been an enduring topic of inquiry and concern for social scientists, philosophers, and policy-makers.

Paradoxically, contemporary social science research suggests that it may be difficult to attain these values simultaneously, especially for developing countries with finite resources and fragile societies. Originally, it was assumed that these values constituted a "virtuous cycle." Indeed, some researchers have claimed that the most affluent or developed societies are on average the most democratic, stable, egalitarian, and pacific. A closer consideration of the processes of economic growth, however, has led many scholars to doubt such a rosy generalization about the progress of developing nations.

In fact, simultaneous improvement on many of the above value dimensions appears to be fairly incompatible. Thus, various economists (for example, Simon Kuznets and Mancur Olson), sociologists (for example, Seymour Martin Lipset), and political scientists (for example, Samuel Huntington) argue that rapid economic growth can destabilize the existing political order, undermine fledgling democracies, exacerbate income inequality, and further marginalize the social marginals. Moreover, influential dependency theorists (for example, Fernando Henrique Cardoso, Andre Gundar Frank, and Immanuel Wallerstein) contend that the very structure of the capitalist world system constrains economic development in the Third World, and precludes even successful industrialization that does occur there from promoting popular affluence, equality, and welfare. Similarly, long-term social and political stability, often considered a prerequisite for economic growth and liberal democracy, may actually exact a cost in economic stagnation and social rigidity (for example, Mancur Olson), whereas policy efforts aimed at income equalization and welfare provision may dampen capital formation and economic productivity (for example, Milton Friedman). As yet another example of policy tradeoffs, the "paradox of voting" (for example, Kenneth Arrow) suggests that unstable mass preferences and shifting winning coalitions can produce incoherent and even contradictory policies in liberal democracies. Thus, these hallmarks of pluralistic politics tend to be incompatible with the requirements of social rationality. Finally, the pursuit of security (in the form of a heavy defense burden) may entail severe opportunity costs in foregone economic growth, reduced welfare provision, and an increasing gap between the haves and the have nots. In short, one cannot but get the impression from the extant literature that "good things don't tend to go together."

These various theoretical arguments imply, therefore, that development sets off a series of tradeoffs since many of the desiderata toward which it is theoretically proceeding appear to be mutually incompatible. Consequently, successful development requires skillful or lucky navigation, analogous to sailing between Scylla and Charybdis. By either default or conscious decision, a country may pursue one value at the expense of another. For example, conservatives tend to argue that democratization is much less important for development than the political stability provided by authoritarian regimes, while liberals tend to argue that economic growth per se should be sacrificed in the pursuit of redistributive social justice. Alternatively, successful socio-economic change may entail only partial accomplishments of the multiple developmental goals or, more ominously, run into obstacles that threaten social, political, and economic break-down — a situation which is actually far more true to the Scylla and Charybdis metaphor.

Taiwan has been one of the very few countries that evidently have been able to defy this generalization. While hardly a paragon of virtue, it can boast of making substantial progress on all the aforementioned major policy values with relatively meager resources during the past four decades. For instance, its record of growth with equity provides a sharp contrast to the experiences of other countries (for example, Brazil, Saudi Arabia) where economic progress or aggregate wealth has not produced major improvements in social equity or physical quality of life for the masses. Furthermore, in comparison with the recent history of Iran, South Korea, and even China, Taiwan has somehow managed to contradict the expectation of rapid growth as a destabilizing force. It has also in the past few years made substantial progress in extending tangible civil liberties and political rights to its citizens, although it still falls quite short of Western standards of liberal democracy. In addition, Taiwan has been relatively successful in the pursuit of physical security. Even though starting from a rather precarious position of military and political vulnerability, it has avoided the ravages of civil strife or foreign war that have befallen some others, such as Israel, Lebanon, and Pakistan. And, despite having borne a rather heavy defense burden historically, it has managed the "guns-versus-butter" tradeoff more successfully than most others as attested by the island's phenomenal economic growth and rising physical quality of life in the past 40 years.

This is certainly not to say, however, that Taiwan's developmental experience has been entirely smooth or devoid of problems. Historically, the price of political stability and a "strong and autonomous developmental state" was a high degree of political repression and persecution, especially during the 1950s; and authoritarian political rule clearly exacerbated ethnic tensions between the 15% of the population who were Main-landers (that is, those who arrived in Taiwan with Chiang Kai-shek in the late 1940s) and the large majority of Islanders. In addition, despite Taiwan's overall good record on income equality, a significant portion of the population among farmers and workers, especially unskilled women, has benefitted only marginally if at all from the "economic miracle" (Gates 1987); and, despite the government's general record of successful developmental policies, problems of rigidity and bureaucratism are easy to discern in specific sectors, such as state controls over financial institutions (Wade 1985). More recently, Taiwan's very success in stimulating economic and political development has created new problems, as several of the theories adumbrated above would predict. Most spectacularly of late, the process of political liberalization has brought about more confrontational and occasionally even violent partisan politics. In the economic realm, rapid growth has created some negative spinoffs of success, such as pollution and gridlocked streets; and skyrocketing house prices and an extremely volatile stock market suggest that having too much money may produce some problems of its own.

Overall, though, Taiwan has clearly been a deviant case in regard to prevailing social science theorizing and cross-national patterns of policy performance. In this book we ask what has been its formula for success. In our inquiry we avail ourselves of the tools of historical analysis as well as those of statistical analysis. Additionally, we relate Taiwan's experience to the concerns of social science theories and developmental statecraft. Thus, we hope to facilitate communication across several scholarly communities that tend to be otherwise insulated by their differences in area specialization, methodological preference, and disciplinary membership.

In particular, this book combines several approaches that are usually used in isolation from one another. First, we present both a qualitative model of Taiwan's political economy and quantitative measures of how economic, social, and political variables are related to each other. We believe that these two methodologies are complementary, not competitive. Statistical relationships are much more meaningful when put within broader interpretive frameworks, whereas macro qualitative models can only benefit from being grounded in micro empirical verifications. Second, while most of the quantitative work on development and political economy has been based on cross-national statistics at one point in time (Bornschier & Chase-Dunn 1985, Jackman 1982, 1975, Mahler 1980), our analysis is based on relationships that emerge within one successful developing country over time. We chose this approach because most developmental theories are really concerned with temporal changes. Moreover, causal inferences are more appropriately derived from longitudinal than cross-sectional studies. The primary disadvantages, of course, are that it is hard to generalize from the experience of just one country, and to distinguish from the time series data for this country the necessary and sufficient conditions for particular policy outcomes. However, the utility of theoretically informed case studies for comparative analysis has been well established — the key is to focus on concepts and relationships rather than idiosyncratic history (Eckstein 1975, George 1979).

We certainly do not wish to assume the self-appointed role of partisan scorekeepers in assigning blame or allocating credit in our analysis of Taiwan's developmental experience. This is not to say that we do not have any normative concerns, because we clearly do as indicated by the opening statement to this chapter. Social scientists can be both objective analysts and concerned citizens. In this sense, we are no different from other analysts who are prompted by normative reasons to investigate the causes of economic underdevelopment, interstate war, or governmental abuse of human rights. We are interested in understanding the conditions that promote those basic values indicated at the beginning of this chapter, and we believe that there is substantial prima facie evidence to suggest that Taiwan may provide an interesting empirical case for studying these conditions.

Because this book undertakes a case-study approach, the readers may perhaps get the impression that we are saying Taiwan represents a unique case. In the scheme of cross-national analyses, Taiwan's policy accomplishments are quite unusual and atypical (as we shall demonstrate in Chapter 4). However, one can easily identify other statistically deviant cases such as Costa Rica, Singapore, Saudi Arabia, South Korea, and Sri Lanka on different dimensions of policy performance. Accordingly, there are a number of exceptional cases to cross-national norms of policy performance, with Taiwan just being one member of this small group.

In particular, Taiwan seemingly represents an "East Asian developmental model" that has produced overachievement on a number of economic and social dimensions during the postwar period. It is by now commonplace to assert that East Asia has been the most dynamic region in the global economy during the postwar era. First Japan, then the "Gang of Four" (Hong Kong, Singapore, South Korea, and Taiwan), and most recently several other neighbors (Malaysia and Thailand) experienced rapid growth and seemingly achieved economic takeoff. That so many countries in a single region have been "overachievers" in developmental performance surely cannot be coincidental. Thus, scholars have devoted increasing attention to delineating an East

Asian developmental model. Rapid development in East Asia, in fact, has evidently exhibited a number of similar economic, social, and political features. Economic strategy has generally emphasized expanding exports and finding niches of comparative advantage in the global economy, rather than using protectionism to pursue import substitution with a reliance upon internal markets. In terms of sectoral phasing, most of the countries have moved upward along the international product cycle from light to heavy to high-technology industries over fairly brief time spans, indicating that their comparative advantages are far from static. The East Asian societies have been marked by comparatively equal distributions of income, opportunities for upward mobility, strong proclivities for entrepreneurship, and a heavy emphasis on education which promotes the creation of human capital. Politically, the state has taken a leading role in structuring the economy and targeting leading sectors (Hong Kong excepted); most of the countries have been marked by a high level of political stability that is remarkable in the developing world; and authoritarian governments of varying hues and rationales have predominated (political life even in democratic Japan and Singapore is dominated by one continuously ruling party). These economic, social, and political characteristics, in addition, are undergirded by the region's Confucian culture whose values promote respect for authority, merit-based mobility, family entrepreneurship, and in Japan "groupist" dynamics that seem perfectly suited for large-scale corporations and bureaucracies.

This is not to say that the East Asian political economies are exactly the same. Japan and South Korea have economies dominated by large-scale conglomerates; Hong Kong is notable for its laissez-faire economics; the role of foreign capital in Singapore is much stronger than elsewhere; South Korea has had much greater internal political conflict and instability than its neighbors; and Taiwan and Hong Kong stand out for the important role of small-scale firms in promoting economic flexibility (Berger & Hsiao 1988, Bradford & Branson 1987, Chan 1990b, Cheng & Haggard 1987, Cumings 1984, Deyo 1987b, Haggard 1990, Hofheinz & Calder 1982, Kuznets 1988, Linder 1986, Pye with Pye 1985). Nevertheless, while featuring some differences from the other East Asian trading nations, the successful developmental experience of Taiwan also reflects the general case of economic dynamism and improving physical welfare in this region. Our explicit attempt to place Taiwan's experience in a cross-national context, then, testifies to our general skepticism about "uniqueness" explanations.

We employ the concept of tradeoff to refer to the substitution effects among alternative public goods (for example, the more defense spending, the less the welfare spending). The presence of policy tradeoffs forces public officials to set priorities and to choose among alternative desiderata. While these tradeoffs constrain policy-making, public officials are hardly their prisoners. Indeed, our premise is that some officials are better at dampening, relaxing and, indeed, skirting the necessary policy tradeoffs than others (Bobrow 1990). This premise in turn leads us to consider a variety of factors — such as the timing and sequence of developmental experience, the strength and autonomy of the developmental state, and the nature of foreign linkages — that influence policy capacity and decisional latitude.

Finally, our selection of the Taiwan case and our research design for studying this case have been motivated by a number of concerns relating to the philosophy of science. To the extent that this island's policy performance constitutes a nonconforming case to cross-national patterns, its empirical deviations offer a fruitful platform from which to search for clues that can be used to solve substantively and theoretically important puzzles. Thus, just as Sherlock Holmes asks "why the dog did not bark," our logic of inquiry focuses on the exception to the norm. Indeed, according to some philosophers of science (Kuhn 1970), attention to empirical enigmas that somehow fail to support the prevailing analytic paradigm has in the past resulted in scientific revolutions in a variety of fields. Thus, the discovery and analysis of deviant cases have served as the critical catalyst for scientific progress.

We do not believe in our case of studying national developmental experiences, however, that the relevant theoretical perspectives are sufficiently articulated and rigorously formulated to lend themselves to the procedures of scientific refutation. In this sense, Taiwan's experience does not provide so much of a critical test as a puzzle. The puzzle stems from the departure of this island's experience from standard analytic expectations and widely accepted "stylized facts" (that is, conventional wisdom buttressed by strong evidence) concerning the pursuit of various

policy goals. Instead of attempting to reach some dichotomous
verdict (true or false) regarding the validity of alternative
theoretical perspectives, we hope to identify the relevant scope
conditions that help to reconcile to some extent these perspectives. That is, rather than presuming that these perspectives are
logical opposites, we focus on the search for possible reasons why
they could all be at least partially right. In the terminology of
philosophy of science, we eschew the validation of universal
truths in favor of deriving possible "nice laws" that are more
context- or domain-specific (Most & Starr 1989).

To summarize the logic of our research design, we start by
taking note of some standard analytic expectations regarding
conditions that affect the successful pursuit of various policy
goals. We then compare Taiwan's developmental experience to
important "stylized facts" about cross-national norms of policy
performance. The observed discrepancy between the prevailing
analytic expectations and the established norms of policy
performance on the one hand, and the island's historical record
on the other hand, poses the central puzzle of our analysis. This
puzzle is then juxtaposed against four dominant perspectives on
development (the developmental, dependency, tradeoff, and
statist perspectives), and both qualitative and quantitative
evidence is introduced to identify and assess areas of convergence
and divergence between the predictions of these perspectives and
Taiwan's actual experience. Finally, our historical and statistical
inquiry leads us to posit in our conclusion several scope
conditions that help to account for the puzzle of "most good
things going together so far" in the case of Taiwan.

The architecture or organization of our book follows closely
the logic of inquiry just sketched. We begin our analysis by
examining the proposition that Taiwan constitutes a fairly
unusual instance of seemingly broad-based developmental success. Chapter 2 reviews the rationales offered by various social
science theories for the proposition that "good things won't go
together." As will be seen, while different paradigms offer
competing hypotheses about why this is so, conflicting theoretical
traditions in political economy reach a surprising consensus that
prosperity, stability, democracy, welfare, equality, and security
do not form a simple, linear, and "virtuous" pattern of
development. The next two chapters consider Taiwan's general

performance on these six dimensions. Specifically, Chapter 3 presents descriptive statistics on some key aspects of Taiwan's policy performance. It shows the progress this island has made during the past four decades on all these dimensions, and strongly suggests that success in one area did not inhibit progress in others. Chapter 4 puts Taiwan's record in a comparative context by assessing the extent to which this performance conforms to or departs from the broad cross-national patterns of other states. This statistical analysis finds that in many (but not all) areas, Taiwan is a significant overachiever in the sense that its policy performance has been far superior to what would be expected given its various resource bases and constraints.

We then attempt to construct a more qualitative model of Taiwan's political economy. Chapter 5 develops this model which incorporates the historical base for rapid growth in Taiwan, the basic stages of its developmental history, the interactions between political and economic variables, and the contemporary prospects and problems facing the island. Chapter 6 then juxtaposes Taiwan's developmental experience against several prevailing perspectives on political economy. Here, we argue that this country is a deviant case in that its economic success contradicts the predictions of all the major theoretical traditions in development studies, again raising the question of how this one political economy has been able to navigate between Scylla and Charybdis. Chapter 7 submits the theories reviewed earlier to statistical examination. It undertakes time series analyses in an attempt to assess the contribution of various alleged factors to Taiwan's economic growth and social outcomes. Again, the results in this chapter show that each theory receives only partial support from the quantitative evidence. None of them is able to account satisfactorily for all aspects of Taiwan's developmental experience.

Chapter 8 synthesizes the conclusions of the earlier analysis. It searches for the major analytic and policy implications of the "Taiwan model." To anticipate our conclusions, three macro factors appear relevant for explaining these felicitous outcomes. First, Taiwan has proved extremely flexible both at the level of macro political and economic change and at the micro level of entrepreneurial behavior in response to the market. The island's developmental history reflects pragmatic eclecticism that eschews rigid adherence to any single economic orthodoxy. Second, its state has proved quite effective in promoting continuing economic and political change. In particular, Taiwan's statecraft has been important in guarding against the sort of foreign penetration prevalent in other Third World countries as well as in overcoming conservative class interests that proved to be the Kuomintang's own undoing on the Mainland. Third, the island has benefitted from several broader structural conditions, such as the legacy of Japanese colonialism, the Cold War ideology of the United States, and the global economic cycle at the time of its initial export drive. As a consequence, economic, social, and political change in Taiwan has followed a sequence that proved to be quite felicitous for the country's ongoing development. In combination, therefore, these three factors produce our title — "Flexibility, Foresight, and *Fortuna* in Taiwan."

Chapter 2
Theoretical Conundra

Since World War II, Taiwan has made considerable progress in economic affluence and growth, income equality, popular welfare, political stability, democracy and freedom, and military security (Chapters 3 and 4 will present data supporting this contention). In addition to the "Taiwan success story" that these achievements imply by themselves, the island's record has also been rather remarkable in view of the prevailing theoretical expectations in Western social science research. The collective evidence from recent cross-national studies in economics, sociology, and political science suggests strongly that it is difficult to achieve many of these values concurrently. The empirical relationships among the pertinent variables often contradict popular hunches that "good things" should go together in a "virtuous cycle," and suggest instead the presence of important value tradeoffs. We present below the major policy paradoxes or conundra indicated by such research and theorizing.

Initially, studies of development assumed that good things would go together, and that economic development was tightly interwoven with social and political progress in the transformation from traditional societies to modern ones. Scholars in this tradition assumed that the industrial revolution in Europe and North America formed a universal model that other societies must follow if they were to develop successfully. Thus, they attempted to isolate the key components of economic change in the West, especially those conditions that sparked the industrialization of Britain and the United States.

This research generally took the central variable to be economic development, defined as sustained growth in national product and structural transformation away from a primary economy. As depicted in Figure 2.1, this development was

12   *Taiwan's Development*

Figure 2.1
Components of capitalist development and
industrialization.

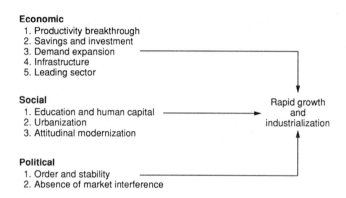

Economic
1. Productivity breakthrough
2. Savings and investment
3. Demand expansion
4. Infrastructure
5. Leading sector

Social   Rapid growth
1. Education and human capital   and
2. Urbanization   industrialization
3. Attitudinal modernization

Political
1. Order and stability
2. Absence of market interference

viewed as being stimulated by a combination of economic, social, and political conditions.

Economically, it depended upon a breakthrough in production techniques and productivity, high and sustained savings and investment to maintain the momentum of productivity gains, expansion of demand for increased production, creation of sufficient infrastructure, and the existence of a leading sector to serve as an "engine of growth" (historically the textile industry). Such economic change usually did not occur in a vacuum. Thus, it was generally assumed that there had to be concomitant social development, such as increased education to provide a trained industrial workforce, urbanization to create developmental centers, and the creation of "modern" attitudes in the population. Moreover, the government needed to provide order and stability, and to refrain from interfering in the private economic sector in order to create an environment conducive to business entrepreneurship. Although the specific direction of causal linkages among many of these factors was somewhat ambiguous and raised "chicken or egg" questions, these elements fit together in a syndrome of capitalist development that was widely accepted by economists such as Simon Kuznets (1976) and

W. W. Rostow (1960), sociologists such as Talcott Parsons (1964) and Seymour Martin Lipset (1963), and political scientists such as David Apter (1965).

This paradigm, then, focused particularly upon two central causal components of industrialization. First, it appeared that development rested upon the social transformation from traditional societies in which stagnant social and political structures prevented economic change to modern ones based on much more individualistic values promoting the social mobility and economic entrepreneurship necessary to stimulate development (Almond & Powell 1966, Bendix 1964, Eisenstadt 1973, Inkeles 1983, Levy 1952, 1953–4, 1986, McClelland 1961, Nisbet 1987, Parsons 1964, Pye 1966, Weber 1958). Second, developmentalists emphasized the role of capitalism or neoclassical laissez-faire economics in promoting growth (Chenery 1979, Chenery & Syrquin 1975, Hagen 1975, Kuznets 1976, Lewis 1955); and several scholars of development explained the rise of capitalism by the social changes produced in modernization (Rosenberg & Birdzell 1986, Rostow 1960). Thus, according to this approach, "the passing of traditional society" (Lerner 1958) would almost inevitably produce "economic takeoff."

Furthermore, this development syndrome was generally seen as promoting progress along the other dimensions under consideration here as well. Thus, empirical research based on aggregate data established that a high *level* of economic development or national wealth promotes political stability, liberal democracy, and social equality (Jackman 1975, Lipset 1959, Neubauer 1967). Few poor or economically under-developed countries have been able to attain the latter desiderata, although not all affluent or economically developed countries are necessarily assured of this attainment. Thus, economic development or national wealth seems to constitute a necessary but insufficient condition for achieving the values of political stability, liberal democracy, and social equality. This generalization is rather robust, although exceptions clearly do exist. These exceptions are furnished by overachievers such as Costa Rica and Sri Lanka whose policy performances on such values as democracy or equality exceed the cross-national norm, and by underachievers such as Saudi Arabia and Brazil whose performances fall below this norm.

Overall, therefore, these relationships imply a long-term "virtuous cycle" of development sketched in Figure 2.2. Sustained economic growth and industrialization should promote social development along a variety of dimensions: (a) education and the development of human capital, (b) growing social and economic equality, (c) increased levels of social welfare, and (d) basic value transformations. In turn, economic and social development should encourage the two basic elements of political development: democratization and political stability. These political conditions should provide a conducive environment for further economic growth and stimulate welfare policies promoting social progress, thus completing the virtuous cycle and implying a model of self-sustaining development (Rostow 1960). This self-reinforcing virtuous cycle is indicated in Figure 2.2 by the two-headed arrows that link economic development to both social and political development. Finally, while the line of argument is not so well developed for the value of security, a positive cycle is also implicit in conventional reasoning. Economic growth and industrialization should enhance military power and national autonomy; and this increased national strength, especially when combined with a democratic polity, should promote security and peace.

This idea of a virtuous cycle of self-sustaining development did not remain immune from debate for very long, if at all, perhaps because of the continued underdevelopment of Africa, Asia, and Latin America. It was challenged at two very different levels. Most fundamentally, dependency scholars argued that its assumptions about developmental phenomena were essentially flawed and that the very processes which this developmental or modernization approach sought to model actually prevented development in the contemporary Third World. In addition, theorists working within the conventional paradigm also began to question the optimistic conclusions of the virtuous cycle and to find more complex and destabilizing relationships among the various dimensions of development.

The conventional theory of development outlined above basically believed that the key to successful growth and transformation lay in the endogenous economic and social processes within a society. This assumption was stood on its head by the dependency paradigm in large part because its optimistic

Figure 2.2
Long-term virtuous cycle of development

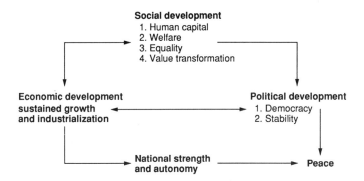

assumptions about economic growth were at substantial variance with the reality of continued poverty and stagnation in much of the Third World.

Dependency theorists argued that, rather than constituting a universal model for development, Western industrialization resulted from locking the developing world into a subordinate position in the global division of labor. This subordination was maintained through a combination of direct political control (that is, colonialism), the exercise of monopoly economic power (that is, neocolonialism), and the formation of alliances with internal elites in the Third World who opposed change because it challenged their dominant economic and political positions. As a result of these dependency structures, industrialization and growth were retarded, the economy was marked by foreign-dominated enclaves that were essentially cut off from the rest of society, little development of human capital occurred (if anything, poverty and inequality increased within the society), and growing political repression was needed to suppress social discontent. Even when significant industrialization did occur in a few countries, such as Brazil, it remained dependent (that is, dominated by foreign multinational corporations) and distorted (that is, involving only a small portion of the indigenous economies and populations), so that no alteration occurred in the periphery's inferior position. Thus, the world was divided into an industrialized core and an underdeveloped periphery (Amin 1974, Baran & Sweezy 1966, Biersteker 1978, Bornschier & Chase-Dunn 1985, Cardoso 1973, Cardoso & Faletto 1979, Chase-Dunn 1981, de Janvry 1981, Emmanuel 1972, Evans 1979, Frank 1969, Galtung 1971, Gereffi 1983, Mahler 1980, Moulder 1977, O'Donnell 1973, Petras 1979, Portes & Walton 1981, Wallerstein 1974, 1979, 1980).

Even scholars not sympathetic to the broader dependency tradition generally assume that an extreme dependence upon foreign markets can have deleterious consequences. A high trade/GNP ratio tends to make a country vulnerable to the vagaries of international markets; and a concentration of exports in a few products or of trade with a few partners reduces bargaining power and leads to unfavorable terms of trade. In some views (Dos Santos 1970, Galtung 1971, Hirschman 1945, Rangarajan 1978), these tendencies of trade dependence account for the economic as well as political vulnerability of the small developing countries to the influences and manipulations of their larger developed trade partners.

Certainly, most countries in the Third World are quite dependent upon the international economy and the capitalist core. This is obviously true of nations selecting an export-oriented growth strategy, such as Taiwan (Galenson 1979a, Kuo *et al.* 1981, Li 1988), but it also applies to a significant extent even for nations that have tried to promote domestic growth through import substitution, such as Brazil (Evans 1979). In either case, if a country's rapid economic growth is based substantially on export expansion and foreign investment, it can entail a loss of national autonomy. Various models of sovereignty at bay (Vernon 1971) point to this loss as a result of a developing country's external trade (as well as other sorts of) dependence and the penetration of multinational corporations into its domestic economy. In some formulations, the dependent state and elite become an agent of the core countries (Galtung 1971) or, at best, one of the partners in an unholy triple alliance of state, local, and foreign capital (Evans 1979). Others have further argued that the dependency syndrome can bring about regime repression, worker marginalization, deteriorating income equality, and falling physical quality of life for the masses (Bornschier & Chase-Dunn 1985, Cardoso & Faletto 1979, O'Donnell 1973). In their external relations, the dependent countries are seen to have little bargaining power and are therefore expected to be easy targets for the core countries' coercion or enticement to obtain political compliance. These expectations regarding the domestic as well as foreign consequences of dependency have been the focus of much lively debate and somewhat contradictory statistical results (Anschuler 1976, Bornschier & Ballmer-Cao 1979, Bornschier & Chase-Dunn 1985, Bornschier *et al.* 1978, Chase-Dunn 1975, Evans & Timberlake 1980, Jackman 1982, Kaufman *et al.* 1975, Mahler 1980, McGowan & Smith 1978, Ray 1981, Richardson 1976, Richardson & Kegley 1980, Rubinson 1976, Walleri 1978, Weede & Tiefenbach 1981).

The above theoretical strands are summarized in the model of the "dependency syndrome" presented in Figure 2.3. Peripheral growth can only occur if a society becomes reliant on foreign multinational corporations (MNCs) and export markets. In the economic sphere, this leads to continued exploitation and extraction of surplus value from the periphery, a tendency that is further compounded by the core's political domination. In the social sphere, it creates substantial distortions (as opposed to social development) because only a small modern sector participates in the industrialization process. Growing inequality, massive poverty, and the absence of human capital development are some of the alleged consequences. Such social dislocations, when coupled with the local elites' class alliances with the core, produce political retrogression in the form of authoritarianism, repression, and instability. Finally, these economic, social, and political factors combine to disrupt and distort development, producing underdevelopment in the very real sense that a country's potential for economic growth and industrial transformation is prevented from being realized because of external structural constraints. Thus, growth in the periphery is marked by sectoral imbalances, the declining position of workers, and vulnerability to economic events in the advanced industrialized nations.

By the 1970s, the dependency paradigm — derived as it was

Figure 2.3
Dependency syndrome.

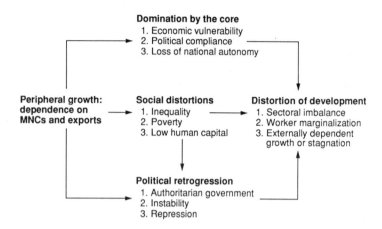

primarily from the Latin American context — was itself increasingly coming under the assault of events. The success of OPEC, the decline of the military and economic hegemony of the United States, and the rapid economic growth of several East Asian developing countries all suggested that the international political economy is not nearly as rigid and deterministic as dependency theorists have implied. This did not so much resurrect the competing developmental approach, however, as stimulate two less sweeping theoretical perspectives — one focusing upon the tradeoffs between developmental goals and the other focusing upon the role of the state in actively promoting development.

Thus, the depiction of development as following a virtuous cycle has not just been challenged by an alternative paradigm decrying the basic premises of developmentalism and arguing that Third World countries actually suffer from a vicious cycle, but also by scholars working within the developmental tradition. Rather than forcing a choice between such starkly different conclusions, this work suggests that development produces a series of tradeoffs in the sense that several of the valued outcomes tend to be mutually incompatible. Thus, success in terms of one desideratum may well cause failure in terms of another. First, there appears to be a very significant tradeoff between growth and stability. Paradoxically, cross-national aggregate research has convincingly demonstrated that while a high *level* of economic development may bring many good things, a high *rate* of economic growth tends to be profoundly destabilizing. Rapid economic growth and the accompanying social mobilization are apt to undermine traditional institutions, destroy existing production systems, and marginalize further the socially marginal (Deutsch 1961, Eisenstadt 1966, Huntington 1968, Lipset 1963, Olson 1963). The forces unleashed by a high rate of socioeconomic change will overload the government's capacity to adapt, and diminish the prospects of political institutionalization (Huntington 1968). Concomitantly, they tend to increase the gap between the rich and the poor (Kuznets 1955). Indeed, as Olson (1963) has put it, while the *average* per capita income in an expanding economy may rise quickly, the *median* per capita income can fall precipitously. The actual economic conditions of the masses may deteriorate because their wages tend to be "stickier" than escalating consumer prices due to rampant inflation.

Of course, rapid socioeconomic change redistributes not only monetary income but also social status. There are bound to be economic as well as social winners and losers in the modernization process as implied by Schumpeter's (1950) reference to industrialization as a process of "creative destruction." This redistributive and destructive process can arouse a widespread sense of relative deprivation among large segments of the population (Gurr 1970), and furnish a fertile breeding ground for potential recruits of anti-establishment movements (Rostow 1965). In short, then, rapid socioeconomic change is likely to have a negative effect on the values of political stability, liberal democracy, and social equality and welfare. The expectations sketched above have been strongly supported by various empirical analyses that show a high rate of economic growth to be correlated with more political instability, more income inequality, lower physical quality of life, less political rights, less civil liberties, and larger communist parties (Adelman & Morris 1973, Ahluwalia 1974, 1976a, 1976b, Benjamin & Kautsky 1968, Chan 1989a, Cutright 1967, Dixon & Moon 1989, Finkle & Gable 1971, Gillespie & Nesvold 1971, Jackman 1975, Kohli *et al.* 1984, Kuznets 1963, Strouse & Claude 1976, Tilly 1978, Weede 1980, 1987).

The pertinent literature shows that social inequality tends to abet political instability and regime repression (Lichbach 1989, Midlarsky 1982, 1988, Midlarsky & Roberts 1985, Muller 1985, 1986, 1988, Muller & Seligson 1987, Russett 1964). Actual or perceived inequality in the distribution of available resources (especially when these resources are in severe shortage or when they are withdrawn after a period of relative abundance) has been a constant source of rebellion from below. Nevertheless, one should not expect a simple linear relationship between social discontent or inequality on the one hand, and instability and insurgency on the other hand. The latter phenomena are not most likely to occur in the poorest or most inegalitarian societies; instead, they occur most often in those middle-level countries undergoing the most rapid *improvements* in their socioeconomic conditions (Benjamin & Kautsky 1968, Gurr 1970, Olson 1963, Rostow 1965). At the same time, it would be reasonable to expect the elites of these transitional societies to resort most intensively and extensively to force and repression as a means to preserve their privileges. Paradoxically, according to Olson (1963), a repressive regime is most vulnerable to being over-thrown when it initiates economic or political reforms. Rebellions and revolutions are not apt to occur during periods of the worst absolute deprivation for the masses, but rather when improving conditions intensify a sense of relative deprivation and arouse the so-called revolution of rising expectations.

These various negative effects of rapid economic growth form what may be termed the "social disruption" perspective. Its main contentions are portrayed in Figure 2.4. Rapid economic growth produces increased inequality and feelings of relative deprivation in the socioeconomic sphere and increased demands upon the authorities in the political sphere. These occurrences, in turn, combine to stimulate political instability and repression, or governmental incapacity due to overload. These "social distor-

Figure 2.4
Social disruption model.

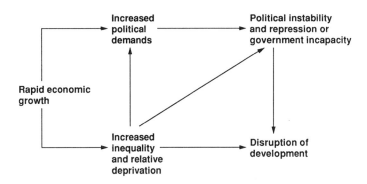

tions" and "political retrogressions" then disrupt and distort the developmental processes. While the underlying premises about ultimate causation are very different from the dependency approach, the posited relationships among economic, social, and political variables are quite similar and produce another pessimistic model of development in the periphery.

The pursuit of security may well have negative implications for the other dimensions of development as well, indicating a second important tradeoff by raising the question "what price vigilance?" (Russett 1970). As is well known to the scholars in this field, the opportunity costs of defense can take two forms. First, a heavy defense burden can dampen capital formation, undermine export competitiveness, produce structural unemployment and inflation, and retard economic growth (Benoit 1973, 1978, Cappelen *et al.* 1984, Chan 1985, Deger & Smith 1983, Frederiksen & Looney 1983, Gleditsch *et al.* 1988, Leontief & Duchin 1983, Lim 1983, Melman 1972, Rasler & Thompson 1988, Rothschild 1973, Russett 1970, Smith 1977, 1980, Starr *et al.* 1984, Szymanski 1973). Second, large defense outlays may curtail a government's ability or willingness to spend on social welfare, education, and health. Whereas recent research has generally failed to establish a strong guns-versus-butter tradeoff among the advanced industrial nations (Domke *et al.* 1983, Mintz 1989, Russett 1982), such a tradeoff may be more likely in developing countries with tighter resource constraints (Dabelko & McCormick 1977). In particular, especially under rightist regimes, income equality and physical quality of life are likely to suffer as a result of heavy defense expenditures (Dixon & Moon 1986, Moon & Dixon 1985). The operationalization of the concept of opportunity costs remains, however, a rather thorny issue in this area of research (Aldrich *et al.* no date, Dabelko & McCormick 1984, Lyttkens & Vedovato 1984).

A number of scholars (Chan 1989a, Dixon & Moon 1986, Moon & Dixon 1985, Weede 1986a) have found that, in contrast to defense expenditures, the military participation ratio (that is, the number of military personnel relative to total population) tends to be positively correlated with greater income equality or fulfillment of basic needs among the developing countries. Some of these analysts, along with Benoit (1973), have argued that military participation in developing countries provides a form of investment in human capital, which in turn facilitates economic growth. Not withstanding the possible contributions of military participation to greater income equality and fuller provision of social welfare, a highly militarized society — as implied by the term "garrison state" — is hardly conducive to the enhancement of a people's political rights or civil liberties. In other words, one would expect a negative relationship between militarization on the one hand, and liberal democratic values and institutions on the other.

Finally, what does the pertinent literature have to say about the conditions for peace? The available evidence does not support the view that democratic countries are necessarily less war-prone, except in the restricted sense of democracies being involved on different sides of a war (Chan 1984, Maoz & Abdolali 1989, Rummel 1983, 1985, 1987, Small & Singer 1976, Vincent 1987a, 1987b, Weede 1984). It also tends to contradict another popular expectation supposing that domestic instability will necessarily encourage foreign conflict (Maoz 1989, Rummel 1963, Stohl 1980, Tanter 1966, Ward & Widmaier 1982, Wilkenfeld 1968, 1969). More recently, however, Hoole & Huang (1989) discovered a reciprocal influence between international war and civil war at the level of the global system. Significantly, this relationship tends to be negative; that is, increases in international war activities tend to dampen civil war activities, and increases in civil war activities tend to reduce international war activities. Concomitantly, one cannot assume that peace and prosperity will necessarily go hand in hand. Russett (1983, 1987) has observed that, historically, countries seem most likely to go to war not when they are mired in the depths of economic recession, but rather when they are on the road to economic recovery. Moreover, the relationship between economic distress and international disputes tends to vary for different types of regimes. A negative relationship between economic expansion and dispute involvement applies to the democratic regimes, whereas a positive relationship between these variables characterizes nondemocratic countries.

These somewhat contradictory effects of defense spending and the pursuit of national security are modeled in Figure 2.5. The ambiguous nature of these relationships is readily apparent. First, defense vigilance produces increased military participation ratios which can promote social development. At the same time, defense vigilance can imply higher military spending, which can in turn produce economic stagnation and smaller welfare programs. Second, while high military participation ratios may promote human capital formation, they may also support authoritarian governments which undercut political development. Third, defense vigilance may stimulate counterarmament by one's adversary. The consequent arms race makes it more likely that diplomatic disputes will escalate into war (e.g., Wallace, 1979, 1982). Fourth, domestic conflict and political instability may diminish the war proneness that economic stress seems to induce in democratic societies.

Yet another basic proposition of the virtuous cycle was that political democracy and stability tend to promote social development (equality, welfare, and human capital creation) and continued economic growth. This proposition was also implicit in both the dependency and social disruption schools which argued that authoritarianism and instability distorted and disrupted economic and social progress. However, even this premise has come under considerable fire, implying another type of tradeoff between stability and growth.

First, it would seem that long-term political stability also carries a heavy price tag. Olson's (1982) theory of distributional

Figure 2.5
Military tradeoffs in developing societies.

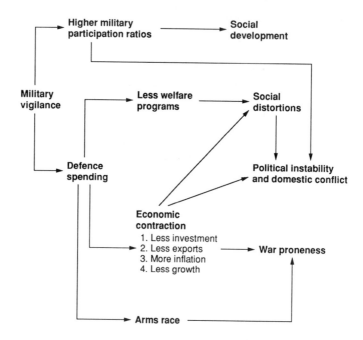

coalitions argues that over time peace and stability can induce economic stagnation, social rigidity, and income inequality. It is hypothesized that stable countries are likely to accumulate more numerous and stronger interest groups or distributional coalitions, which seek to fix prices, restrict supply, and resist technological changes that can threaten their vested interests. These countries therefore tend to suffer from slower economic growth. At the same time, since distributional coalitions tend to be formed by small groups with selective incentives, their efforts at redistributing income and status to their own members have the effect of widening the social gap between the haves and the have nots. These hidden costs of political stability have received some limited support from recent empirical research (Chan 1987a, 1989b, 1990a, Choi 1983, Goldsmith 1986, Gray & Lowery 1988, Kugler & Arbetman 1989, Mueller 1983, Weede 1986a, 1986b). According to these studies, those countries that have suffered traumatic upheavals such as foreign occupation or civil war (which would destroy or weaken their distributional coalitions) tend to feature more vibrant economies and more egalitarian societies in the subsequent period than others that have escaped this fate. Concomitantly, countries that feature a tradition of pluralistic politics and competitive party systems are more likely to experience distributional coalitions — which in turn are likely to induce the tendency toward policy cycling and socioeconomic stagnation.

Second, it would seem from some studies that political instability — especially in the form of protest movements — may have a therapeutic effect on certain desirable social, economic, and political outcomes. For instance, a recent cross-national analysis by Dixon & Moon (1989) reported a positive correlation between domestic conflict intensity and the provision of basic human needs in the relative long term (that is, in 20 years) after controlling for the effect of GNP growth rate. As a second example, Zimmerman (1980) showed similar results about the relationship between domestic conflict and economic development. Furthermore, Popper (1971) argued that domestic conflict can facilitate political development, if the violence involved is sufficiently high to stimulate social change but not so high as to cause severe social disruption.

Third, it has long been widely accepted in conventional scholarship in the United States that multiple cross-cutting social cleavages and fluid political coalitions among many small interest groups provide the basis for liberal democracy. It is less well recognized, however, that these very hallmarks of pluralistic politics may not be conducive to stable or rational social choices. These features imply that it is difficult to reach a single-peaked distribution of policy preferences because the voters' individual values tend to be unstable and intransitive. This situation has been popularized as the paradox of voting by Arrow (1951). Thus, the very conditions that are supposed to promote and sustain pluralistic democracies have the effect of undermining social rationality and inducing policy drift (Miller 1983). Incoherent and even contradictory policies are often the result of the politics of compromise (for example, log rolling, pork barrel, vote trading, issue linkage, constant coalition building and splitting). Accordingly, social choices in pluralistic democracies tend to be suboptimal and haphazard because various competing group interests are combined in an erratic manner.

Fourth, some observers have also questioned the efficacy and wisdom of governmental efforts to promote social equality as a means of encouraging faster economic growth. Conservative economists would generally object to governmental intervention in the marketplace — including policies aimed at income redistribution — on the ground that such intervention tends to distort economic incentives and undermine productive efficiency (Friedman & Friedman 1980). If they are right, an egalitarian ethos such as that proclaimed by the socialist countries would tend to impede economic growth.

This argument obviously raises the question of whether democracy really does stimulate social welfare policies as is normally assumed; and the available evidence may surprise some people. Several earlier studies have been unable to demonstrate that the *level* of political democracy is a significant and positive determinant of income equality cross-nationally (Bollen 1980, Bollen & Grandjean 1981, Bollen & Jackman 1985, Hewitt 1977, Jackman 1975, Rubinson & Quinlan 1977). A more recent study by Muller (1988), however, has shown that the *duration* of democracy is positively correlated with income equality. It also seems that regime strength and ideology combine to have a major impact on the provision of basic human needs in the Third World. Strong leftist regimes appear to have a positive effect in the fulfillment of these needs, whereas strong rightist regimes appear to have a negative effect (Dixon & Moon 1986). Thus, democratization does seem to have an impact on social equality and welfare, although one that is weaker than normally supposed and mediated, especially for developing countries, by regime ideology.

These various relationships are sketched in Figure 2.6 which models the "spinoffs of stability." Political stability and democracy promote the growth of distributional coalitions and, in combination with a leftist ideology, the growth of welfare spending which may improve social development (some distributional coalitions push up welfare spending as well). The increased power of distributional coalitions and the paradox of voting, in contrast, lead to policy instability and cycling. Policy cycling, the distorting effects of interest group activities, and the drag of social welfare

Figure 2.6
Spinoffs of stability.

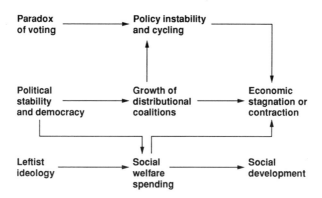

spending culminate, therefore, in the "British disease" that undercuts economic dynamism. This perspective, hence, implies a cruel paradox for development. Political stability seems to be a necessary (although far from sufficient) condition for a vibrant economy. However, long-term stability creates a political environment that inhibits economic performance.

The preceding review indicates that the pertinent empirical relationships are often neither linear nor continuous. Kuznets's (1955) well-known inverted U-curve hypothesis regarding the association between economic development and income equality offers one such example. That is, economic growth initially produces greater inequality but, if sustained, ultimately results in a more egalitarian society. As another example, Goldstein (1985) and Russett (1978) have demonstrated that the relationship between per capita income and physical quality of life is asymptotic curvilinear. That is, small increases in a poor country's per capita income can contribute substantially to its people's welfare. On the other hand, among the affluent countries further increases in their already high per capita income have only marginal effects on physical quality of life. Finally, Neubauer's (1967) statistical analysis found a threshold in the relationship between affluence and democracy. That is, up to a certain point greater affluence facilitates democratization, but once this level of wealth is reached, the two variables become uncorrelated.

There are various perspectives that try to derive theoretical and policy implications from the empirical patterns reviewed above. *Dependentistas* argue that the virtuous cycle in the core was, in fact, based upon an integrated world capitalist economy that directly prevents similar development in the periphery. The social disruption model argues that relationships which exist for countries at the beginning and end of the developmental processes do not hold for others at the middle that are experiencing rapid growth. It also contends that developmental transformation is inherently destabilizing. In addition, the relationships between the pursuit of national security and other dimensions of development appear somewhat contradictory; and even the almost universally sought-after goals of democracy and political stability may have some negative side-effects. Taken together, these theories certainly create a strong impression that "good things don't tend to go together."

Thus, to the extent that the pursuit of one policy goal may jeopardize that of another, government officials must obviously engage in *policy tradeoffs* and *value suboptimization*. They typically adopt rules of "satisficing" and attend to alternative goals sequentially (March & Simon 1958). To be consistently successful, they must be agile in juggling various policy priorities and be capable of working their way out of the apparent policy dilemmas implied by the cross-national patterns reviewed above.

Nevertheless, some countries have obviously been much more successful in managing these policy dilemmas than others. Given the preceding discussion that the developmental experience is likely to involve complex tradeoffs and choices between competing goals, it is not surprising that recent theorizing has emphasized the role of the state in directing development (Evans *et al.* 1985), in contrast to the previous disdain for the state by both developmentalists who believed that governmental interference perverts the market and *dependentistas* who viewed the capitalist state as the "handmaiden for the bourgeoisie" (Smith 1985). This new theoretical tack stems from two general sources. First, the role of the state is seen by many as central to the development of East Asia which recorded the most rapid economic growth in the world during the postwar period (Alam

1989, Amsden 1985, 1989, Cheng & Haggard 1987, Gold 1986, Hofheinz & Calder 1982, Johnson 1982, Jones & Sakong 1980, Prestowicz 1988, Vogel 1979, Wade 1990, White 1988). Second, a broader theoretical framework is provided by scholars such as Charles Tilly (1975, 1984) and Theda Skocpol (1979) who conceptualize states as important and at least semi-independent actors in social history.

This approach invokes the primacy of the state's autonomy, strength, and policies in explaining a variety of phenomena encompassing the defeat of the United States in the Vietnam War, the re-industrialization of Japan, and the development of the newly industrializing countries, especially in East Asia (Amsden 1989, Deyo 1987b, Evans 1979, Haggard 1990, Hofheinz & Calder 1982, Johnson 1981, 1982, Kugler & Domke 1986, Organski & Kugler 1978, Tilly 1985, Wade 1990, White 1988). The dominant roles and activities of the state's "techno-bureaucracy," however, have sometimes been studied within the dependency framework (Duvall & Freeman 1981, 1983, Freeman 1982, Freeman & Duvall 1984).

In contrast to dependency theorists who are inclined to explain the underdevelopment of the Third World by their external conditions, statist theories try to bring back the focus to domestic conditions (Evans *et al.* 1985, Lockwood 1965, Trimberger 1978). They tend to treat as variables those factors that are often taken by the *dependentistas* as constants (for example, the impact of foreign capital, the influence of multinational corporations, the terms of external trade). In the statists' view, these are variables that are at least in principle subject to the influence of the strength, autonomy, and perspicacity of the state authorities; this contrasts to the general disdain for the state as an independent actor by both the dependency and developmental approaches (Smith 1985). That is to say, developing states are not always hopelessly boxed in by oppressive external structural conditions; there is instead considerable room for policy choice and conduct. Thus, the emerging statist theory both views the state as an independent variable that shapes economic outcomes and as a dependent variable affected by its environment. It seeks to develop "institutionalist" explanations of state policy and behavior in terms of a country's basic political structures and how they react to internal pressures and external factors (Haggard 1986,

Figure 2.7
Alternative statist paths to development.

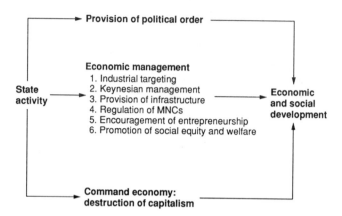

1990, Katzenstein 1978, Krasner 1978, Lake 1988, Zysman 1983). Views about the state's contribution to development (summarized in Figure 2.7), however, tend to differ radically. At one extreme, the state is viewed as valuable if it can impose order and stability to facilitate capitalist markets (Huntington 1968, von Mises 1983). At the other extreme, it is argued that only a socialist state which destroys capitalist relations and imposes a command economy can overcome the structural contradictions of dependency (Chase-Dunn 1983). Between these two polarities, a variety of theories impute an important role of economic leadership to the state. Some focus primarily on economic policy-making and management, such as industrial targeting and promotion, Keynesian countercyclical policies, provision of socioeconomic infrastructure, and regulation of MNCs (Encarnation 1989, Gerschenkron 1962, Johnson 1982, Myrdal 1968), but others argue that the state (including public corporations) plays an important role in mediating relations between economic activities and the general civil society, such as supporting private entrepreneurs and promoting social equity (Bradshaw & Tshandu 1990, Evans *et al.* 1985, Freeman 1989, Gold 1986, Katzenstein 1985, Trimberger 1978). This last perspective, then, provides a theoretical foundation for conceptualizing the tradeoffs that seem necessary because "good things don't tend to go together."

Taiwan's past policy performance looks especially impressive because it has been able to achieve multiple policy values that, according to Western social science research, are unlikely to co-occur. Accordingly, this island has been frequently labelled as an outlier or deviant case in cross-national generalizations. Our basic questions, therefore, are: was simultaneous or sequential progress actually made in terms of growth, equality, welfare, stability, freedom, and security? And, if so, were these happy outcomes the results of broader socioeconomic forces and processes? Or was Taiwan's elite particularly skillful in managing the various competing policy goals? Explaining either alternative should make an interesting contribution to the evolving models of the political economy of development in the modern world.

Chapter 3

From Rags to Riches

Taiwan tells a story of "rags to riches." In 1950, it was quite a political, economic, and military basketcase, ready to be consigned to the garbage heap of history. The island had lost its chief prewar export market and source of capital and entrepreneurship, namely Japan. Much of its industrial and transportation infrastructure was in disarray due to wartime destruction or neglect. The Kuomintang's (hereafter KMT) defeat in the Chinese civil war on the Mainland further saddled the island with a bureaucracy and an army of a continental size. Rampant inflation and political demoralization threatened the KMT's demise in its last territorial remnant, even in the absence of an impending invasion by the People's Liberation Army across the Strait. The KMT regime was, figuratively speaking, only saved by the bell when the Korean War broke out. The U.S. intervention in the latter conflict led to a concomitant decision to neutralize the Taiwan Strait and subsequently to provide the KMT with massive economic as well as military aid.

Taiwan's situation, moreover, would have appeared dismal from the perspective of *all* four paradigms of development summarized in Chapter 2. Dependency theorists would have expected catastrophe in view of its extreme economic and political dependence upon the core of capitalism (the United States), its backward agrarian economy, and its authoritarian capitalist ruling class divorced from the sullen masses. Developmentalists would have been quite dismayed by the island's economic chaos, hyperinflation, and the heavy hand of the state which controlled over half of industry, as well as by the alleged anti-market biases in a Confucian culture. The statists, for their part, would have pointed to the economic failures of the KMT on the Mainland and the existence of a garrison state dominated by the military as reasons for being extremely pessimistic about the emergence of a developmental state. From the tradeoff perspective, the heavy commitment to defense by an authoritarian regime would be seen as almost inevitably precluding progress in terms of growth, welfare, and democratization which, in turn, could well sow the seeds for future instability. In short, Taiwan seemed to be saddled with many liabilities and to possess few assets for undertaking successful economic modernization.

The rest, as they say, is history. In the ensuing four decades, Taiwan has had one of the most dynamic economies in the world. Its gross national product (GNP) has grown by approximately 9% per year after adjustment for inflation. Thus, the island has been transformed from an agricultural backwater sundered from its traditional markets in Japan and China with a GNP per capita of $100 to an industrial society with a GNP per capita of $7,600 (in 1989) that appears to be on the verge of entering the developed world (some estimate the 1990 figure to be close to $10,000 if the subterranean economy is counted). Taiwan's "economic miracle," furthermore, has been associated with performances on other dimensions of development that, according to one or more of the theoretical perspectives discussed in the last chapter, are inconsistent with rapid growth: its society was marked by growing equality, a rising standard of living, social mobilization, political stability, and (with a significant time lag) political liberalization. Moreover, in terms of factors normally assumed to inhibit economic growth, Taiwan has been burdened with heavy defense expenditures, severe dependence upon foreign economic capital and markets, and an intrusive state sector. In sum, the island so far has navigated between the Scylla and Charybdis of different threats to successful development, thereby escaping or lessening the tradeoffs between "good things" expected by most theories of development.

We review Taiwan's policy performance over time in this chapter. We offer some "then versus now" comparisons in order to gain a historical perspective on the island's achievements during the past three and a half decades. Much of what we have to say forms the standard scripts of the Taiwan success story. The next chapter will place these observations in a cross-national context, thus evaluating Taiwan's policy performance in relation to those of other countries. We report the time series data pertaining to this chapter in the Appendix, so that we will not have to interrupt the discussion with many tables. The tables in the Appendix follow the order in which the data are discussed below.

Surely, one of the most basic indicators of economic transformation is the rate of change in GNP per capita. Taiwan's performance on this dimension of development is nothing short of spectacular as its GNP per capita doubled in real value (that is, after controlling for inflation) every 10 to 12 years (1952 to 1966 to 1976 to 1987). As shown in Figure 3.1, in current (or unadjusted) U.S. dollars, Taiwan's GNP per capita skyrocketed almost 40 fold from $153 in 1952 to $3,841 in 1986 and was expected to top $7,600 at the end of 1989. However, the rising value of the New Taiwan dollar in foreign currency exchange accounted for much of the increase in U.S. dollar-denominated GNP per capita between 1986 and 1989.

Such a rapid growth in national income implies, of course, that Taiwan has achieved consistently high rates of real GNP growth and industrial expansion, which have averaged respectively 8.9%

Figure 3.1
GNP per capita (current US dollars) by year.

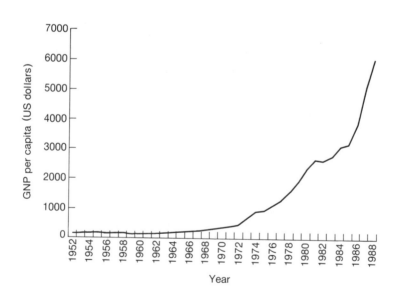

Year

and 12.7% annually between 1952 and 1988. GNP growth has been fairly steady as it fell below 5% in only three years. The figures for industrial growth show a more cyclical pattern with peak values in the mid 1960s to the late 1970s and a bottoming out in the recessions of the mid 1970s and early 1980s as a result of surging oil price. Few countries, developed or developing, can match this record of *rapid and sustained* growth.

The structural transformation of Taiwan's economy is indicated by the major shifts in agriculture's and industry's shares of total production. Overall, between 1952 and 1988, agriculture's proportion of total production plummeted from 36% to 6%, while industry's share jumped from 18% to 46% (that of manufacturing alone more than tripled from 11% to 38%). The most dramatic stage of this change from a primary to a secondary economy occurred between 1961 and 1972 when agriculture's share of net domestic product (NDP) was more than halved from 32% to 14%, while industry's jumped from 25% to 40%. Thus, Taiwan now has one of the most industrialized economies in the world, suggesting that it will soon follow the more advanced industrial societies in expanding its tertiary (service) sector (Schive 1989).

Such rapid economic growth depends upon an equal expansion of demand. That is, there has to be a market for the increased production of goods. One commonly accepted explanation is that Taiwan's economic growth has relied heavily upon exports to create demand for its products (Galenson 1979a, Kuo 1983). Overall, exports increased at an average annual rate of 15.5% between 1952 and 1988, substantially higher than the rates of industrial and GNP growth. Figure 3.2 also confirms this image of export-oriented growth, at least for the period after the early 1960s when the island's growth really took off, by highlighting the trends in the island's exports as a percentage of its GNP and in its industrial products as a percentage of exports. Exports were relatively unimportant for the overall economy until 1962 (composing between 6% and 11% of GNP). However, they then skyrocketed to 26% in 1970, 42% in 1973, and rose more gradually to 54% in 1987. At the same time, the composition of the island's exports changed dramatically. Before 1958, industrial products composed less than 15% of total exports. However, they dominated the export surge of the 1960s. Their share in

Figure 3.2
Export as per cent of GDP and industrial content of exports
(per cent) by year.

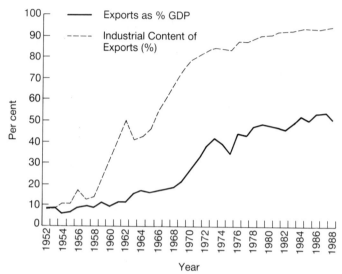

Taiwan's export mix rapidly escalated to 50% in 1962, 79% in 1970, 88% in 1976, and 95% in 1985.

Taiwan's successful export drive, moreover, changed the chronic trade deficit of the 1950s and 1960s into a comfortable trade surplus during most of the 1970s. This trade surplus rapidly escalated from $3.3 billion in 1982 to $18.7 billion in 1987. By the late 1980s, though, this success was creating major frictions with the United States which accounted for at least 85% of Taiwan's trade surplus throughout the 1980s. In response to the U.S. pressure, this surplus was almost halved to a still very healthy $11 billion in 1988 (Copper 1989).

The expansion of internal demand should also be important even for a country with a relatively small population (about 20 million in 1988). The average growth rates for private and government consumption were only half as much as for exports (8% and 7% respectively), but were still high enough to be quite stimulative. All three series follow fairly similar patterns, although exports were by far the most volatile in the 1950s. They all rose dramatically during the 1960s and early 1970s (with exports leading the way), and fell significantly during the two recessions of the mid 1970s and early 1980s. Following the second oil-induced recession, exports recovered more strongly than domestic demand in the mid 1980s, thus exacerbating Taiwan's dependence on foreign trade. However, for 1987–8 domestic demand grew more rapidly than exports, in part because of Taiwan's attempt to pacify U.S. trade pressures, suggesting that the island may be forced to move toward more internally oriented growth.

Inflation and unemployment often represent serious problems in mature industrialized countries that are afflicted with the phenomenon of "stagflation." Their impact on developing countries — even those with high economic growth — can be even.more traumatic. High inflation eats up apparent economic gains, while large-scale unemployment denies many people the benefits of economic growth. Moreover, there appears to be a substantial tradeoff in fighting these two economic dangers because improvement on one usually comes at the expense of retrogression on the other. Naturally, mismanagement of these economic conditions increases the danger of social unrest and political instability.

Given the KMT's inability to cope with the runaway inflation on the Mainland and given the island's vulnerability to externally introduced price pushes, Taiwan's record on taming inflation (as measured by annual changes in wholesale and consumer prices) has again been quite remarkable. The hyperinflation of the late 1940s was brought under control fairly quickly (Kuo 1983, Li 1988); and since the late 1950s inflation has remained well under 10% except for the two price surges induced by the energy crises of 1973–4 and 1979–80. As shown in Figure 3.3, Taiwan's inflation rate is negatively associated with GNP and industrial growth. That is, growth is higher when inflation is low and falls drastically during inflationary surges. Thus, Taiwan's ability to keep price increases fairly mild is clearly a key ingredient in its economic success story. However, with an increasingly cash-laden economy, it remains to be seen whether the island will be as successful in containing inflation in the future as it has been in the past.

A major reason for Taiwan's very successful inflation record has been its conservative monetary policy. For example, except during the oil-induced inflationary surges, money supply has

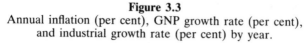

Figure 3.3
Annual inflation (per cent), GNP growth rate (per cent),
and industrial growth rate (per cent) by year.

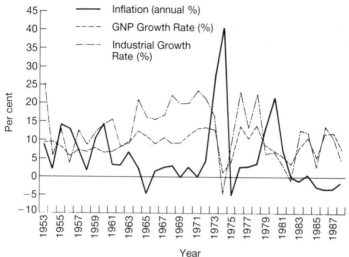

generally not expanded much faster than the overall economy. However, the rapid rise of 51% in money supply in 1986, triggered in part by the island's huge trade surplus, raised an ominous threat of inflation yet to come. While the government subsequently succeeded in dampening this escalation of money supply, huge increases in housing and stock prices in the late 1980s (Seymour 1989) indicated that the inflation danger was far from over.

Especially in developing countries, the price of low inflation is usually economic austerity programs which produce substantial unemployment. High unemployment in turn creates an industrial reserve army whose competition for jobs keeps wages exploitatively low. This situation produces a comparative advantage in cheap labor. In Taiwan, in very sharp contrast to this Third World norm, rapid growth created a steadily expanding job market with major spurts in total jobs occurring in the late 1960s and early 1970s, late 1970s, and late 1980s. Consequently, the unemployment rate has generally been quite low, averaging 4% during the 1950s and early 1960s. It then fell to 2% or less in the 1970s, rose back to about 3% in the mid 1980s, before dropping under 2% again at the end of the decade. Low unemployment, furthermore, has stimulated steadily rising wages throughout much of the postwar period. For example, real manufacturing wages, after stagnating from the mid 1950s to the mid 1960s, grew by 5% a year during 1965–72, 10% a year for 1975–9 (after falling 4% a year in the 1973–4 recession), 6% a year during 1980–6, and a strong 9.5% annually in 1987–8 as the tight labor market at a time of economic expansion pushed up salary levels. Taiwan, therefore, has generally had low rates of both inflation and unemployment.

Sustained investment is seen by many as a prerequisite for economic growth, and an amount of 10% of GNP has been suggested as a threshold necessary for economic takeoff (Rostow 1960). Obviously, the inability of subsistence societies to produce the requisite savings presents a formidable brake on their economic potential. Taiwan's high savings and investment rates, then, suggest a proximate cause of its "economic miracle." Even during the 1950s, when the island was quite poor, its savings rate was just below the 10% level. This relatively high level perhaps reflects the Chinese "cultural propensity to save" (Greenhalgh 1988a). Another possible explanation is the regime's relative success in dampening inflationary psychology, which would otherwise encourage consumption and speculation at the expense of savings. Yet a third set of factors includes the institution of year-end bonuses, the relative absence of social welfare and retirement plans, and the easy accessibility of the postal savings system (Myers 1984). Finally, favorable government tax and interest policies have encouraged the public's incentive to save. In particular, the high real interest rates that the government used to attack inflation during the 1950s provided a major stimulus for savings when the island was still quite poor (Myers 1984).

When combined with the massive amounts of aid from the United States, Taiwan was actually able to achieve investment rates of 12% to 20% during the earlier years. Once its rapid growth began, the savings rate quickly escalated from about 13% at the beginning of the 1960s to over 30% at the beginning of the 1970s where it has remained ever since (except in 1975). The investment rate rose a little more gradually to 25% in the late 1960s and over 30% in the late 1970s, thus becoming one of the highest in the world. In contrast, during the 1980s, it fell back to

16% despite continued high savings as substantial amounts of entrepreneurial capital began to flow out of Taiwan. The investment rate did rebound considerably to 24% in 1988, but much of this increased domestic investment probably went into the highly speculative stock market. Furthermore, Taiwan's trade success resulted in a rapid escalation of its foreign reserves from $2 billion in 1980 to $79 billion in 1988, the second highest absolute amount in the world next to Japan ($98 billion) at that time.

Up through the late 1960s, savings were stimulated by high interest rates (indicated here by the rediscount rate after 1960); and increased interest rates were used to fight the inflationary trends set off by the two oil-price leaps in the 1970s. However, interest rates dropped greatly during the 1980s (for example, the rediscount rate fell from 11.75% in 1981 to 4.5% in 1985) and were not increased in response to the price increases of the late 1980s, suggesting that popular pressures for "loose money" had become strong enough to curtail the government's usual counter-cyclical use of monetary policy. Ironically, then, Taiwan's excellent performance in trade and savings may have led it into a "success trap." The island is facing an embarrassing situation of a large cash surplus and dwindling domestic investment opportunities which may well prove inflationary. In addition, its recent process of democratization may limit the government's ability to take the corrective actions that it would have in the past, calling to mind Olson's (1982) theory about the growth of distributional coalitions.

Impressive as some of the foregoing statistics on economic performance may appear, they say little about the well-being of the people. The benefits of rapid economic growth may not trickle down to the masses as shown by the Brazilian case, where growth failed to promote development as defined by income equity and physical quality of life (Evans 1979). In fact, as discussed in Chapter 2, it is generally assumed by developmentalists and *dependentistas* alike that rapid growth will initially exacerbate inequality and thus fail to produce improvement in the popular standard of living.

In regard to the desideratum of an egalitarian society as indexed by income distribution, Taiwan presents one of the most impressive cases in the world. Rapid growth on the island was accompanied by decreased, rather than increased, income inequality (although the high levels of inequality in 1953 and 1961 could well be overstated because of the restricted samples from which they were calculated). Income inequality declined steadily and markedly in Taiwan until 1980 (Fei *et al.* 1979, Greenhalgh 1988b). For example, the ratio between the income share of the richest fifth of the population and that of the poorest fifth fell from 5.33 in 1964 to 4.17 in 1980; and the Gini index of inequality declined from 0.321 to 0.277 over the same period. During the 1980s, this trend was reversed, and the gap between these two income groups increased to the level of the early 1970s (for example, the income ratio was 4.85 in 1988). Thus, fears about growing inequality began to emerge as a political issue by the end of the 1980s (Song 1990). Despite this setback, however, Taiwan still has one of the most egalitarian systems of income distribution in the capitalist world. In addition, fears about rural–urban disparities in income (Chu & Tsaur 1984) appear to have been unfounded. While industrialization in the mid 1960s led to a big jump in the advantage of city dwellers, the rural–urban income disparity has remained fairly constant since then. In particular, Taiwan's record on income distribution has stood on its head the normal pattern or stylized fact described by Kuznets (1955) in which development first exacerbates inequality and only produces a more egalitarian society after a considerable time lag.

As another indication of egalitarianism, let us consider the pattern of ownership of agricultural land. Land inequality has been seen as a major causal link in models of underdevelopment and domestic violence (Midlarsky 1988, Prosterman & Riedinger 1987). As suggested by many scholars, Taiwan's land reform of the late 1940s and the early 1950s was instrumental in promoting rural equity and in providing an economic stimulus for subsequent industrialization (Ho 1978, Kuo 1983, Thorbecke 1979). Our figures clearly bear out the former part of this suggestion. Farmers who were full owners of their land climbed from 38% of the agricultural population in 1952 to 85% in 1988. During the same period, the relative size of part owners went down from 26% to 11%. And, whereas 36% of the rural population were tenants in 1952, this number was only 4% in 1988. Thus, except for a small minority, the slogan of "Land to the tiller" has become a reality in Taiwan's countryside.

The popular standard of living rose considerably as well, although at somewhat different rates in specific areas, as illustrated by the graphs in Figure 3.4. Central measures of the standard of living are provided by the three components (literacy, infant mortality, and life expectancy) of the physical quality of life index (PQLI) developed by Morris (1979). On these scores, Taiwan has surely come a long way. Between 1950 and 1988, its literacy jumped from 56.0% to 92.6%, its infant mortality rate declined from 35.16 deaths to 5.34 deaths per 1,000 live births, and its people's average life expectancy increased from 55.57 years to 73.51 years. This caused the island's PQLI rating to rise from 63 to 95, with 100 being a hypothetically perfect score. By comparison, the PQLI score for the United States stood at 93 in 1979 (Morris 1979).

Taiwan's dramatic improvements in standard of living are also reflected in other basic indicators of popular welfare. The quantity and quality of food consumption, as measured by caloric and protein consumption respectively, rose by 50% or more

Figure 3.4
Physical quality of life index (PQLI), literacy rate (per cent),
infant mortality (per 1,000 live births), and life expectancy by year.

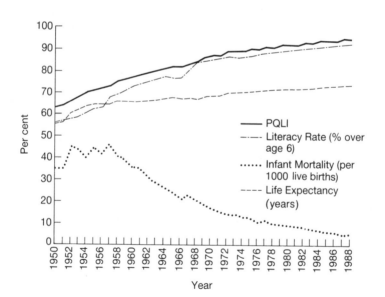

Year

during the postwar period. Between 1952 and 1988, for example, the daily food consumption of the average citizen jumped from 2078 to 3017 calories and from 49 to 90 grams of protein. Moreover, the rate of communicable disease fell from about 15–20 to 1 per 100,000 people between the 1950s and the 1980s; the share of household earnings spent on food, beverages, and tobacco (a central indicator of disposable income) was nearly halved from 62% to 32.4% between 1952 and 1987; the proportion of employees covered by labor and farmer insurance skyrocketed from 7% to 82%; and by the late 1980s almost all the population had electricity and over 80% was served by running water.

The rapid rise in standard of living is also indicated by the marked improvement in housing facilities between the mid 1970s and late 1980s. For example, housing space per family increased by 40% between 1976 and 1988, while the average number of family members decreased from five to four. Over the same period, there was also a tremendous increase in the percentage of homes having many amenities — 39% to 84% for washing machines, 74% to 98% for refrigerators, 3% to 34% for air conditioners, 23% to 97% for color televisions, and 1% to 51% for video recorders. Last and by no means least, over three quarters of the population owned their homes by 1988 which meant that most of the population benefitted from the huge increases in the prices of housing in the late 1980s.

Another important element in social development is what Karl Deutsch (1961) has termed social mobilization, or the acquisition of skills and facilities that permits a population to participate in the industrialization and democratization processes. The general educational achievements of a population form a central dimension of social mobilization. The rapid improvements in literacy noted above, for example, denote the development of an important skill for both industrial and political communication. In addition to literacy, Taiwan's advancement in education is spectacular in several other regards. Between 1952 and 1988, for instance, the percentage of population with a secondary-school education level leaped five fold from 10% to 54%; the proportion of primary-school graduates going on to junior high school tripled (from about a third to almost all); real spending per primary-school student jumped seven fold; and college students as a

proportion of total population leaped 20 fold (from 0.12% to
2.49%).

Communications infrastructure and facilities are another important component of social mobilization; and the island's record
was outstanding here as well. Taiwan displayed many-fold
increases during the postwar era on two indicators of communications. Mail per capita rose from 7.7 to 77.4 letters and packages;
and telephone subscribers per 100 people rose from 0.3 to 26.7.
In strictly economic terms, the real growth of transportation and
communications averaged nearly 10% a year throughout the
postwar period with the greatest increase occurring between the
mid 1960s and late 1970s. Thus, the growth of this key sector
kept pace with overall economic expansion.

Taiwan, therefore, has manifested tremendous progress on
many important dimensions of the popular standard of living and
social mobilization. However, the time series for the various
indicators (e.g., literacy, infant mortality, food as a proportion of
household spending) show quite different patterns of change.
Evidently, progress first occurred in basic areas and was
significantly delayed along more qualitative dimensions. For
education, major gains in literacy and percentage of students
going on to junior high school occurred in the 1950s, but the big
jump in college and even high-school enrollments did not occur
until the 1960s and early 1970s. Additionally, the real spending
per student in primary school remained almost constant during
the 1950s but then took off after the early 1960s, doubling
between 1963 and 1972, doubling again by 1979, and almost
doubling yet again by 1984.

This pattern is replicated by most other indicators. Quantity of
food consumption, as measured by calories, rose rapidly from
1952 through 1970, and then increased only slowly as demand
was evidently satisfied. In contrast, the quality of diet as
indicated by protein consumption, rose steadily but more slowly
than caloric consumption during the 1950s, accelerated from the
mid 1960s to the early 1970s, increased gradually through 1983,
and jumped again in the mid and late 1980s.

This pattern implies that the first stage of improvement in the
standard of living involved simply the increase in food consumption, but that later prosperity permitted a changed focus
from dietary quantity to quality. The change from quantity to

quality in food, moreover, was associated with major health improvements as well since the rates of infant mortality and communicable disease did not display major improvement until the early 1960s, but then dropped dramatically. This interpretation is bolstered by the fact that disposable income, as measured by the proportion of household income spent on nonfood items, did not manifest much improvement until the early 1960s but has increased steadily since then.

The increase in welfare protection signaled by expanding the coverage of workers insurance was even later in coming. The proportion of employed people who were covered by this insurance increased gradually to 36% in 1979 before more than doubling over the next decade, in part because farmers became eligible in the late 1980s. The latter expansion was perhaps viewed by the government as something of a "frill" which was not emphasized until the society became fairly prosperous.

Finally, major improvements in housing quality did not really take off until the mid 1970s. In the communications realm, mail flow began its rapid growth in the 1950s. Telephones, in contrast, did not become widespread until the late 1970s but then increased five fold from 5 to 25 per hundred people in little more than a decade after 1975, suggesting a communications revolution.

The pattern of differential growth in standard of living and social mobilization noted above is suggestive in several regards. First, gains in popular welfare lagged behind the beginning of rapid economic growth by a decade and even longer for many of these indicators. Thus, the benefits of growth took some time to appear. Second, immediate progress did occur in basic education and diet which set the stage for social mobilization promoting development and later gains in health. Third, the pattern of first emphasizing quantitative and then qualitative improvements seems providential, but is only so if the time lag between the two is fairly short, as it was on Taiwan. In summary, while Taiwan has made continuous and concurrent progress on multiple (but not all) policy dimensions over the past four decades, it is also important to recognize the presence of sequences and stages that denote especially rapid improvements in particular components or aspects of general policy values.

A more directly political dimension of social mobilization involves membership in civic organizations which provides a picture of how people are mobilizing themselves. Very significant progress occurred here as well. While the number of civic organizations grew fairly evenly over the postwar period from 2,560 to 12,605 (with the exception of a period of stagnation during most of the 1960s), there were two very distinct spurts in the growth of total members. Memberships in civic organizations as a percentage of the adult population rose steadily from 29% to 40% between 1952 and 1961, stayed almost constant during the 1960s and 1970s, and then jumped from 40% in 1980 to 52% in 1986 and 69% in 1988. The first growth spurt probably represented mobilization of the population by the regime, in contrast to the second which was almost certainly stimulated by the political liberalization of the 1980s, especially the major democratization reforms that commenced in 1986 (see Chapter 5).

The availability of published materials and political news forms another related dimension of social mobilization. Because martial-law regulation prohibited the founding of new newspapers, the number of newspapers stayed at about 30 from 1952 to 1987 before jumping four fold in 1988 after martial law was lifted. A more valid picture of expanding social communications, though, is presented by the number of periodicals and journals — which encompass both political (including opposition) and undoubtedly a large majority of wholly nonpolitical publications. Their number expanded over 15 fold between 1952 and 1988 with big growth spurts in the early 1950s, the early 1960s, and most of the 1980s. These three periods represented both times of political liberalization and of significant changes in what might be called social modernization. Thus, the publishing industry seemed to be responding to both political and social change.

Several strands of theory discussed in Chapter 2, however, argue that rapid economic growth and social mobilization tend to be politically and socially destabilizing. Recent events in Brazil, Iran, South Korea, and China (specifically the pro-democracy movement and the regime's crackdown in the summer of 1989) bear this line of reasoning out. Taiwan, in contrast, has been fairly stable politically in terms of the most common indicators of political unrest. Thus, the data for 1948–77 on these variables demonstrate that, while some instability existed in the first half of the 1950s, the island has been remarkably stable since the early

1960s. While most of these indicators undoubtedly understate political instability because they are based on foreign press reports, they do show that popular protest, as measured by demonstrations, riots, and political strikes, has been quite limited (although demonstrations have become almost daily occurrences following the liberalization of the late 1980s). In contrast, deaths from political violence were quite high before the mid 1960s, but most of these came from Communist shellings of the offshore islands.

The government itself was quite stable. There were no attempted coups or irregular transfers of political power; and the number of "executive adjustments" (that is, a major change in the top leadership) was relatively low, especially after 1967. However, the number of political executions was very high through the late 1950s; and the government imposed a significant number of restrictions on and sanctions against its citizens during the postwar period, although this frequency declined significantly over time (especially in the late 1980s after the lifting of martial law). This decline has been accompanied by the emergence of competitive party politics. The Democratic Progressive Party (DPP) has emerged as a major political opposition of the KMT. This process toward political liberalization and partisan competition, however, has also produced a concomitant increase in the incidence of violent protests and mass demonstrations. Consequently, the island's political stability (which has previously been enforced by an authoritarian government) is undergoing a period of challenge.

These more recent changes are perhaps better described by more indirect measures of social instability such as labor disputes, emigration, and the crime rate. For example, despite the high rate of economic growth between 1983 and 1988, the number of workers involved in labor disputes almost tripled; the emigration rate more than doubled; and the crime rate nearly doubled. In comparison, the economic stress brought on by the first oil-price crisis in the early 1970s also brought an upsurge in labor disputes and emigration (but not crime). Thus, there is some evidence that at long last the social disruption model may have some applicability for Taiwan.

One reason for Taiwan's relative stability so far, of course, is that the island has been ruled by the dominant and authoritarian

Kuomintang Party — which is certainly at variance with the values of democracy and liberty. However, even here, Taiwan's performance has shown some encouraging signs. Qualitatively, as will be discussed in greater detail in Chapter 5, it has undergone substantial liberalization and democratization along three primary dimensions: (a) broadening the elite composition of the regime, (b) providing increasing opportunities first in the economy and then in the polity for the Taiwanese majority, and (c) greatly expanding the role of elections and electoral competition, especially in the late 1980s (T. Cheng 1989, Chou & Nathan 1987, Copper 1988, Gold 1989, Tien 1989).

These changes are reflected in quantitative scores that assess the level of political rights and civil liberties prevailing on the island. These ratings by the Freedom House indicate some overtime improvements. On a scale of 1 (best) to 7 (worst) applied to all countries, Taiwan's score on the political rights enjoyed by its people changed from 6 in 1972 to 4 in 1989. There has also been a greater improvement in its people's civil liberties, for which the score decreased from 5 to 3. Similar conclusions are produced by an examination of more direct indicators of electoral competition — for example, the ratio of winners to candidates and the electoral prowess of the KMT in contests for the Provincial Assembly, a directly elected body where politics has traditionally been much more open than at the national level (Lerman 1978). There have generally been almost twice as many candidates as seats, but until the DPP gains of almost ten percentage points in the 1989 election (Jiang 1990) the KMT had easily dominated these elections, winning about 70% of the vote and 80% of the seats. Thus, while Taiwan evidently is still far from achieving the democratic standards taken for granted in the United States and Britain, it has made some progress in comparison with its own past.

The island's accomplishments in terms of economic and social development, furthermore, have occurred despite several conditions that one or more of the four paradigms of political economy consider to be gravely deleterious for such development. First, Taiwan's dependency upon foreign sources for its economic growth naturally brings to mind the island's consequent economic as well as political vulnerability to outside influences. Dependency theories, as well as several nondependency approaches to unequal relations in international political economy (Hirschman 1945), presume that this situation produces the economic and political exploitation of and distortions within the periphery. Taiwan constitutes an interesting case study in this regard. Although it is often cited as a prime example of a strong and autonomous developmental state (Amsden 1985, Gold 1986, Wade 1988), its autonomy vis-à-vis the internal population contrasts sharply with its political, military, and economic dependence externally, especially upon its patron the United States, thereby creating a complex structure of strength and weakness (Chan 1988b).

We review, therefore, some pertinent data reflecting Taiwan's dependence upon foreign aid, capital, and trade. This island has been considerably dependent at one time or another on all three dimensions, but it has also managed to mitigate most of these dependencies as well. First, up through the early 1960s, U.S. aid (over 80% of which was in the form of grants) provided almost 40% of gross domestic capital formation (GDCF), explaining the fact that the investment rate was much higher than the savings rate during those years. In particular, U.S. aid financed much of the key investment in agriculture and infrastructure, and covered Taiwan's trade and budgetary deficits (Jacoby 1966). Yet the island was able to wean itself from this heavy aid dependence in relatively short order. The U.S. aid was terminated in 1965 without any adverse effect on the growth and investment rates as seen above. Thus, Taiwan belongs to a very select club of developing countries that have graduated from this kind of foreign dependence. Indeed, it has even undergone a role reversal in this regard; Taiwan is now an aid donor to other developing countries (for example, in Central America).

In contrast to U.S. aid, foreign investment was never dominant in Taiwan's economy. It did, however, play an important role in the export surge of 1963–73. In addition to the investors from United States and Japan, overseas Chinese communities have been an important provider of imported capital as each of these three sources provided between 18% and 28% of the cumulative foreign investment in Taiwan over the postwar period. Foreign investment peaked at just under 10% of GDCF in 1968–71, and then fell back substantially to about 3% during the 1970s and early 1980s before climbing again to about 7% in the late 1980s.

Foreign capital has dominated a few important export industries, such as electronics, but even here the positions of multinational corporations have eroded considerably over time (Ranis & Schive 1985, Schive 1990). They never became strong enough to denationalize the economy. Indeed, Taiwan has been comparatively successful in unpacking the investment package that foreign companies have to offer. It encourages some components of this package (such as capital, technology), while regulating or shunning those other components that threaten to undermine its economic or political autonomy (Huang 1989). Instead of submitting to "sovereignty at bay," it has been practicing "sovereignty *en garde*."

Dependency theorists charge that over the long term, debt repayments and profit remittance by multinational corporations lead to the decapitalization of industries in the developing countries. Taiwan's record is somewhat different. The KMT government had brought to the island its gold reserve from the Mainland. Because much of the U.S. aid was in the form of grants, the 1952–62 period saw heavy net inflows of foreign capital equal to well over one third of domestic investment. With the end of foreign aid and the rise of foreign investment, the amount of net inflows dropped drastically. Yet, Taiwan ran a positive cumulative balance of capital flows during 1963–71. In the 1970s, this balance turned negative. However, outflows occurred during years of strong growth and investment (1972–3 and 1977–8), when huge corporate profits and foreign investments by Taiwan's prosperous businesses would have been expected. On the other hand, there was actually a net capital inflow during the recession of 1974–5.

Capital outflows began to escalate during the 1980s, reaching the level of total domestic investment by mid decade. This development, however, represents the rising foreign investments made by Taiwan's businessmen, who have been motivated by the desire to preserve overseas sales against protectionism in the developed world, particularly in the United States, and to exploit cheap labor in the developing world (for example, Taiwan is now the largest foreign investor in the Philippines). It does not indicate the extraction of indigenous surplus by the core, although it does have the negative implication that the local business community is losing confidence in the government's ability to preserve political stability and a good investment environment. Certainly, the fact that tiny Taiwan has managed to accumulate the second highest *absolute* amount of foreign reserves in the world (as mentioned earlier, about $79 billion in 1988) demonstrates that decapitalization is far from a problem for its economy. In addition, capital outflows fell to half of total investment, although this may not be an entirely favorable development to the extent that it reflects vastly increased speculation in the stock market and real estate.

Whereas some recent dependency writers (e.g., Bornschier & Chase-Dunn 1985) have emphasized the Third World's financial dependence and the consequent deleterious effects of this dependence, other more traditional proponents of the dependency perspective have been primarily concerned with its trade dependence. Most developing countries are expected to exhibit three characteristics of trade dependence: (a) a high ratio of trade to GNP, (b) a high concentration of exports in a few products, and (c) a concentration of trade with just a few countries (Doran 1983).

Taiwan's record in these areas is mixed. As seen above, the export surge of the 1960s initiated a dramatic upward trend in the export/GDP ratio that is now over 50%. Moreover, Taiwan's two largest foreign markets, the United States and Japan, have almost always accounted for about 50% or more of its exports, and this figure jumped to almost 60% in the mid 1980s, although it fell back to 53% in 1988 as the U.S. share in Taiwan's exports dropped from 48% in 1986 to 39% in 1988. In sharp contrast, Taiwan's two largest traditional exports, rice and sugar (agricultural products which tend to be the most vulnerable to market distortions), fell from 70% of total exports in the early and mid 1950s to one third in the early 1960s and then to minuscule levels by the mid 1970s.

On the other hand, Taiwan has been marked by substantial dependence upon foreign markets, although the degree of this dependence has varied considerably both over time and among specific subdimensions. Its successful export drive from the early 1960s to the late 1980s certainly indicated that these ties to international markets were not necessarily deleterious. However, growing trade conflicts with Washington and increasing competition from other NICs (newly industrializing countries) also demonstrate that trade dependence may entail future vulnerability. Taiwan, therefore, has certainly been economically dependent (not to speak of its military and political dependencies upon the United States). However, its policy performances thus far have proved quite successful in limiting such vulnerability or, conversely, in protecting the island's national autonomy. Foreign aid was obtained at little cost and utilized efficiently; foreign capital was channeled into priority sectors and prevented from assuming a dominant role in the economy; and economic performance kept the country internationally competitive so that it benefitted from its market dependence. Dependency management, therefore, vitiated this particular threat to economic growth.

A heavy defense burden constitutes another potential drag on the economy. While developing countries can use participation in the military to mobilize and modernize their populations, military spending should normally dampen capital formation and export competitiveness (through the diversion of funds and human capital) which would, in turn, slow overall economic growth. Taiwan's economic and welfare accomplishments, therefore, are even more remarkable because it has borne a rather heavy defense burden historically. Until the early 1970s, military expenditures consumed nearly 10% of GNP and about 4% of the island's population was under arms. During the 1970s and 1980s this burden declined significantly with defense spending averaging 7% of GNP and the ratio of military personnel to total population declining gradually but steadily to 2%. By 1988, defense spending had dropped to 5.2% of GNP, therefore presaging a much more normal level of expenditures for national security in the future. Still, compared to other countries, Taiwan has had to bear a very heavy defense burden throughout most of the postwar period.

These quantitative data fail to report, however, what is probably the most important indicator of Taiwan's security performance, which is after all concerned with the deterrence of an outside attack. In this respect, the absence of a major external attack or foreign war is significant. Considering the military plight of the KMT regime in the early 1950s and the experiences of other states (for example, Israel, Pakistan, South Korea, Syria) facing comparable security threats, the preservation of peace was no small feat. The nonoccurrence of the expected (that is, a

Communist military assault, although shellings of the offshore islands in the earlier years did produce significant casualties) in the security sphere is as remarkable as the occurrence of the unexpected (that is, Taiwan's industrial takeoff and export expansion) in the economic sphere. To mix analogies, the island's policy performance presents one with the puzzles of "the dog that did not bark" as well as "the mouse that roared."

The impact of the state upon development is more controversial among the theoretical traditions. Statists see it as positive; developmentalists as negative; and *dependentistas* as probably negative (for example, a socialist state would promote development but a capitalist one probably would not). It is perhaps fitting, then, that the three basic indicators of the state's economic role in Taiwan presented here vary considerably in what they show about the state's power over and intervention in the economy.

The most intrusive activity is direct state control of production through what has been called "state entrepreneurship" (Duvall & Freeman 1983, Freeman 1989). In Taiwan this has been quite substantial. Because the government seized Japanese assets at the end of World War II, state corporations accounted for almost half of all industrial production until the early 1960s, a figure higher than in many "socialist" developing nations. The industrialization of the 1960s and 1970s was primarily based on new private industries, so that the state's share in industrial production fell dramatically to 20% in the early 1970s where it has stayed since. This is equivalent to about 9% of GNP which places Taiwan within but at the lower end of the 7%–15% range that Jones and Mason (1982) consider the normal level of state entrepreneurship in developing countries. The state's share in just the manufacturing sector showed a similar decline through the early 1970s but, unlike total industrial production, continued to decrease to about 10% at the end of the 1980s (the figure for total industrial production is higher because of the state monopoly in utilities). State entrepreneurship in Taiwan may also decline even further in the future due to the increasing political controversy over the "inefficiencies" of public corporations.

The state (both the government and public corporations) has also played a major role in investment, although its investment rate has been quite cyclical ranging from 30% to 60% of gross domestic capital formation (GDCF) depending upon economic circumstances. In general, state investment was highest during the 1950s and, subsequently, during periods of economic downturn when it was used to substitute for private resources. The final indicator of the government's economic role concerns the relative weight of the government in the total economy. The size of government involvement has been fairly moderate and stable. Public employees have averaged an almost constant 6.5% of the workforce over the last 30 years; and the ratio of the public budget to GNP has only varied between 20% and 25% throughout the entire postwar period. This great stability over time is particularly noteworthy since development usually produces "bigger government." It also has meant that the tax burden has been fairly moderate and stable, gradually increasing from about 15% to 20% of personal income between 1960 and 1980 and then declining slightly during the 1980s. This, in turn, has permitted both a substantial amount of private investment and growing popular consumption. Thus, Taiwan has clearly practiced fiscal conservatism (for example, it has almost always run a budgetary surplus).

Other aggregate data on the public sector suggest some positive conclusions about the state's role as well. First, the government is becoming more professionalized (Liu 1987, Lu 1984). For example, the percentage of government employees who passed civil service examinations jumped four fold from 11% in 1962 to 45% in 1988; and over just the 1970s the percentage of government employees who had a college education rose considerably from 38% to 58%. Second, despite the regime's image for a hands-off approach to social welfare, a growing commitment in this area is evident. For example, the share of social welfare and social security spending in the total budget jumped from 11% in 1980 to 17.5% in 1988 after growing slowly from 6% in 1954 to 8% in 1964 to 10% in 1971. Third, a charting of the real growth rate in government spending implies that it has been used to promote countercyclical adjustment. Thus, spending has been moderated at times of inflationary threats (the mid 1950s, the early and late 1970s, and the mid to late 1980s) and expanded during times of economic stress (the mid 1970s and early 1980s). The one possible exception here — a 13% jump in public spending in 1988 despite looming inflation — can be explained by the government's hope of counteracting the flight of private capital.

Finally, the ratio of direct taxes to total revenue is often used to measure a government's capacity to extract resources from society. Weaker governments tend to depend more upon indirect taxes such as customs duties and license fees which are easier to collect than direct taxes based on personal income (Snider 1987). In addition, this variable should tap a regime's redistributive potential. Generally speaking, indirect taxes impose a flat rate on consumption, whereas direct taxes on personal income adopt a progressive rate. Consequently, the more a government's revenues rely on direct as opposed to indirect taxes, the less unfavorable its tax system is toward the poor people — and, hence, the less adverse is this system in regard to the achievement of an equitable distribution of income. Taiwan's proportion of direct taxes remained fairly low at about 25% until the mid 1970s when it commenced a fairly sharp rise to 45% in 1988. Thus, the regime appears to have significantly increased its economic and redistributive capacities at a time when the island is facing the challenge of fundamental economic and political transformation.

The role of the state in Taiwan, therefore, has something to both succor and offend the contrasting developmental and statist perspectives. The former can praise the relatively small size of the budget and the depoliticization of production that occurred, while the latter can cite the evidently stimulative effects of state investment and countercyclical fiscal policy, the professionalization of the bureaucracy, the still significant degree of public entrepreneurship, and the recent expansion of the welfare budget as the hallmarks of a developmental state. Whether Taiwan's rapid development occurred because of or in spite of state activities, then, depends upon the specific activity and one's theoretical perspective.

We do not mean to suggest that Taiwan's policy record is without blemishes. Certainly, there is room for further improvement, especially in the political realm. On the other hand, the island's economic, social, and security achievements are quite impressive by any standard. It has made remarkable strides in the people's economic, social, and physical well-being in a span of four decades. Its progress in these regards would be the envy of most of the Third World. Indeed, given the KMT's dismal record on the Mainland, few would have expected such glowing policy performance from a regime that was once totally discredited. Comparing then with now, one may justifiably use the "phoenix factor" to describe the KMT's resurrection on Taiwan.

More importantly for our basic thesis, Taiwan's story of "rags to riches" has involved more or less continuous and concurrent policy progress along a variety of dimensions that are viewed as incompatible by major social science theories. At the same time, however, one can notice some periodicity in the time series data indicating sequences and stages when majors spurts in particular components or aspects of general policy values took place. Thus, in the 1950s, the regime focused on staving off its imminent demise. The pursuit of internal stability and external security received its top priority and was its major achievement. During this period, the successful land reform also laid the foundation for an egalitarian system of income distribution, while facilitating at the same time economic development and state power (see our discussion in Chapter 5). The 1960s and 1970s saw the island's turn to export-led growth and its economic takeoff. These decades also witnessed major improvements in the people's living standards; first in quantitative terms and then in qualitative terms. Finally, in the 1980s, the island underwent a period of major and rapid political liberalization, while undergoing a process of industrial adjustment as a result of its declining comparative advantage in cheap labor and the rising wave of foreign protectionism. This rough chronology would then suggest a policy sequence of focusing first on the pursuit of military security, political stability, and a basic level of education and living standards to dampen discontent, second on the quest for economic growth, third on using the resources generated by growth to improve physical quality of life and to sustain the gains in socioeconomic equality, and finally on the initiation of democratic reform. The ability of the KMT state to pace the speed of socioeconomic change and to engineer this temporal order of progression may in large part account for the Taiwan success story. This attempt to influence the rate and sequence of development (by first emphasizing political stability, then economic growth, and only recently democratization) seems most sensible from the tradeoff perspective.

Chapter 4

Comparative Performances

Policy performance is more than just a matter of how far one has come relative to one's own recent past. It also involves evaluations of how well one has done with the national assets and liabilities dealt by nature and history, and of how fast others are running. Accordingly, if Taiwan's development record (which seems so glowing based on the national statistics described in Chapter 3) is really to be considered a success, the country should have shown more rapid progress than most others and, in particular, done better than nations facing similar conditions.

In this chapter, we put Taiwan's policy performance in a comparative context. The first part of the analysis examines its international ranking on several dimensions of development. For Taiwan's record to be considered out of the ordinary, it should display significant upward mobility over time and/or have consistently high rankings on a variety of developmental indicators. The second part of the chapter uses ordinary least-square regression to establish cross-national patterns of policy performance. Taiwan's achievements are then compared with these international norms in order to assess its policy performance relative to that of other countries. Thus, we follow through our stated intention of examining Taiwan's deviation from some "stylized facts" about policy performance based on aggregate data analysis.

Table 4.1 provides an overview of Taiwan's performance over the last three decades on a variety of developmental dimensions — economic growth, inequality and welfare, social mobilization, external dependency, defense burden, political stability, and democratization. Data are presented for several indicators at three points in time — approximately the middle of the 1960s, the middle of the 1970s, and the middle of the 1980s. The exact time of measurement for each variable is reported in the table's source references and noted in the text if it is out of the ordinary. For each time point, the table includes both the actual value of the indicator for Taiwan (for example, in the mid 1970s, the country had a GNP per capita of $930 and a literacy rate of 87%), and its percentile ranking among all countries for which data on the variable are available (for example, the 49th for GNP per capita and the 70th for literacy rate). The percentile score indicates the percentage of countries having values lower than Taiwan's. For most of these indicators, higher percentiles denote better rankings, but on "bad" characteristics (for example, inflation, income inequality, and political instability), the lower the percentile, the better the policy performance. Parenthetically, Gastil's (1988) ratings of political rights and civil liberties range from 1 (best) to 7 (worst). Therefore, for these two indicators lower percentile figures mean greater liberal democracy.

Taiwan's record on economic growth is certainly exceptional by any standard. For each of the last three decades, the island has ranked in the top 10% of all nations in terms of real (that is, inflation adjusted) growth of GNP, perhaps the most central indicator of economic success. Consequently, it has recorded rapid and sustained economic development. It moved from approximately the 33rd to the 80th percentile between the mid 1960s and the mid 1980s on two central indicators of economic development — GNP per capita and nonagricultural production as a percentage of GDP (gross domestic product). For example, its projected GNP per capita of $7,600 in 1989 had already exceeded New Zealand's figure ($7,460) for the same year (World Bank 1988). The average income of Taiwan's citizens approximately quadrupled over each of these two decades. The island also turned in solid, if less spectacular, performance in its management of investment and inflation during the 1960s and 1970s. In the 1980s, its inflation rate improved to the 15th percentile (low inflation is good), but its investment rate fell to well below the cross-national average.

Taiwan's upward mobility in the international system is underlined by Cline's (1980) ratings of national power in the late 1970s. He first constructed an index of each country's objective resource base, including measures of its population and territory, economic development, and military capability. On this index,

Taiwan ranked 25th among the 77 countries in the sample. Cline then added the more subjective measures of strategic policy and national will to the index in order to create an overall measure of national power. On this overall measure, Taiwan ranked 12th in the world. While this latter ranking may overstate Taiwan's real power, its score on even the objective index was no mean accomplishment for a small island with few natural resources.

The initial reservoir of human capital in Taiwan was much greater than in most developing countries, a factor that could well have made a considerable contribution to its exceptional growth record. As early as 1960 it ranked in approximately the top third of the world on literacy rate and on number of college students per million population, although its rankings on these factors improved only gradually over the next two decades. Taiwan has also featured a high degree of social mobilization. The island's rankings on communications exposure, as indicated by domestic mail and television ownership, was also high compared to its development level.

Taiwan's rapid economic growth, moreover, was accompanied by substantial progress in welfare. In view of the tendency for rapid economic growth to exacerbate income inequality (Kuznets 1955), the island's achievement on an egalitarian system of income distribution is especially remarkable. It ranked in about the top 10% of the world on income equality in both the mid 1970s and the mid 1980s (that is, only 10% of all countries had less income inequality as measured by the ratio of the income share of the richest 20% of the population to that of the poorest 40%). For example, in 1985 the poorest 40% of Taiwan's population took 21.96% of the national income, whereas the richest 20% claimed 37.64%. By comparison, the share of national income going to the bottom 40% of the population was 18.5% and 18.9% for the United Kingdom and Norway respectively, whereas the proportion taken by the richest quintile in these countries was 39.70% and 38.20% (World Bank 1988).

There was also very significant growth in Taiwan's popular standard of living, as indicated by daily calorie consumption, infant mortality, and the physical quality of life (PQLI) index. On average, the island jumped from about the 40th to the 70th percentile between the mid 1960s and the mid 1970s on these indicators, a much higher ranking than its level of GNP per

Table 4.1 Taiwan's rankings on development indicators.

	Mid 1960s Value	Mid 1960s Percentile	Mid 1970s Value	Mid 1970s Percentile	Mid 1980s Value	Mid 1980s Percentile
Economic development						
Real GNP growth	9.2%*	94	10.3%*	93	6.7%*	96
GNP per capita	$153*	28	$930	49	$3143*	73
Nonagricultural product/GDP	67%*	36	89%*	62	93.1%*	73
Investment/GDP	23%*	76	28%*	78	17.6%*	39
Inflation	3.1%*	42	9.8%*	31	4.3%*	16
National power						
Resource index†	—	—	29	68	—	—
Overall index†	—	—	49	84	—	—
Social mobilization						
Literacy rate	75%	62	87%*	70	85%‡	65
College students/ million population	3304*	67	17922*	88	22254*	—
TVs per 1,000 population	5	35	152	73	—	—
Mail per capita	33.0*	52	49.5*	74	68.2*	—
Social welfare						
Income ratio	—	—	1.79	7	1.71*	11
Daily calorie intake	2350	41	2805	69	2874*	62
Infant mortality	31	58	25	27	11.1*	18
PQLI			86	77	90.4	77
External dependency						
Trade/GNP	36.0%*	45	73.7%*	75	67.0%‡	74
Export concentration	.116	22	.153*	35	.141*	—
Partner concentration	.178	55	.217	71	.265*	—
Foreign capital inflow	—	—	8484	67	—	—
Foreign capital stock	—	—	1842	22	—	—
Defense burden						
Military expenditure/ GNP	11.6%	94	7.3%	93	4.6%	74
Military size (1000s)	544	94	504	94	365	82
Military/1,000 population	40.7	100	31.3	96	18.5	90
Political stability						
Protest demonstrations	0	1	4	36	—	—
Political strikes	5	65	3	62	—	—
Riots	11	40	3	28	—	—
Deaths from political violence	4876	89	473	77	—	—
Political executions	318	92	4	63	—	—
Irregular executive transfers	0	1	0	1	—	—
Executive adjustments	11	56	6	25	—	—
Democratization						
Political rights	—	—	5.6	57	5	53
Civil liberties	—	—	4.7	54	4	41
Government sanctions	66	53	38	44	—	—

* Data for Taiwan not in cited source and taken from official government statistics: Council for Economic Planning and Development (1989) for real GNP growth and wholesale price increases, 1960–70, 1970–81 and 1980–5 (p. 2); GNP per capita 1960 and 1985 (p. 29); exchange rate between US $ and NT $ (p. 208); nonagricultural production as a percentage of GDP, 1960, 1978 and 1985 (p. 41); investment as a percentage of GDP, 1965, 1978 and 1985 (p. 43); mail per capita, 1960, 1975 and 1985 (p. 140); college students per million population, 1960, 1975 and 1985 (pp. 4 and 286); income ratio, 1985 (p. 62); daily calorie consumption, 1985, and daily protein consumption, 1974 and 1985 (p. 301); and foreign trade (imports plus exports) as percentage of GDP in 1965 and 1975 (pp. 23 and 208). Ministry of Finance (1988) was the source of data for export concentration index 1975 and 1985 (pp. 63–76); and trade partner concentration index, 1985 (pp. 215–62).

When data for Taiwan is from the sources listed above, the figures may differ slightly from the official Taiwan reports contained in the Appendix tables.

† The index of resource power is based upon a nation's population, territory, economic development, and military capabilities. The index of overall power modifies the resource base for power by estimates of strategy and national will.

‡ Official Taiwanese data show significantly higher values. For literacy, this occurs because Taiwan measures it for population over the age of six, while Sivard (1985) measures it for population over the age of 15; and in Taiwan most illiterates are the elderly. The under-estimation of Taiwan's trade/GNP ratio by the USACDA (1989) is not readily explicable.

Sources: Taylor & Jodice (1983, vol. 1) provided the data on GNP per capita, 1978 (pp. 110–12); nonagricultural production as a percentage of GDP, 1960 and 1978 (pp. 217–19); investment as a percentage of GDP, 1960 and 1978 (pp. 46–8); literacy, 1960 and 1975 (pp. 169–71; 1960 figure for Taiwan comes from raw data not reported in table); televisions per 1000 population, 1965 and 1975 (pp. 181–4); domestic letter mail per capita, 1960 and 1975 (pp. 191–3); college students per million population, 1960 (raw data not included in book) and 1975 (pp. 166–9); income ratio of richest 20% to poorest 40% of population, late 1960s to mid 1970s (pp. 134–5); daily calorie consumption per capita, 1960 and 1977 (pp. 142–4); daily protein consumption, 1965 (raw data not included in book) and 1974 (pp. 146–8); infant mortality rate, 1960 and 1975 (pp. 156–8); trade as a percent of GNP, 1965 and 1975 (pp. 226–8); index of export commodity concentration, 1965 (raw data not included in book) and 1975 (pp. 230–2); index of export partner concentration, 1965 (raw data not included in book) and 1975 (pp. 233–5); average political rights index, 1973–9 (pp. 58–60); and average civil liberties index, 1973–9 (pp. 62–4). Taylor & Jodice (1983, vol. 2) provided the data on protest demonstration, 1948–62 and 1963–77 (pp. 22–5); political strikes, 1948–62 and 1963–77 (pp. 30–2); riots, 1948–62 and 1963–77 (pp. 33–6); deaths from political violence, 1948–62 and 1963–77 (pp. 48–51); political executions, 1948–62 and 1963–77 (pp. 73–5); irregular executive transfers, 1948–62 and 1963–77 (pp. 92–4); unsuccessful irregular executive transfers, 1948–62 and 1963–77 (pp. 89–91); executive adjustments, 1948–62 and 1963–77 (pp. 96–9); and imposition of government sanctions, 1948–62 and 1963–77 (pp. 64–7). The World Bank (1987) provided the data on GNP per capita, 1985, and inflation, 1980–5 (pp. 202–3); real GDP growth, 1980–5 (pp. 204–5); nonagricultural production as a percentage of GDP, 1985 (pp. 206–7); investment as a percentage of GDP, 1985 (pp. 210–11); income ratio of richest 20% to poorest 40% of population, late 1970s to mid 1980s (pp. 252–3); daily calorie consumption per capita, 1985 (pp. 260–1); and infant mortality rate, 1985 (pp. 258–9). The World Bank (1983, pp. 148–9) is the source of the inflation data for 1960–70 and 1970–81. The United Nations (1983) provided the data on real GDP growth for 1960–70 and 1970–9, and GNP per capita for 1960 (pp. 144–50 and 156–62). For 1966 figures of military expenditures as a percentage of GNP, military size (in 1,000s of personnel), and military personnel per 1,000 population, the data source is United States Arms Control and Disarmament Agency (1976, pp. 19–54). The 1975 data for the same variables came from USACDA (1988, pp. 48–84), and those for 1987 from USACDA (1989, pp. 32–68). USACDA (1989, pp. 32–110) also provided the data on trade as a percentage of GNP in 1985. The physical quality of life index (PQLI) for the early 1970s is derived from Morris (1979, pp. 138–45). The 1982 PQLI is based on the data for 1982 literacy, infant mortality, and life expectancy given by Sivard (1985, pp. 38–43). It is computed according to the formula originally provided in Morris (1979). Bornschier & Chase-Dunn (1985, pp. 156–9) gave the index of foreign capital stock, 1967 and index of foreign capital inflows, 1967–73. The rankings of national power are from Cline (1980, pp. 138–9 and 173–4). Gastil (1988, pp. 26–7) was the source for the ratings of political rights and civil liberties for 1987.

capita at that time. The summary PQLI rating rose fairly steadily
through the 1950s and 1960s, and then its rate of progress slowed
down as it moved toward the upper end. By comparison to
Taiwan's PQLI of 86 in the mid 1970s and 90 in the mid 1980s,
the same index stood at 93 and 97 for the United States and
Norway, respectively, in 1979. Thus, in contrast to the so-called
trickle-down theory of economic growth, improvements in
Taiwan's cross-national rankings on social welfare, income
equality, and quality of life tended to accompany and even to
lead the rise in average income during the 1960s and 1970s (thus,
these trends differ somewhat from the trends based on the
comparisons of the island's own over-time accomplishments
noted in Chapter 3). However, in the 1980s, progress in social
mobilization, welfare provision, and income equality showed
signs of stagnation and even regression; it failed to keep pace
with the more rapid advance in average income.

A heavy defense burden and external dependency are two
factors that one or more of the theoretical paradigms discussed in
Chapter 2 posit as constituting substantial drags on economic
growth. Clearly, Taiwan has had one of the highest defense
burdens in the world; and even though this burden decreased
noticeably in the 1980s, the island still ranked in the top 25% of
all countries. In terms of external economic dependency, the
record is more mixed. Taiwan has been moderately dependent
upon foreign capital. For example, on Bornschier & Chase-
Dunn's (1985) indices for MNC (multinational corporation)
penetration in the mid 1970s, the island ranked in the top third of
all developing countries in current inflows of capital but was
relatively low in total capital stock because of the recency of
major MNC investments. The concentration of Taiwan's export
mix has been fairly low since the industrialization drive got off
the ground, but it has ranked in the top quarter of the world in
trade partner concentration and trade/GNP ratio since the mid
1970s. To the extent that Taiwan has had to labor under these
comparative disadvantages of a heavy defense burden and a high
dependency upon foreign trade and selective markets, its rapid
and sustained economic growth seems all the more remarkable.

Political stability and liberal democracy are two other "good
things" that may bear a contradictory relationship to rapid
economic growth. Countries undergoing rapid change are espec-

ially susceptible to unstable or authoritarian politics. The data on political stability are somewhat questionable because they are based on media reports whose coverage varies greatly among nations (for example, the United States and the United Kingdom have the most reported protest demonstrations). Still, it is clear that Taiwan's political stability increased greatly from the first (1948–62) to the second (1963–77) period both in absolute level and relative to the rest of the world. However, this stability was greater in government composition than in regime–society relations. Finally, although there were hundreds of political executions during the 1950s, the large number of deaths from political violence was mainly a result of the unfinished civil war with the Chinese Communists (Clough 1978).

Democratization in Taiwan as measured by the Freedom House's indices of political and civil rights and by the imposition of government sanctions against dissident groups has lagged well behind economic and social development. The island's averages on these indices for 1973–9 lagged behind its ranking for GNP per capita. By 1987, although its democratization ranking had improved slightly in absolute terms as well as relative to the rest of the world, the gap between this ranking and the country's rapidly rising status on economic development widened further. However, the process of political liberalization discussed in Chapter 5 may portend a catching up on this dimension as well.

The data discussed so far reinforce the impression of the "Taiwan miracle," both because of this country's absolute accomplishments and because of the rare condition of "good things going together" so far along most dimensions of development. However, the question still remains as to whether this island's achievements are exceptional. Alternatively, one may ask whether these achievements might be expected on the basis of various conditions that either facilitate or constrain policy performance. To answer these questions, we performed a series of regression analyses in order to establish cross-national norms of policy performance, norms that can in turn be used as a benchmark for determining exceptional accomplishments.

A regression equation describes an empirical relationship, such as the tendency for the richer countries to be more democratic or for economies that invest more to grow faster. It is stated in the following general form:

$$Y = a + b_1X_1 + b_2X_2 \ldots$$

where: Y is the value of the dependent variable
       X is the value of an independent variable
       a is a constant
       b is the constant "slope coefficient" measuring how
          much Y changes when X increases by one unit
          controlling for the effect of the other Xs (if any)
      $\ldots$ indicates that other Xs may be added to the equation

The precise nature of the empirical relationship may take several forms. Here, we are concerned with three possibilities. First, a change in X may produce a linear change in Y. For example, each 10% increment of investment as a share of GNP raises the growth of GNP by an additional 3%. Second, the effects of X may diminish after it reaches a certain value. For example, whereas increases in GNP per capita have a significant positive impact upon the quality of life among the people of the poorest countries, this impact declines precipitously among the most affluent countries. Third, the direction of a relationship may change at different values of the independent variable. For example, countries with very low and very high levels of GNP per capita have relatively equal distributions of income, whereas countries at middle levels of GNP per capita have relatively unequal distributions of income. These three types of relationships are modeled as follows:

Linear: $Y = a + bX$

Diminishing effect: $Y = a + b \text{ LOG } (X)$

Changed direction: $Y = a + b_1X + b_2X^2$

The effect of an independent variable on a dependent variable is indicated by the regression coefficient b. In addition, the coefficient R^2 indicates the percentage of variance in the dependent variable that is statistically explained by the independent variable(s). The higher this percentage, the greater is the empirical fit of the regression equation with the observed data. To guard against unwarranted confidence, tests of statistical significance are undertaken to determine the probability that a relationship as strong as the one observed would occur by random chance. When this probability is low (conventionally 5% or less — the 0.05 level), a relationship is considered statistically significant.

When a relationship is strong enough to establish a cross-national pattern, the policy performance of an individual country can then be assessed by comparing its actual value on Y with the value that would be predicted for it given its values on the Xs. If the actual and predicted values are close, the country conforms to normal national performance. If the actual value is much higher than the predicted value, the country is an "overachiever." Conversely, if the actual value is much lower than the predicted value, the country is an "underachiever."

We focus upon Taiwan's deviations from cross-national norms rather than the exact nature of the norms themselves. The analysis of deviations, or regression residuals, can serve various purposes (Kugler 1983). In our case, we are investigating whether the Taiwan success story can be explained by the customary relationships among developmental variables or whether it truly reflects anomalous policy performance (Chan 1987c, 1987/88). Finding that Taiwan has been an overachiever or underachiever may prove helpful in subsequent attempts to establish more complete theories or valid generalizations about developmental relationships. By calling attention to anomalies or exceptions to the rule, one can help to stimulate the search for scientifically more satisfying explanations (Kuhn 1970) or for lessons to inform more effective policy.

Most of the regression data were taken from Taylor & Jodice (1983). This data set was supplemented by other sources identified in Table 4.2. The form of each regression relationship (linear, diminishing, or changed direction) was reached inductively on the basis of its empirical fit with the observed data.

Our first analytic question is whether Taiwan's rapid growth during the 1960s and 1970s is explicable in terms of its characteristics or whether it represents overachievement. Thus, a series of socioeconomic conditions from the early 1960s were used to predict the average annual growth rate of GNP per capita between 1960 and 1975. In particular, these explanatory factors included four economic conditions (the GNP per capita level, the

Table 4.2 Taiwan's performances regarding the determinants of economic growth.

Equation	R^2	n
Economic context		
1. 1960–75 GNP pc Grth = 2.71 + 0.002† 1960 GNP pc − 0.0000005† (1960 GNP pc)^2	0.11†	103
2. 1960–75 GNP pc Grth = 1.33 + 0.102† 1965 Invst/GDP	0.08†	87
3. 1960–75 GNP pc Grth = 0.0022 + 0.729* Log 1960 Litrcy + 0.0029 Col St/Pop − 0.00000002 (Col St/Pop)^2	0.14†	117
4. 1960–75 GNP pc Grth not affected by 1960–70 Inflation		
External dependency		
1. 1960–75 GNP pc Grth = 3.64 + 0.03† 1965 Trd/GNP − 3.69† 1965 Export Conc − 4.23 1965 Partner Conc	0.18†	102
2. 1960–75 GNP pc Grth = 1.32 + 0.00014* 1967 For Cap Stck + 0.000076† 1967–73 For Cap Inflow	0.19†	81‡
3. 1970s Income Ratio = 3.53 + 0.000197* 1967 For Cap Stck + 0.00054 1967–73 For Cap Inflow	0.12†	52‡
Defense Burden		
1. 1960–75 GNP pc Grth not affected by 1965 Mil Expds/GDP		

* Statistically significant at 0.05 level.
† Statistically significant at 0.01 level.
‡ Analysis conducted for developing countries only.

Taiwan's relative performances

	Taiwan's value	Predicted value	Residual	Standard-ized residual	Percentile
Growth					
GNP per capita	6.3	3.0	3.3	1.40	91
Investment/GDP	6.3	3.0	3.3	1.87	95
Human capital	6.3	3.9	2.4	0.89	88
Market dependency	6.3	3.5	2.8	1.06	93
Foreign capital	6.3	2.2	4.1	2.10	95
Inequality					
Foreign capital	1.8	4.4	−2.6	−1.03	10

Sources: Taylor & Jodice (1983, vol. 1, pp. 110–12) for average annual 1960–75 GNP per capita growth rate. For other variables, see sources listed in Table 4.1.

investment rate, the inflation rate, and human capital formation as indicated by the literacy rate and the ratio of college students to general population), two types of dependency (on foreign capital and foreign markets), and the defense burden. Table 4.2 reports these results. The upper half of the table describes each cross-national norm by presenting the actual regression equation, the R^2, the statistical significance of the regression coefficients, and the number of countries in the sample. The lower half assesses Taiwan's comparative performance. It contains this island's actual growth rate (6.3%), its predicted growth rate on the basis of the independent variable(s), the "residual" or difference between the actual and predicted values, the "standardized" form of this residual (which allows different residuals to be more directly compared), and Taiwan's percentile score on this residual. Taiwan can be considered an overachiever when its percentile is high.

The four developmental perspectives suggest different expectations about the nature of empirical relationships examined in Table 4.2. All would agree that affluence, investment, and human capital should have a positive impact and that inflation and defense burden should have a negative one. However, their interpretations of these effects diverge. Dependency theory argues that the rich countries have a permanent advantage, so that the assumed association between growth and economic characteristics reflects the lasting structural inequalities in the global economy. Therefore, dependence upon foreign trade and capital should slow growth and exacerbate inequality. Developmentalists, in contrast, believe that the relative growth of wealthier nations slows down after their initial economic takeoff, and that countries which industrialize later can benefit from the backlog of their predecessors' experiences. Thus, the latter countries have a chance to catch up, and international status mobility is possible. Developmentalists furthermore argue that the domestic factors (especially a free market) are the primary determinants of economic growth, even though the pursuit of comparative advantage in foreign trade is also relevant. Statists agree with this internal focus but stress the capacity of state policy to promote development. They argue in particular that the state must take an active and leading role in today's developing countries in order to offset their relative weakness as late industrializers. Finally, the tradeoff perspective would stress the opportunity costs of a heavy defense burden and high inflation. Given these various expectations, the relationships reported in Table 4.2 are surprisingly weak. The R^2 values for the 1960 GNP per capita level, the 1965 investment as a percentage of GNP, as well as the 1960 literacy rate and the ratio of college students to total population all range between only 0.08 and 0.14. The 1960–70 inflation rate turned out to be totally unrelated to economic growth. Still, these relationships follow the predictions that countries with more investment and greater human capital tended to grow faster, and that economic growth was highest among the middle-income nations. More importantly, Taiwan's growth rate clearly indicated overachievement in terms of its objective assets and liabilities. Thus, one would have predicted from the regression analysis an annual growth of 3% to 4% on the basis of its prior GNP per capita level, investment rate, and human capital, instead of the much higher 6.3% that actually occurred. Comparatively, Taiwan rated in the top 10% of nations in this overachievement.

The results in Table 4.2 are somewhat mixed with regard to the expectation that economic growth will be depressed by high levels of trade dependence, concentration of export commodities, and concentration of trade partners. Dependencies upon foreign markets and capital have only a slightly larger impact than the internal factors on economic performance. The R^2 is a moderate 0.18. While both export concentration and partner concentration had a negative impact upon economic growth, a high trade/GNP ratio was associated with a better growth record. This empirical pattern tends to validate the distinction made by McGowan & Smith (1978) between market dependence which may not necessarily be harmful (especially in the expanding international markets of the 1960s and early 1970s) and power dependence (tapped by the two concentration scores) as a result of which low bargaining leverage produces economic losses.

Recent reformulations of the dependency perspective tend to focus upon international capital flows rather than international trade flows. They stress the control that MNCs can exercise over the economies of Third World countries and the ill effects that this foreign penetration can produce for the developmental potential of these countries (Biersteker 1978, Bornschier &

Chase-Dunn 1985, Evans 1979). In contrast, developmentalists and statists believe that MNCs can provide an important stimulus for development, at least under certain circumstances (Haggard & Cheng 1987, Moran 1974, Vernon 1977). Unlike the other relationships examined here which apply to all nations, the logic of dependency analysis is that MNC activities are qualitatively different in the developed and developing nations. Thus, the analysis of the impact of foreign capital excludes Western Europe, North America, the USSR and Eastern Europe, and three developed countries in the Pacific region (Australia, Japan, and New Zealand). The independent variables are Bornschier & Chase-Dunn's (1985) indices of foreign capital penetration in terms of 1967 capital stock and 1967–73 capital inflows. In addition to GNP growth rate, foreign capital penetration is also used to predict income inequality since, according to dependency theory, the former should induce or exacerbate the latter.

Dependence on foreign capital has a significant, though moderate, impact upon both economic growth rate and income inequality with R^2s of 0.19 and 0.12 respectively. As predicted, the more dependent countries had higher income inequality, with long-term foreign capital stock rather than recent inflows being the primary determinant. More surprisingly, both measures of foreign penetration are positively associated with GNP growth, although adding other statistical controls shows that the 1967 capital stock actually depressed growth quite significantly (Bornschier & Chase-Dunn 1985). Thus, while these results generally support dependency theory, critics of that approach can find some solace as well.

Turning to the central question of Taiwan's policy performance given its actual dependence upon foreign capital and foreign markets, the island again emerges as a considerable overachiever. For example, a typical country with its degree of market dependence would have grown by 3.5% a year — in comparison to Taiwan's actual historical achievement of 6.3% a year. More spectacularly, the prediction for its growth rate on the basis of foreign capital penetration is 2.2% or about one third of its actual success. The predicted ratio of the income of the richest 20% to the poorest 40% of the population is 4.4, more than double the actual figure of 1.8. Overall, Taiwan ranked in the top 10% of overachievers on all these dimensions (a lower percentile denotes greater income equality).

Finally, defense burden is generally regarded as inimical for growth. The prevailing view argues that a heavy defense burden tends to discourage capital formation, dampen civilian research and development, impair export competitiveness and, in short, stifle economic growth. However, the 1965 ratio of defense spending to GNP had no impact upon the 1960–75 growth rate whatsoever. The failure of defense burden to extract economic costs is a bit surprising, although it is consistent with some studies that have found the relevant empirical relationship to be highly variable across countries and time periods, with military spending in some cases playing only a statistically negligible role in economic performance (Chan 1988a, Rasler & Thompson 1988, Starr *et al.* 1984).

This set of regression results has demonstrated that Taiwan is an overachiever in the sense that its economic growth rate was much higher than for other countries with comparable economic resources or handicaps. It is also appropriate to assess the island's performance in terms of the social and political consequences of this growth. To do this, we use affluence or GNP per capita in the late 1970s or early 1980s to predict several important sociopolitical outcomes — such as income inequality, educational opportunity (as measured by the literacy rate and college students as a percentage of their age group), the standard of living (as measured by the PQLI rating, infant mortality, life expectancy, and calorie consumption), and political repression (as measured by the sum of the Freedom House's indices of political rights and civil liberties). What we are asking, then, is whether Taiwan's "good" performances on these items were simply a function of its outstanding economic growth, or whether they represented a second type of overachievement — in attaining better-than-average sociopolitical outcomes given the island's relative economic resources.

The regression results in Table 4.3 pertain to this question. Two quite distinct empirical patterns emerge. All six quality-of-life and education variables were strongly influenced by GNP per capita during the early 1980s as indicated by R^2s ranging between 0.47 and 0.66. In addition, all these equations show a tendency toward diminishing impact, thus confirming the results from previous studies on cross-national patterns of physical quality of

Table 4.3 Taiwan's performances regarding the consequences of economic growth.

Equation	R^2	n
1. 1970s Inc Ratio = 4.78† − 0.00016 1975 GNP pc − 0.0000000024 (1975 GNP pc)^2	0.16†	66
2. 1982 Col St/Age Group = −31.15† + 6.02 Log 1982 GNP pc	0.53†	114
3. 1982 Lit = −33.97† + 13.75† Log 1982 GNP pc	0.48†	137
4. 1982 Inf Mort = 271.95† − 27.38† Log 1982 GNP pc	0.55†	137
5. 1982 Life Exp = 16.08† + 6.06† Log 1982 GNP pc	0.60†	137
6. 1982 PQLI = −36.52† + 13.87† Log 1982 GNP pc	0.57†	137
7. 1982 Cal/Req = 30.70† + 11.03† Log 1982 GNP pc	0.66†	134
8. 1980 Dictator = 10.69† − 0.00061† 1980 GNP pc + 0.000000015† (1980 GNP pc)^2	0.24†	138

* Statistically significant at 0.05 level.
† Statistically significant at 0.01 level.

Taiwan's relative performances

	Taiwan's value	Predicted value	Residual	Standard-ized residual	Percentile
Income ratio	1.79	4.51	−2.72	−1.11	3
College students	28.0	16.4	11.6	1.44	93
Literacy rate	85.0	74.5	10.5	0.52	70
Infant mortality	9.0	55.9	−46.9	−1.35	5
Life expectancy	72.0	63.9	8.1	1.15	93
PQLI	90.4	72.9	17.5	1.03	90
Calorie/require- ment	121.0	117.7	3.3	0.29	61
Dictatorship	10.0	8.85	1.2	0.33	57

Sources: GNP per capita data for 1975, 1980, and 1982 are from USACDA (1989, pp. 32–68, 1988). For other variables, see sources listed in Table 4.1.

life (Alcock & Kohler 1979, Goldstein 1985, Kohler & Alcock 1976, Russett 1978). For the poorest countries, a small increase in per capita income can contribute significantly to their citizens' physical well-being. On the other hand, for the richest countries even a large increase in per capita income can only make a small marginal contribution to their already very high standards of living. In contrast, income inequality and political repression are only moderately affected by GNP per capita (with R^2s of 0.16 and 0.24 respectively), and tend to be the highest among the middle-income countries.

Taiwan's record on almost all these dimensions has been outstanding, to say the least. The island's excellent record on income inequality is readily apparent as it made the top 3% of overachievers with an income inequality ratio about two and half times smaller than the predicted level. Likewise, it did well on the two indicators of human capital: there were 1.7 times as many college students as predicted, and the literacy rate was about ten points higher than expected. Taiwan's overachievement was just as spectacular for the infant mortality rate (seven times less than the predicted value), average life expectancy (eight more years than predicted), and the overall PQLI index (24% greater than the norm). The island's policy performance on dietary nutrition (calorie intake as a percentage of daily requirement) was somewhat less exceptional, putting it among the top three fifths of all countries examined here. In short, the quality of life on Taiwan has generally exceeded that found in comparable countries, so that the phrase "Taiwan miracle" appears well merited.

We do not intend to suggest that Taiwan has excelled on all dimensions of policy performance, especially since the descriptive data in Table 4.1 strongly imply that political development on the island has lagged well behind economic and social progress. Unfortunately, the comparability of the political stability data among countries is questionable enough (see above) to preclude statistical data analysis. However, the Freedom House's indices of civil and political rights provide a good measure of democratization. Thus, we added the two together for 1978 to provide an index of political repression or dictatorship (freer nations receive lower scores). The overall impact of development level upon dictatorship is moderate ($R^2 = 0.24$); and, as expected, the fast-growing middle-income countries are likely to be the least democratic. In terms of Taiwan's relative performance, it had done less well on this dimension than the cross-national norm, putting it at the 57th percentile for political repression and, thus, an underachiever for democracy. The major political reforms that began in 1986 (see Chapter 5), then, appear overdue.

Thus, Taiwan's policy achievements have not been uniformly

exceptional. Clearly, its political development has fallen behind its social and economic achievements. Nevertheless, the island's experience has proven to be a sufficiently deviant case on a number of normative values to warrant classification as a major overachiever in several important senses. The country has now attained levels of industrialization that put it on the verge of entering the developed world; it has experienced extremely rapid upward mobility in world rankings on most dimensions of economic and social development; given its objective circumstances in the early 1960s, its overall growth during 1960–75 was far greater than would have normally been expected; and its policy performance relative to its development level has been truly exceptional in almost all areas except democratization. Thus, a comparative evaluation of Taiwan reinforces the conclusion that this island represents a relatively unusual case of successful pursuit of most — if not all — important values.

Chapter 5

The (Other) Long March

Taiwan has had one of the most successful economic records in the world during the post-World War II era as it has been transformed from a poor agricultural society to a thriving industrial one seemingly poised to enter the developed world. Political development and liberalization, while lagging well behind the impressive economic growth for most of this period, have been significant; and the democratization reforms of the late 1980s have wrought considerable change in the previously authoritarian political system. Chapter 3 presented descriptive data about Taiwan's generally impressive achievements on a variety of values such as growth, welfare, and equality. Chapter 4, moreover, demonstrated that Taiwan has been an overachiever on most such desiderata in terms of its performances compared to relationships that hold cross-nationally.

The "Taiwan miracle" can be seen as analogous to another "miracle" in recent Chinese history — the Long March of the Chinese Communists in the mid 1930s when they escaped near annihilation and retreated to lick their wounds and wait for more auspicious times. Taiwan in the early 1950s seemed to be an economic and political basketcase whose very survival was dependent upon the security umbrella and large-scale economic aid provided by the United States. Yet, almost imperceptibly at first, the country began its movement toward industrialization, popular welfare, military security, and finally political liberalization. While not as dramatic as the Communists' Long March, this other Long March has proved just as momentous in the long run for the transformation of a society and the creation of a vibrant political economy.

The statistical data presented in the last two chapters describe what happened but do not really provide an explanation for the

Long March on the eastern side of the Taiwan Strait. This chapter, therefore, offers a qualitative account of the political economy of rapid growth in Taiwan, focusing upon the two primary factors of economic strategy and elite composition. It begins by discussing the pre-1949 foundation upon which Taiwan's subsequent transformation was based. It then describes three basic stages in the economic and political development of the island: (1) the first steps of the 1950s, (2) the industrial transition of the 1960s and 1970s, and (3) the mature political economy that seemingly emerged in the 1980s. Finally, the conclusion argues that the core of the Taiwan model rests upon economic flexibility and elite expansion.

As illustrated by the relief map in Figure 5.1, Taiwan is a large island (about 250 miles long and 100 wide at its widest point, about the size of New Jersey) on the Tropic of Cancer 100 miles from Fujian Province of China. Taiwan also controls several smaller islands, but none of them have been important for its developmental history (although Quemoy and Matsu certainly made the headlines in foreign policy). Because the main island is quite mountainous, only about a quarter of the land is arable. Intensive farming over the centuries has gradually depleted the land and necessitated the increasing use of fertilizer. The island is generally poor in natural resources except for some coal deposits which are now not commercially viable (Hsieh 1964). Thus, Taiwan would not appear particularly well situated for an almost stunning industrialization drive.

The island's historical experience before World War II had both positive and negative implications for its developmental potential. After a brief period of Dutch colonial rule in the 17th century, Taiwan was governed by China for the next 200 years. In general, the island remained a frontier of little interest to the central government. The governorship of General Liu Ming-ch'uan from 1884 to 1891 witnessed a brief flurry of reforms as part of China's "self-strengthening movement," but Liu's dynamism departed with him. Four years later, Taiwan was ceded to Japan as a result of the Sino-Japanese War; it remained a Japanese colony for the next 50 years. Before the imposition of Japanese colonialism, therefore, there was little specific economic development strategy. Even the brief period of progress that occurred at the end of the 19th century was primarily the result of

Figure 5.1
Map of Taiwan.

external forces — Beijing's response to imperialist threats against the island (Chu 1963, Gold 1986, Ho 1978, Knapp 1980, Kuo 1973, Myers 1972a, 1972b).

Japan's two major goals regarding its colony were to control the indigenous population and stimulate agricultural output to help feed the metropole. These goals interacted to provide a mixed legacy. Japanese investment in infrastructure, education, and agricultural technology stimulated substantial economic growth, an innovative agricultural sector, some increase in the standard of living, and a population with some rudimentary skills necessary for industrialization. More indirectly, the base for an integrated economy rather than a disarticulated enclave was laid by the creation of a geographically-dispersed light industry linked to agriculture. To facilitate rural extraction, the *sotokufu* (Japanese colonial government) undertook an extensive cadastral survey and altered the traditional system of absentee landlords with its three-tier tenancy. These reforms clarified property rights regarding land, thus facilitating tax collection as well as commercial farming under a capitalist system (Amsden 1979, Wickberg 1981). The exclusion of Taiwan people from significant political and business positions under the *sotokufu* also had a lasting influence. Class formation was stunted, and the state assumed commanding heights in its relation with civil society. As well, the extensive police apparatus, the tax bureaus, and the state enterprises created by the Japanese paved the way for a strong state under the Kuomintang (KMT). Finally, Japan's extraction of resources from the island was quite high compared to other colonial powers, even though Tokyo did export more industries and processing plants to its colonies (Taiwan as well as Korea).

The above combination of positive and negative implications, in turn, can be explained by the nature of the colonial elite and development strategy. The Japanese were willing to promote the development of Taiwan along certain dimensions and up to a certain point because it benefitted the metropole. However, once these limits were reached colonial hegemony prevented the rise of business and administrative skills by the indigenous people and the expansion of industrial activities into areas that might compete with Japan, such as textiles (Barclay 1954, Chang & Myers 1963, Chen 1972, Cumings 1984, Gold 1988a, Ho 1978, Kerr 1974, Kublin 1973, Lee 1971).

This mixed colonial heritage was affected by the way in which the Japanese left Taiwan. United States bombing destroyed over half the island's industrial capacity and infrastructure; the Japanese evacuation took away most of the administrators and businessmen; the Chinese Nationalists (Kuomintang) stripped many of Taiwan's resources to finance their civil war with the Communists; and massive inflation was imported from the Mainland. Thus, prewar production levels were not attained until the 1950s. This dismal economic picture was exacerbated by repressive Nationalist rule that stimulated an uprising on February 28, 1947 which led to massive reprisals and the slaughter of up to 10,000 Taiwanese. While a more conciliatory administration was quickly appointed, a legacy of distrust between the Nationalists and the native Taiwanese had been created (Gold 1986, Kerr 1965, Mendel 1970).

Another mixed legacy certainly derived from the nature of the Nationalist regime which evacuated to Taiwan in 1949. The Nationalists had been a revolutionary party fired by the vision of a new China contained in Sun Yat-sen's "Three Principles of the People" or *San Min Chu I* (nationalism, democracy, and people's livelihood). Yet once in power, the KMT under Chiang Kai-shek did little to improve the economic and social well-being of China; and this failure obviously paved the way for its defeat in the Chinese civil war. While how much of the failure should be blamed upon its own incompetence, corruption, and dictatorial tendencies and how much can be attributed to events beyond its control (that is, foreign invasion, uncontrollable warlords, and the global Great Depression) is a matter of great contentiousness among historians (Bedeski 1981, Botjer 1979, Coble 1980, Crozier 1976, Eastman 1974, 1984, Hoyt 1989, Johnson 1962, Pepper 1978, Seagrave 1985, Sheridan 1975, Sih 1970, Tien 1972), the KMT would hardly appear in 1949 as a good candidate for realizing Taiwan's developmental potential.

The Nationalist government which set up shop in Taipei in 1949 was clearly dominated by its military and security sectors, as reflected by its declared commitment to "Mainland recovery" as the regime's raison d'etre and by the widespread repression directed against opponents of the Mainlander-dominated government. It would not be an exaggeration to describe Taiwan in the early 1950s as a garrison state. In addition to the disaffected majority of native Islanders (who constituted 85% of the population), the Nationalists faced Communist infiltrators from the Mainland and dissident KMT factions. To counter these threats, then, a strong security apparatus was created under Chiang Kai-shek's son, Chiang Ching-kuo, which essentially operated outside the law during the early 1950s and only gradually relaxed its grip over the next two decades. Even in the 1960s, tolerance for political opposition was quite limited as evidenced by the arrests of Chen Lei in 1960 for trying to organize an opposition party and Peng Ming-min in 1964 for writing pamphlets advocating the overthrow of the KMT.

More broadly, martial law was imposed under the Temporary Provisions of the 1947 Constitution. It permitted the suspension of constitutional rights, giving rise to an extensive security apparatus and censorship activities (for example, many opposition political journals were suspended or harassed even in the 1980s). Moreover, the formation of new political parties, in addition to the KMT and two politically inconsequential parties that came to Taiwan from the Mainland, was prohibited, although opposition political figures ran as independent candidates (Clough 1978, Mancall 1964). In addition, ethnicity was clearly intertwined with class differences to the disadvantage of the Islanders (Gates 1981).

Unlike many authoritarian regimes in similar circumstances, however, the KMT did not try to hang onto power simply through repression and terror. Rather, during the 1950s the regime tried to generate some popular support and legitimacy both by promoting economic development and an increased standard of living, and by introducing political reforms that involved creating a new elite segment and allowing very limited mass participation. This change in policy undoubtedly had several causes. Chiang Kai-shek and many KMT leaders realized the need for reform in the wake of their humiliation on the Mainland; Taiwan's patron, the United States, applied significant pressure as well; the regime was no longer hampered by ties to local economic elites and, in fact, probably saw their destruction as politically beneficial; and industrialization was promoted to create defense production.

In the early 1950s, the government took three major economic initiatives which helped to stimulate the first stage of Taiwan's phoenix-like postwar growth. The regime believed that the raging inflation of the late 1940s had been a major reason for its defeat in the Chinese civil war, and moved quickly to stem inflation in Taiwan (which had escalated to a stupendous rate of 30 fold in 1949). Interest rates were increased to realistic levels; the New Taiwan dollar was depreciated; strict regulation was imposed on the financial system to control the growth of money supply and credit; and the government adopted a policy of fiscal conservatism and balanced budgets. These policies proved quite successful in taming inflation as consumer price increases dropped precipitously to 30% in 1951–2 and 10% or less a year by the mid 1950s, creating an environment for renewed economic growth (Kuo 1983, Li 1988, Lundberg 1979).

Perhaps the most momentous changes came from the radical land reform that was implemented in three stages between 1949 and 1953: (1) rent reductions of 25%, (2) sale of public farming land to the peasants, and (3) enforced sale of all farms exceeding approximately 3 hectares. The land reform itself was supplemented by sizeable investments in agriculture and by a large-scale agricultural extension program to stimulate innovation in farming. These various endeavors dovetailed well; and the result was a sustained increase in agricultural production averaging 5% a year in the 1950s and 4.5% a year in the 1960s. Agricultural growth, in turn, created enough surplus to help finance the initial spurt of industrialization. During the 1950s capital outflows from the agricultural sector through such mechanisms as "the hidden rice tax" (that is, the enforced barter of rice for fertilizer at state-dictated prices) equaled approximately one quarter of total farm production. In addition, agricultural exports (which dominated Taiwan's trade throughout the 1950s) increased rapidly enough to keep the trade deficit tolerable. While agriculture was serving as a major source of capital for the rest of the economy, increased production was sufficient to support a rising standard of living among farmers. Moreover, the deconcentration of land holdings produced substantial increases in income equality. Thus, for about two decades Taiwan's agriculture was quite successful, although it became a lagging sector in the 1970s and 1980s (Gallin 1966, Gallin & Gallin 1982, Ho 1978, Huang 1981, Johnson *et al.* 1987, Lee 1971, Thorbecke 1979, Yager 1988, Yang 1970).

The land reform implemented during 1949–53 also had

profound and lasting political implications. It defused the threat of rural discontent stemming from the thirst for land by the poor peasants, who were the main supporters of the KMT's Communist rivals on the Mainland. At the same time, land reform undermined the social and political position of the indigenous landlord class, which could also have posed a challenge to the transplanted KMT regime. The KMT regime used stock certificates of the confiscated Japanese properties to pay the landlords for the land sold to the poor peasants at nominal prices. This step encouraged the island's gentry class to venture into modest manufacturing activities (for example, cement and paper), which marked the inception of Taiwan's industrialization. Thus, the land reform had the far-reaching effect of eventually converting the traditional landowners into modern industrialists.

In the industrial realm, Taiwan made a conscious effort to promote what is called "import substitution" for light industrial products — that is, to replace previously foreign manufactures with domestic production by means of high tariffs, restrictive quotas, and manipulated exchange rates to discourage imports. This import substitution proved quite successful at least in the short run. Real industrial growth, while quite cyclical, averaged over 10% a year during the 1950s; the ratio of imports to total production in manufactured goods fell drastically; and Taiwan expanded its industrial base from food processing to other light industries (Lin 1973, Ranis 1979).

In addition to simply promoting economic growth, the regime reached out toward the population in several other significant ways. First, universal education through the sixth grade was introduced. It had several salutary results. The literate and increasingly well-educated population both formed a reservoir of human capital for future development and permitted individuals to experience rapid upward socioeconomic mobility. Furthermore, the National Language Movement of using Mandarin as the language of instruction helped to promote social integration between Mainlanders and Islanders, although the political indoctrination of the system was certainly questioned (Appleton 1976, Chen 1981, Huang 1984, Wei 1973).

Second, the regime moved rapidly to create a system of elections for local governments and the Provincial Assembly, while leaving the "national" bodies under the control of officials elected on the Mainland in the late 1940s. To be sure, the KMT dominated these elections, and the prohibition against forming an opposition party certainly violated the basic tenets of democracy. Still, electoral competition among competing KMT factions was quite intense in many localities, and "independents" were able to win important elections (for example, they won the mayorships in three of the five largest cities in 1964). Thus, local politicians were forced to become more responsive to their constituencies, and a considerable Taiwanization of the lower levels of the party and government occurred because Mainlanders had a hard time winning at the polls (Copper with Chen 1984, Riggs 1972, Tai 1970).

Third, the attempt to gain popular support through promoting economic development entailed a significant broadening of the elite segments included in the regime. The push for rapid growth necessitated bringing technocrats and administrators, many of whom had been educated at leading U.S. universities, into the top levels of government (Ho 1987, Winckler 1988).

Thus, during the 1950s the government implemented a coherent economic development strategy based upon controlling inflation, stimulating agricultural productivity, and promoting light industries through import substitution. In the political and social realms, authoritarian controls were supplemented by limited liberalization in local politics; and the agricultural reform and expanded educational opportunities provided routes for upward mobility for a significant proportion of the population. These economic and political changes were buttressed finally by the fact that the leadership had been expanded from a primarily military regime to include technocrats who had a vested interest in preserving and broadening these liberalization efforts.

However, by the late 1950s, the initial surge of import substitution began to subside as the domestic market became saturated with locally produced goods and as rising imports of capital goods and industrial raw materials increased the trade deficit. Consequently, overall growth began to decline (from 9% in the early 1950s to 6.5% in the late 1950s), while inflation and unemployment began to increase. Moreover, Taiwan had become highly dependent on U.S. aid, especially for balancing its budget, providing infrastructure and agricultural investment, and paying for the trade deficit. For example, because of this aid the investment rate averaged 15% of GNP during the 1950s, while the savings rate was only 9% (Jacoby 1966).

As the 1950s ended, therefore, Taiwan was clearly facing a threat to its continued economic development, forcing a choice among economic strategies. The government could continue as before and hope that the situation would not get out of hand; it could attempt to move to second-stage import substitution in heavy industry; or it could adopt an export-oriented strategy in the hope that its light industry based on low-cost labor would be competitive on international markets. The third strategy was ultimately selected, but it was far from an easy or obvious choice. Few other developing countries had taken this path in the recent past; many leaders doubted that Taiwan could sell its manufactured products abroad; and this strategy challenged the interests of the military sector, which wanted to develop defense industries, and middle-level bureaucrats, who were forced to yield much of their direct power over the economy.

Still, a coalition of technocrats and U.S. advisors convinced Chiang Kai-shek of the necessity for radical reform. A comprehensive set of measures was rapidly implemented to encourage exports and investment. Exchange rates were made more realistic; cheap credit and rebates on imported components and raw materials were made available to exporters; export-processing zones were established; the protectionist trade system was liberalized since most export industries relied on imports; tax reform and decreased regulation encouraged domestic entrepreneurship; and foreign investment was solicited (Kuo *et al.* 1981, Li 1988, Lin 1973, Scott 1979).

This new economic strategy proved to be phenomenally successful, probably far more so than even its ardent advocates had anticipated. Real GNP growth accelerated to a very high average of 11% annually during 1963–73. Furthermore, this rapid growth resulted from a fundamental industrial transformation of the island's economy. For example, between 1958 and 1973, manufacturing's share of net domestic product more than doubled from 16% to 36%, while that of agriculture suffered a corresponding decline from 31% to 14% (Ho 1978, Lin 1973, Ranis 1979, Wu 1987).

The export-led nature of this economic growth and structural transformation is also very clear. Exports surged by an average of

15% a year even in inflation-adjusted terms for most of the 1960s; and then skyrocketed by 30% annually for 1969–73. Consequently, their share in gross domestic product almost quadrupled from 11% in 1962 to 42% in 1973, indicating that the economy had become extremely export-oriented. Taiwan's export mix became overwhelmingly industrial in composition (industrial goods rose from 14% to 85% of total exports between 1958 and 1973), proving that its manufactured products were internationally competitive. Most of these exports went to developed countries, with the U.S. market being by far the largest (rising from 6% in 1958 to 37% of Taiwan's total exports in 1973). The export surge also caused a dramatic change in the country's balance of trade as the large deficits of the late 1950s and early 1960s were turned into surpluses by the early 1970s (Kuo & Fei 1985, Scott 1979).

The nature of Taiwan's industry changed fundamentally as well. First, the country began to produce a wider range of products that became increasingly sophisticated over time as the leading domestic production and export sectors advanced from food processing to textiles to electronics assembly and chemicals. Thus, even though labor-intensive industries still dominated the economy, a gradual upgrading occurred in the utilization of capital and technology (Ho 1978, Kuo & Fei 1985, Schive 1987). Second, Taiwan's industrial structure has been marked by a much greater role for small and medium family-based enterprises than elsewhere in Asia. It spawned complex subcontracting relationships among small entrepreneurs, reflecting what has recently been called "Confucian capitalism." This structure of production allowed businessmen to respond very quickly to market demand and reduced problems of excess capacity, thus promoting internal competitiveness and external flexibility. The strong role of small business, in addition, helped promote the geographic dispersion of industry in Taiwan that in turn facilitated socioeconomic equality by enabling underemployed agricultural workers to seek part-time factory work (Fei 1986, Greenhalgh 1984, 1988a, Ho 1979, Hsiao 1988, Lam 1988, 1990, Li 1986, Sutter 1988).

Third, there was both stability and change in the role of the state in Taiwan's economy. On the one hand, the industrialization drive of the 1960s was associated with a privatization and

Taiwanization of the business elites. Before 1960, state corporations mostly based on confiscated Japanese assets accounted for
about half of industrial production, and Mainlanders dominated
their management. In contrast, Islander entrepreneurs accounted
for most of the business expansion of the 1960s, so that the
private sector accounted for over 80% of industrial production in
the early 1970s (Fei 1989, Gold 1986). In other areas, though,
state activity remained fairly constant. The state continued to set
macroeconomic strategy and the public sector as reflected by
government budgets consumed just over one fifth of GNP.
Finally, the defense burden remained quite heavy in the face of
the threat from across the Taiwan Strait (Chan 1988a, Clough
1978).

   A principal reason for Taiwan's rapid industrial transformation
was the country's extremely strong investment record. Savings as
a proportion of GNP, which had averaged about 9% in the 1950s,
skyrocketed from 12% in 1962 to 22% in 1968 to 35% in 1973 —
one of the highest in the world. This great jump in the savings
rate, in turn, permitted the investment rate to rise from 18% of
GNP in the early 1960s to 25% over the rest of the decade,
despite the termination of U.S. aid which had financed over 40%
of the island's investment during the import-substitution period.
Taiwan's remarkable record for savings and investment derived
from a variety of factors — the popularity of opening small
businesses, a cultural emphasis on family advancement, the very
low social-security safety net, limited consumer credit, the
widespread use of bonus payments, policy incentives regarding
tax and interest rates, and a loosening of controls over loans to
private business (Myers 1984).

   These increased domestic savings were augmented by Taiwan's
successful measures to stimulate and manage foreign investment.
Private foreign investment, which accounted for less than 1% of
total investment during the 1950s, rose to just over 4% during
1960–7 and to 9% at the beginning of the 1970s. Multinational
corporations (MNCs) are generally credited with a key role in
stimulating the export drive, unlike the experience of many other
developing nations where foreign capital simply displaces domestic
businessmen. This resulted from the regime's explicit attempts to
harness MNCs to the island's developmental objectives. Thus,
the government channeled foreign investment into the dynamic

export sector, integrated MNCs into the overall economy with domestic-content legislation, and maintained state monopolies in those heavy industries usually dominated by foreigners (Gold 1988b, Haggard & Cheng 1987, Huang 1989, Ranis & Schive 1985 but see Schive 1990 for a primarily nonstatist interpretation of foreign capital's contribution to Taiwan's development).

Finally, rapid economic growth in Taiwan had a profound effect on improving living standards and reducing socioeconomic inequality for the population at large. The ratio of the income of the richest fifth of the population to the poorest fifth fell rapidly during the 1950s because of the land reform program and then declined further from 5.33 in 1964 to 4.49 in 1972 (a level approximating that of most developed countries) as the rapid growth of labor-intensive industries stimulated real wage increases of over 5% a year during this period (Fei *et al.* 1979, Greenhalgh 1988b). Consequently, many indicators of the standard of living (see Chapter 3) showed substantial improvement. Taiwan, then, had instituted a takeoff toward becoming a middle-class society (Galenson 1979b, Li 1984, Wei 1973).

This dramatic economic expansion was brought to a sudden halt by the oil crisis of 1973–4 which disrupted the global economy in general and hit Taiwan hard in particular. The inflationary surge was quickly transferred to the domestic economy as consumer prices jumped by nearly 50% in 1974, and Taiwan's trade performance plummeted. Real exports, which had grown by 30% a year during 1970–3, actually fell by 6% a year in 1974–5, creating a new deficit in the country's balance of trade. As a result, in 1974 real GNP growth slumped to 1.1%, and real industrial production fell by 4.5%. Savings also fell by 9% a year in 1974–5 in inflation-adjusted terms, a situation that was further exacerbated by a precipitous decline in foreign investment from 8% to 2.5% of total investment. Not surprisingly, rapidly deteriorating economic performance hurt the popular standard of living as well. Real wages in manufacturing grew by a minuscule 1% in 1973 and then fell sharply by 9% the next year. More broadly, while there were only slight dips in many indicators of the absolute standard of living, their previous upward trend was clearly interrupted.

Taiwan responded to this crisis of "stagflation" with an innovative combination of deflationary policies to tame inflation and state investment to take up the slack of decreased economic activities. Deflationary policies included a sharp increase in interest rates, cutbacks in government spending from 23% to 18% of GNP between 1973 and 1974 that created a budget balance of 22% of total revenues, and a radical drop in the expansion of money supply from 50% in 1973 to 10.5% in 1974. Together these policies proved highly effective in dampening inflation as the growth rate of consumer prices dropped to 5% in 1975 and 2.5% in 1976. In addition to applying the brake of a conservative fiscal policy, however, the regime also pushed down the accelerator of state investment to reinvigorate the economy in the face of a devastated private sector as the state provided 58% of total investment in 1975.

As a result of Taiwan's decisive policy initiatives, its economy came out of the inflationary crisis sooner than most others, so that the relative prices of its exports fell considerably on world markets. This increased export competitiveness finally bore fruit in 1976 when real exports shot up by 46% and ushered in a new period of rapid growth in the late 1970s. During 1976–8, real GNP growth averaged 13%, real industrial production 20%, real savings 23%, and real manufacturing wages 11%. With this renewed economic dynamism, the private sector reasserted its primacy in leading economic growth. The second oil crisis in 1979–80 again derailed Taiwan's double-digit growth, and the government responded with the same policy mix as before. Both the economic impact of escalating energy prices and the policy response were milder than in the mid 1970s, though, as inflation was tamed fairly easily (Clark 1989a, Kuo 1983).

Politically, significant changes in the authoritarian style of rule began to evolve in the 1970s. On the one hand, the island's successful modernization and creation of an Islander business community stimulated pressure for increased popular participation and government responsiveness. On the other hand, when Chiang Ching-kuo became premier in 1972, he instituted a more liberal program that included bringing younger and more educated officials into top leadership positions, gradually increasing the power granted to Islanders in the government and party, cracking down on regime corruption, and forcing the government to be more open. These two trends were also reinforced by popular concerns over the country's increasing loss of international status such as its expulsion from the United Nations in 1971 and derecognition by the United States in 1979. The latter events induced a sense of urgency for the regime to take effective action and helped bring Islanders and Mainlanders together in a common fear of impending disaster (Copper 1988, Durdin 1975, Lerman 1977, 1978).

These intersecting trends from above and below resulted in the gradual liberalization of Taiwan's politics over the 1970s and the first half of the 1980s in terms of increasing the scope of free speech and electoral competition and reducing the power of conservatives within the regime. This liberalization was generally cumulative, although setbacks periodically occurred (for example, a conservative comeback in the KMT following an embarrassing showing at the polls in 1977, a crackdown on dissidents following the Kaohsiung demonstrations in 1979, and the fairly conservative administration of Premier Yu Kuo-hwa in the mid 1980s). A very important component of this liberalization was that the position of the opposition began to improve. While the formation of an opposition party was still illegal, an informal association of opposition politicians called the *tangwai* (literally, "outside the party") began to grow after the late 1970s and used the more liberal atmosphere of the 1980s to stretch the limits of political discourse. It used three primary techniques: (a) publishing dissident journals that proved fairly successful in avoiding the regime's attempts at censorship (for example, by changing their names when closed down), (b) conducting vigorous and highly critical election campaigns, and (c) using legislative interpellation sessions to ask embarrassing questions (C. Cheng 1989, Chou & Nathan 1987, Copper 1988, Domes 1981, Lu 1985, Winckler 1981, 1984).

The transition to industrialization that occurred in Taiwan over the two decades between the early 1960s and early 1980s, therefore, was based on a sea-change reorientation in economic strategy that was intertwined with considerable change in regime and elite composition. The state imposed a fundamental struc-tural shift in the island's economy that was somewhat ironically premised upon what John Fei (1989) has called a "de-politicization" of the economy. Taiwan's elite structure was also broadened quite significantly. First, as a consequence of the privatization of the economy, a dual elite structure had evolved by the early

1970s in which Mainlanders dominated the top political and Islanders the top economic positions, with the latter acting as a link between the regime and general populace. Second, liberal elements within the regime expanded both because of Chiang Ching-kuo's recruitment policies and because of the growing role of elections. Finally, an increasingly articulate opposition subjected the government to competition in the marketplace of ideas. These new elites both contributed vital skills and resources to the island's economic and political development and helped restrain opponents of the ongoing changes (Cole 1967, Gold 1986, Ho 1987, Moody 1988, Winckler 1988).

Taiwan's economic strategy and gradual political liberalization between the early 1950s and early 1980s probably flowed to a significant extent from the KMT's broad doctrine of Dr. Sun Yat-sen's "Three Principles of the People" (*San Min Chu I*). In the political realm, Sun advocated the idea of tutelary democracy in which a vanguard party would gradually educate the people so that they could finally exercise full self-government. In the economic sphere, Sunist doctrine believed that the state should play a leading role in promoting economic growth and change, controlling the business sector (especially foreign capital) to ensure its contribution to national development, and stimulating a rising standard of living and equitable distribution of income. The state, therefore, should play a powerful role in directing society, but one that should be devoted to the national welfare and that should become more "inhibited" and "accommodating" over time (D. Chang 1989, C. Cheng 1989, Gregor with Chang & Zimmerman 1981, Metzger 1987, Myers 1987). This is not to say that *San Min Chu I* provided an operational guideline for Taiwan's policies. However, it certainly did constitute a broad guidepost and legitimating motif for the considerable economic and political reforms which the regime implemented on Taiwan (and which might be considered quite surprising, given the record of the interwar Republic).

The 1980s witnessed the creation of what appears to be a mature political economy. A renewed growth spurt brought further industrial transformation and prosperity; major political reforms pushed the country well along the road toward democratization; and Taiwan's growing economic clout even translated itself into enhanced international status. Thus, while several significant threats to the island's success were easy to discern, Taiwan had found a "place in the sun" where, for the moment at least, it seemed to have safely transversed between Scylla and Charybdis into the calmer waters of a viable industrialized society.

The economic recovery of the United States in 1983 provided an outlet for another export drive. Real exports leaped by 14% in 1983 and 19% in 1984, stagnated in 1985, and then jumped again by 25% a year during 1986–7. The centrality of the U.S. market is indicated by the fact that its share of Taiwan's exports jumped from 34% in 1980 to 48% during 1984–6. The island's trade surplus burgeoned as well to the $15–$20 billion a year range in the late 1980s, and by 1988 Taiwan had the second largest foreign reserves in the world of approximately $79 billion. These latter figures, however, were not entirely positive since they helped to stimulate trade disputes with the United States that threatened Taiwan's primary export market. Rapid trade expansion, in turn, revved up the economy which grew by 9% a year during 1983–4, 5% in the "mini-recession" year of 1985, 11% during 1986–7, and 7% during 1988–9. Real industrial growth was somewhat higher, indicating the increasingly industrial nature of the island's economy. GNP per capita rose rapidly from $1,600 in 1978 to $3,000 in 1984 to $6,000 in 1988 and $7,600 (estimated) in 1989, although much of this growth after 1986 was caused by the 40% appreciation of the New Taiwan dollar. Thus, Taiwan appeared on the verge of entering the developed world (Copper 1988, Seymour 1989, Simon 1986).

This new growth period involved an evolution away from labor-intensive industries as Taiwan was gradually pricing itself out of the low-cost labor niche in the international division of labor (Wu 1985). In a structural sense, the emerging industries were diverse. For example, steel was based on a state corporation; petrochemicals involved a complex triple alliance among state enterprises, MNCs, and domestic private businesses; and much of the high-tech industry was centered on relatively small, innovative firms. This restructuring of Taiwan's economy possesses both advantages and dangers. On the one hand, it represents industrial upgrading and a positive response to international competition from other developing countries. On the other, it threatens the position of small enterprises which have contributed so much to the island's economic flexibility and success in the past (Chu 1989, Gold 1986, Greenhalgh 1988a, Ho 1980, Lam 1988, Liang & Liang 1988).

The standard of living continued to improve. Between 1978 and the mid 1980s, for example, the number of health personnel per capita and real spending per primary student approximately doubled, and the proportion of household spending devoted to food fell by one fifth. On the other hand, income inequality increased significantly due to the decline of the agricultural sector and the reorientation away from labor-intensive production. Many workers were unable to sustain the earlier rate of improvement in their socioeconomic conditions. Still, substantial socioeconomic mobility continued even for the poorest segments of society, although significant disagreement exists over how far social development has really proceeded (Chu & Tsaur 1984, Gates 1979, 1987, Hsiao 1989, 1990, Li 1984, Shack 1989, Tsai 1987, 1988, Wang 1981).

The cumulative movement toward political liberalization over the 1970s and early 1980s reached a more dramatic crescendo during 1986–9. The first step was the open formation of an opposition party. In early 1986, President Chiang Ching-kuo formed a special KMT Task Force to propose political reforms and directed the KMT to open negotiations with the *tangwai*. These negotiations broke down, and in September the opposition proclaimed the formation of the Democratic Progressive Party (DPP). Chiang then declared that martial law would be ended and that new parties could be formed as long as they supported the Constitution and renounced Communism and Taiwan independence. The December elections, therefore, marked the first time that the KMT faced an actual opposition party. The ruling party won handily with its normal 70% of the vote, but both the KMT and DPP seemed pleased with the outcome (Chou & Nathan 1987, Copper 1988, Myers 1987, Sutter 1988, Zeigler 1988).

The next step was the formal abolition of martial law and the Emergency Decree that had been applied to Taiwan ever since the seat of government had been moved to Taipei. After some evident lobbying of KMT conservatives by Chiang, the Emergency Decree was formally repealed in July 1987 and replaced by a National Security Act. While the abolition of martial law had little direct impact on Taiwan's politics, it marked a symbolic break with the past and opened the way for many of the recent reforms to be institutionalized (for example, the legalization of new political parties). It also helped create a more open and even raucous style of politics. Street demonstrations that had been unthinkable before 1986 became a common occurrence, and debates in the Legislative Yuan became quite strident with the regular breaking of microphones (Chira 1988, Gold 1989, Seymour 1988). Furthermore, the balance of power within the KMT appeared to be moving in a more liberal direction. Chiang Ching-kuo's sudden death in January 1988 threw this trend into some question, but the new president, Lee Teng-hui (who is an Islander), appeared to be consolidating power, moving younger and more liberal leaders into top positions, and pushing through innovative domestic and foreign policies (Chang 1986, T. Cheng 1989, 1990, Copper 1990, Domes 1989, Gold 1989, Harrison 1988, Hsiao 1989, Lu 1989, Seymour 1989, Tien 1989, Weng 1988).

The competition in the legislative elections in December 1989 and the election of president in March 1990 raised some questions about the direction of the prevailing political winds. In the legislative elections for the national and provincial assemblies and the two major city councils, the KMT saw its vote drop about ten percentage points (from about 68% to 58%). This was interpreted as a significant loss which was generally seen as strengthening the hands of reformists within the dominant party. However, in the factional infighting surrounding the presidential election, Lee Teng-hui chose conservative Mainlanders connected with the military and security apparatus to be his new premier and vice president, ostensibly for the goals of restoring law and order, enhancing national security, and discouraging the "Taiwan independence" movement. Presumably, the real reason was that the president is chosen by an electoral college which is still dominated by delegates elected in 1947 from Mainland constituencies. This raised many fears on Taiwan that political liberalization would be reversed (Dreyer 1990, Jiang 1990, Ling & Myers 1990, McGregor 1990).

Nevertheless, following the election, President Lee reiterated his commitment to continuing political reform, and pledged to revoke the Temporary Provisions within two years (Wu 1990).

The cancellation of the Temporary Provisions would be extremely significant, because it would end the domination of the national legislature (Legislative Yuan) and electoral college for the president (National Assembly) by Mainlander senior legislators elected to their seats in the late 1940s — arguably the principal barrier to the full realization of democracy in Taiwan. In 1990, Taiwan's Supreme Court (the Judicial Yuan) ruled that all senior legislators must retire by the end of 1991; and at the end of 1990 a plan was announced to elect a new National Assembly in 1992 that would revise the 1947 Constitution. In addition, the new premier, Hau Pei-tsun, has seemingly overcome initial fears of his military background and has become quite popular for his decisive leadership style (Chen & Wu 1990, *Free China Journal* 1990). Thus, while the KMT and DPP have yet to fully accept each other's legitimacy, major changes in the basic assumptions about how government affairs should be conducted have occurred. These changes seem to be inexorably pushing Taiwan toward greater political liberalization (T. Cheng 1989, Cheng & Haggard 1991, Metzger 1987, Myers 1987).

Undeniably, this process toward greater democratization has been accompanied by a more contentious and even confrontational style of politics. As already mentioned, mass street demonstrations and raucous parliamentary debates, led by the DPP but also involving escalating infighting among KMT factions, have increasingly become a common sight recently. There have been frequent episodes of physical violence among rival political factions, and between demonstrators and the police. At the same time, as part of the inevitable modernization process, the social order previously maintained by an authoritarian state has come under increasing strain as evidenced by the rising incidence of violent crimes, teenage gangs, drug addiction, and teenage pregnancy. Thus, political and social liberalization has arguably led to some decline in social tranquility and political stability. It may presage a period of greater uncertainty and turbulence ahead as the island seeks to make the necessary political and social adjustments.

Taiwan has made considerable progress in solidifying its international status which had suffered so grievously during the 1970s (Feldman *et al.* 1988). Despite the loss of diplomatic recognition by the United States, informal relations between

Taipei and Washington became institutionalized as each country set up a quasi-official representative in the other. Taiwan also used commercial offices to unofficially upgrade its relations with many important countries such as Canada, France, the United Kingdom, West Germany and, more recently, even the Soviet Union. It has also made some progress toward regaining its position in leading international organizations. Relations with China even improved in the late 1980s as Taiwan's willingness to permit increased contacts unleashed a "China fever" of tourism and indirect trade and investment that was only slightly disrupted by the Tiananmen Square massacre in China (Ignatius 1990, Tseng 1990b, Wu 1989). In short, the policy of "flexible diplomacy" initiated by Lee Teng-hui after he assumed the presidency in 1988 seems to be bearing considerable fruit (Copper 1990, Gold 1987, Hickey 1988, Kau 1988, Lee 1988, Seymour 1988, 1989, Shaw 1985, Wang 1990, Weng 1984).

This is not to say that the political and economic picture on Taiwan is entirely rosy. In fact both external and internal threats to the island's stability and prosperity are discernible. Externally, China's retreat to orthodoxy and hostility obviously created uncertainty and threat for Taiwan, especially in view of China's clear concern over Taiwan's growing stature in the world community (Chen & Wu 1989, Murray 1990). Moreover, while the direct fallout from Tiananmen Square seems to have faded away in Taiwan's relations with China, this relationship remains potentially unstable because it intimately involves the legitimacy claims of the two governments (Clark & Chan 1990a). In addition, Taiwan's very economic success brought trade frictions with its primary patron and market, the United States (Chu 1988, Haggard & Cheng 1989, Moon 1989b, Seymour 1989). While the crisis in trade relations seemed to be considerably ameliorated at the beginning of the 1990s (Clark 1991, Ho 1990), the threat of growing protectionism in international markets is certainly a severe one for such an export-dependent economy as Taiwan's. At the same time, other newly industrializing countries (for example, Thailand, the Philippines, and even China) are catching up and threatening to erode the island's export competitiveness.

Internally, rapid growth threatens to unleash inflation, especially in the housing market (Tseng 1990a); and the clearly antiquated financial system is coming under increasing stress (Fields 1989, Seymour 1988, 1989, Wade 1985, Wu 1985). The volatile stock market fluctuated wildly, first losing about 85% of its peak value in the first three quarters of 1990 and then rebounding strongly in the last quarter. The economy, however, is still relatively robust; it has been projected to expand by 5% for the year (Liu 1990, Wu 1990).

In the political realm, the generally successful democratic transition so far could be negated by a conservative reaction, especially in the face of a rising security threat from across the Taiwan Strait. Moreover, the very success of democratization may make it hard for the government to take the decisive economic actions that it did in the past for fear that they will be reversed "in the streets." Finally, the decline of KMT power and the introduction of partisan politics have led to greater political confrontation and turbulence. They presage perhaps more political instability in the future.

Despite these caveats, though, Taiwan's Long March must be rated as quite successful thus far. Rapid growth has been sustained for four decades; structural transformation toward a fully developed economy continues apace; the population has clearly benefitted from the "Taiwan miracle" in terms of welfare and equality; the island currently appears stable and secure; the state has played a positive role in development; and external dependencies have been managed so as to contribute to the development project. In short, a qualitative evaluation of Taiwan's developmental history certainly indicates that the country has evaded almost all of the threats that can be raised during the processes of rapid socioeconomic change (Hsiung 1981).

In sum, Taiwan has experienced very rapid growth and industrial transformation over the last four decades. While it is facing some very real challenges at present, it seems set to enter the developed world as the 21st century opens. This economic success represents a combination of both state leadership and private entrepreneurial initiatives that has created an extremely flexible economy along the Japanese model (Friedman 1988). The island's economy has been thus far able to undertake continuous restructuring in order to retain its competitiveness (Myers 1984). This economic flexibility, in turn, has been promoted by periodic regime changes which bring into power new elements (for example, economic technocrats, Islander businessmen, elected politicians, and now even some opposition intellectuals). These new elite elements are not wedded to the economic or political status quo, and possess at the same time the necessary aptitude for meeting the evolving economic and political challenges. A key component of the Taiwan story, therefore, has been the willingness of dominant groups to forego maximizing their own power and material positions in order to promote national development, thereby creating a more differentiated elite with a much broader sharing of political power and economic resources.

Chapter 6
The Taiwan Puzzle

We have tried to demonstrate in the previous chapters that Taiwan offers an interesting developmental case that departs in a number of ways from customary theoretical expectations and established "stylized facts." In this chapter, we juxtapose this case against four major perspectives on the political economy of development — the developmentalist, dependency, tradeoff, and statist paradigms. Additionally, a summary time series analysis of the major influences upon Taiwan's economic growth is presented. We do not suppose that the experience of one country can necessarily validate or invalidate any one of these scholarly traditions. Nevertheless, we hope to use Taiwan's experience to assess the analytic viability and scope of some of the postulates and assumptions of these paradigms (Clark 1987).

As described in Chapter 2, the initial developmental paradigm argued that free market economics and cultural modernization constituted a universal prescription for industrial transformation. Dependency theory soon presented a direct challenge to this perspective with its basic contention that the global capitalist order perpetuated underdevelopment throughout the Third World. More recently, the dialogue of the deaf between these two conflicting models has been joined by two other approaches whose less sweeping conclusions offer some possibility of bridging the chasm between developmentalism and *dependencia*. The tradeoff model argues that several of the central goals of development are mutually incompatible, while the statist perspective contends that a strong and activist government can overcome many of the impediments to economic and social progress.

Taiwan's rapid development can be viewed as paradoxical because it is at variance with the expectations of all four theoretical traditions. On the one hand, Taiwan's developmental history clearly contradicts important aspects of all these traditions; on the other, each theory contains major insights about its political economy (Chan & Clark 1991, Chan 1990b, Clark 1987, 1989b, Winckler & Greenhalgh 1988). Juxtaposing this island's experience against these theories, then, might not only point to their overly restrictive postulates but also suggest how to integrate their insights.

Taiwan's inconsistency with theoretical predictions is perhaps most obvious for dependency theory which would predict continued subordination and stagnation for a country, like Taiwan, whose economy was dominated by primary activities and which was highly dependent upon a capitalist patron (the United States) both economically and militarily. The island's rapid upward mobility in the world system between the 1960s and the 1980s (described in Chapter 4) certainly shows that the structural conditions emphasized by dependency theorists do not necessarily constitute an unalterable system that locks Third World countries into a permanent position of inferiority. Upward mobility and role graduation are possible even in a hierarchical world system dominated by the core countries.

Specifically, comparative advantage certainly did not lock Taiwan into a permanent position of exporting primary products and importing manufactures with much higher value added in what Galtung (1971) has called "vertical trade." In the Pacific area, the United States, Canada, Australia, and New Zealand have come to depend on the export of agricultural and mineral products — they are the ones pressuring the Asian NICs (as well as Japan) to import more beef, tobacco, fruits, grain, lumber, and iron ore. On the other hand, the Asian NICs have graduated from being producers of cheap toys and fabrics to become exporters of expensive home appliances, electronic goods, and automobiles. Orthodox dependency theorists would hardly expect this role reversal on the part of Taiwan as well as its other Asian counterparts (South Korea, Singapore, Hong Kong) over just a couple of decades.

Thus, while a few theorists interpret Taiwan's development from a dependency perspective (Crane 1982, Hamilton 1983), the usual conclusion is that this country's experience refutes the dependency approach (Barrett & Whyte 1982). Even scholars sympathetic to the dependency approach view Taiwan as deviating from the paradigm's normal assumptions. For example, Amsden (1979, 1985) emphasizes the role of the state in promoting rapid growth; and Cumings (1984) focuses upon Taiwan's ability to benefit from the international product cycle.

However, several recent studies analyzing the structural and external forces emphasized by the *dependentistas*, but ignored by the other approaches, found them to be central for explaining the island's economic and social success, albeit in ways that contravene the conventional dependency perspective (Gereffi & Wyman 1989, Haggard 1990, Hsiao 1990, Winckler & Greenhalgh 1988). In particular, Taiwan's extreme dependence upon the United States and its giddy thrust into the world capitalist economy are viewed as crucial determinants of the successful economic and social outcomes on the island.

Indeed, without the U.S. connection, it is hard to imagine the "Taiwan miracle." In the 1950s, the United States provided the critical military protection and political support for the survival of the KMT state. The massive U.S. aid helped to alleviate the island's crushing defense burden, and enabled the regime to stabilize and then to revive its economy. According to one estimate, in the absence of the U.S. aid, Taiwan's annual GNP growth rate would have been cut by half, its per capital income would have been reduced by three quarters, and it would have taken the island 30 more years to reach its 1964 living standards (Jacoby 1966). Even after the termination of the official aid programs, the United States continued to provide less direct but still rather tangible subsidies mainly in the form of granting preferential market access to Taiwan's products.

Unlike their alliance with reactionary economic interests elsewhere in the Third World, U.S. officials apparently used Washington's aid package as a leverage to encourage various social and economic reforms on the island. For example, while the land reform program began before there was much of an American presence in Taiwan, U.S. officials during the 1950s played a significant role in constructing the large-scale extension program which helped the new landowners to increase their production and lobbied, although not always successfully, for more extensive reforms favorable to Islander farmers and small businessmen (Barrett 1988, Simon 1988, Yager 1988). In addition, U.S. AID (Agency for International Development) officials strongly supported American-educated technocrats in Taiwan in a coalition that was instrumental in turning the country in the direction of an outward, export-oriented strategy of development after the initial stage of easy import substitution was exhausted in the early 1960s (Gold 1986). Thus, in this case, foreign political and economic penetration seemed in retrospect to have actually facilitated rather than retarded the island's economic growth and movement toward greater socioeconomic equality.

Rather ironically from the dependency perspective, the KMT state has actively sought to integrate Taiwan into the capitalist world economy. Contrary to the oft-voiced fear that a small developing country may be stunted, stifled, and even suffocated in its economic and political relations with a dominant power, Taiwan's worst nightmare is that it will be shut out of core markets and abandoned by its ideological sponsor and military protector. It has rather conscientiously hitched itself to the U.S. economic, political, and military coattail. Exploiting its real as well as symbolic value in Washington's global containment policy and domestic partisan politics through the strength of the China lobby (Koen 1974, Tucker 1983), Taipei was able to extract considerable economic subsidies from its political dependence upon the United States in the 1950s and 1960s (Chan 1988b). It also made a virtue of the necessity of depending upon the U.S. market, and developed a highly successful strategy of hitching its export-dependent growth to the pocketbooks of American consumers. And, just as the Korean War provided a much needed stimulus to the moribund Japanese economy of the early 1950s, Taiwan (and South Korea) eagerly seized the business opportunities provided by the massive U.S. spending related to the Vietnam War.

This raises the obvious question of why the factors central to dependency theory have had benign, rather than malign, effects in the case of Taiwan. Some *dependentistas* have argued that their structural models provide the answer and that the East Asian experience simply serves as good reason for discarding overly simplistic vulgar versions of the paradigm. For example, Evans (1987) focuses upon the much less extensive penetration of foreign capital into these societies and the facets of economic structure and class formation that are related to it. In addition, one could certainly cite other historical facts, such as that U.S. goals regarding Taiwan stemmed from Cold War competition rather than economic gain, that Japanese colonial policies of using Taiwan as a rice and sugar basket for the metropole fortuitously laid the base for an integrated economy, and that Taiwan's export drive began when the global economy was rapidly growing (Clark 1989b).

What this suggests is that there is no single or universal "dependency syndrome." Rather, the specific nature of developing countries' dependency upon external economic and political factors may vary considerably. For example, situations of political clientelism may be quite different from dependent economic relations because economic and political penetration of the developing world may follow quite different logics in the postcolonial world (Evans 1985). In addition, McGowan & Smith (1978) make the valuable distinction between "market dependence" in foreign trade and "power dependence" on the decisions of specific external actors, such as MNCs and governments — with the latter obviously creating more dangerous vulnerabilities. More broadly, Gereffi & Wyman (1989, 27) present a model based on "natural resource endowments and internal market size, geopolitical factors, transnational economic linkages, state structures, elite policy preferences, prevailing development ideologies, and social coalitions . . . to better identify the conditions under which specific situations of dependency have positive, negative, or mixed consequences for national development."

Developmentalists, of course, would take issue with this dependency interpretation; they would argue that the "Taiwan miracle" occurred because that country simply allowed the "magic of the market" to operate. This occurred both in terms of an ongoing depoliticization of the domestic economy and of integrating the economy into the global division of labor, thereby allowing comparative advantage to dictate production strategy (Balassa 1981, Fei 1989, Linder 1986). There is certainly substantial evidence that market forces and individual entrepreneurship have played a key role in transforming the internal economy and in making Taiwan extremely competitive in international trade (Lam 1988, 1990, Li 1988, Myers 1984, Schive 1990). In comparison with the Latin American nations, Taiwan, as well as the other East Asian trading countries, has shown much more adaptability to market conditions (Morawetz 1981). Quite apart from the concern with competitive pricing, the East Asians have been more attentive to matters such as quality control, labor productivity, design innovation, product upgrading, and prompt delivery. In terms of the role of the public budget in the overall economy, Taiwan has had a fairly small government by international standards. In addition, the importance of public corporations in industrial production dropped precipitously during the export drive of the 1960s and early 1970s from over a half (based on confiscated Japanese assets) to under a fifth, indicating the over-time privatization of the economy.

However, it is clear that rapid growth in Taiwan also contradicts developmentalism, though perhaps less blatantly than in the case of dependency theory. This paradigm is at a loss in explaining why some countries (for example, Argentina, Australia, South Africa) — that are evidently endowed with an abundance of natural wealth, European settlers, and relatively advanced social and industrial infrastructure — failed to do nearly as well as others without such apparent advantages. The answer to this puzzle is surely more than just a matter of pursuing one's comparative advantage in international trade and of "getting the prices right." In particular, Taiwan's developmental history is far more complex and variegated than the predictions of modernization theory.

First, Taiwan's very developmental success raises questions about the theory of comparative advantage on which conventional neoclassical economics gives much stress. Taiwan has moved rapidly up the international product cycle (Vernon 1966) by producing and exporting ever more sophisticated products with increasing value added (Myers 1984). As noted above, this example of dynamic comparative advantage challenges the dependency arguments that free market exchange is simply an ideological excuse for perpetuating underdevelopment. However, Taiwan achieved this success by ignoring the advice of conventional economists that it should be content with the momentary comparative advantage that it had at different times in agricultural goods or low cost, labor-intensive production (Little 1979). More broadly, Taiwan's success supports Gilpin's (1987) contention that comparative advantage in international trade is becoming increasingly arbitrary in the sense that it can be manipulated by national development and industrial policies. If this is true, more is obviously needed for economic success than simply hitching one's fate to the "magic of the market." It also raises the point discussed in more detail below that the state has played a major role in leading the island's development project (Amsden 1985, Cumings 1984, Gold 1986, Haggard 1986, 1990, Wade 1988, 1990) — which directly contravenes the prescriptions of developmentalism.

Additionally, traditional Confucian culture — rejected not so long ago by Chinese and Western observers alike as an obstacle to modernization (Weber 1951) — has seemed more important than social change in promoting entrepreneurship and economic growth (Fei 1986, Greenhalgh 1984, 1988a, Hofstede & Bond 1988, Kahn 1984, Li 1986, McElderry 1986, Pye with Pye 1985, Silin 1976, Sutter 1988, Tai 1989, Winckler 1987, Wong 1986, 1988a, 1988b, Wu 1985). Confucianism has contributed to entrepreneurship and economic growth in several ways. First, by emphasizing the importance of learning and education, it has helped the development of the island's human capital. Second, by stressing the virtues of hard work and deferred gratification, it has encouraged the formation and investment of physical capital. As noted previously, Taiwan has historically featured a very high rate of savings. Third, Confucianism buttresses managerial paternalism, which has in turn facilitated labor peace in a number of East Asian countries. Practices such as a pay scale based on seniority, long-term (if not always lifetime) employment, periodic bonuses as an institution for profit sharing by employees, and company-provided social amenities (ranging from dormitories and schools to vacation homes) all tend to enhance the workers' identification with and loyalty to their business firm.

Such identification and loyalty are particularly strong when the firm is a family enterprise, where the owners and employees are blood relatives. Whereas the traditional Confucian emphasis on the primacy of family as a social unit is well known, its role as an economic unit in Taiwan has been stressed less often. Medium and small family-owned and -operated enterprises form the backbone of the island's economy, and indeed have been the main source of its export dynamism. Termed "guerrilla capitalism" by one analyst (Lam 1988), this sort of industrial organization stresses production flexibility and commercial adaptability as a key to economic success as opposed to the Western textbooks' emphasis on Fordism — the mass assembly-line production of standard models intended to capture the economy of scale (Friedman 1988, Piore & Sable 1984).

Moreover, Taiwan's experience challenges the various theories about the inevitability of tradeoffs in pursuing developmental goals in a manner that is quite ironic in view of dependency theory's charge that the "good things" produced by development are not possible in the periphery because the very economic success of the North described by the modernization approach rests upon the underdevelopment of the South. This is, as we have seen, that in Taiwan progress on multiple policy goals has occurred more or less concurrently in the face of predictions that they should be incompatible. First, a heavy defense burden is generally believed to constitute a drag on the overall economy. Yet, rapid growth in Taiwan was sustained over four decades despite very high defense spending. Second, rapid economic growth and social change are generally believed to cause increasing inequality and instability in the short term. Yet, Taiwan has remained quite stable both politically and socially during the postwar period and has been marked by a rising popular standard of living, declining income inequality, and the emergence of a middle-class society (Cheng 1990, Hsiao 1989). Third, a reliance on export-led growth creates a dependency upon powerful external nations and multinational corporations which would be expected to use their leverage for ultimately exploitative purposes, not just by dependency theorists but also by more conventional analysts of unequal international relations (Baldwin 1985, Hirschman 1945, Myrdal 1971, Prebisch 1950). Yet, Taiwan is often cited as an example of an autonomous state that has successfully promoted development (Amsden 1985, Gold 1986, Wade 1990) and, in particular, regulated and channeled the activities of MNCs on the island (Cheng 1987, Gold 1986, 1988b, Gregor with Chang & Zimmerman 1981, Haggard & Cheng 1987, Huang 1989, Ranis & Schive 1985).

Finally, state activities and the operation of the free market are generally seen as antithetical. Yet, Taiwan has seemingly escaped the assumed contradiction between state and market in economic development. Its economy has proved extremely competitive on international markets, while being subjected to fairly strong state intervention and leadership. For example, the state (both public corporations and the government) has played a considerable and continuing role in financing Taiwan's economic expansion, providing between 35% and 60% of gross domestic capital formation each year, mostly in infrastructure and heavy industry projects. The government has also used its strong control over banking and financial institutions to pursue conservative monetary and fiscal policies and to produce the country's excellent record on price stability described in Chapter 3 (Kuo 1983). It has combined this with an investment stimulus to overcome the oil crisis of the mid 1970s in an innovative attack on "stagflation" (Clark 1989a). More broadly, the state has led the restructuring of the economy through such policies as agricultural reform and import substitution in the 1950s, export promotion in the 1960s, and technological upgrading and financial reform in the 1980s (Alam 1989, Chu 1989, Clark 1989b, Gold 1986, Haggard 1990, Ho 1978, Pang 1990, Wade 1988, 1990).

This brings us to the statist theory which asks how officials deal with the structural conditions facing their nation. In the game of interstate relations as well as in the game of poker, the strength of one's hand dealt by luck, nature, or history surely matters for alternative outcomes. However, the skill with which one plays this hand is also critical in shaping these outcomes. This line of reasoning introduces the importance of statecraft. Except for Israel and South Korea, few of Washington's clients have been as successful as Taiwan in coping with their dependent relationships with the United States. Why some countries have been more successful than others in overcoming their external dependencies or in seizing conducive opportunities is clearly an important question, but one that only the statist paradigm takes seriously.

Taiwan's statecraft is considered important in two different yet interconnected respects. First, the state has been able to set economic strategy, move the economy foward along "market conforming" lines (Amsden 1985, Chu 1989, Gold 1986, Johnson 1981, Pang 1990, Wade 1988), and preserve a good business climate through the repression of labor (Deyo 1989). This pattern confirms Gilpin's (1987) contention that state and market, rather than being antithetical, must be integrated to promote development in the contemporary world political economy. Second,

Taiwan's success has also been attributed in no small measure to its ability to bargain in the broader international system, especially with its patron, the United States (Bobrow & Chan 1986, 1987, Chan 1987b, Yoffie 1983). From this perspective, therefore, the actions of Taiwan's strong state help to explain why structural dependency worked for, not against, national development and why most of the predicted tradeoffs between developmental goals have not yet had to be made.

Yet the statist perspective is also not entirely satisfactory in explaining the "Taiwan miracle." The much acclaimed strong and autonomous KMT state on the island owes its origin to the legacy of Japanese colonialism, Chinese Communist victory on the Mainland, and U.S. patronage. More specifically, the Japanese colonial administration's exploitative and repressive policies had the effect of helping to lay the socioeconomic infrastructure for later industrialization as well as the political foundation for subsequent authoritarian rule (Amsden 1985, Cumings 1984, Gold 1988a). Class formation was stunted under this regime. Similarly, the institutionalization of the strong and autonomous KMT state received its roots in earlier experience. Defeat in the Chinese civil war tore the KMT from its political base on the Mainland, consisting of the Shanghai compradore class and the large landlords. Whereas thus unable to undertake any meaning-ful socioeconomic reform on the Mainland, the transplanted KMT owed no such allegiance to any group on Taiwan and was finally able to carry out various essential reform programs (especially the Land-to-the-Tiller reform). Finally, U.S. patron-age provided tangible as well as intangible assistance to buttress a strong, autonomous, and rightist state, standing aloof and above society. Without the Seventh Fleet preventing a Communist invasion, it is doubtful that there would have been *any* KMT state at all.

In short, Taiwan's history challenges statist theory as well. First, contrary to the contention of some statist theorists, the role and power of the KMT state in the domestic context has very much been shaped and buttressed by conditions external to the island; and in its foreign relations, this state has hardly been either autonomous or strong (Chan 1988b). In the latter regard, the dependency analysts are closer to the mark. Taiwan's economic well-being and military security have been extremely dependent upon its relationship with Washington. Access to the U.S. market and technology — if no longer to a direct military shield that used to be provided by the Seventh Fleet — continues to be vitally important. And, with regard to this access, Taiwan continues to be a price taker and not a price maker.

Second, one does not have to look too far to see that the regime does not necessarily form a unified actor regarding developmental policy. For example, different parts of the leadership stress national security, economic development, and democratization in their policy prescriptions (Domes 1981). Even among the economic technocrats, the Ministries of Economic Affairs and Finance, the Council for Economic Planning and Development, and the Central Bank disagree over whether economic growth, trade expansion, price stability, a balanced budget, or improved popular welfare should be the principal policy objective (Liang & Liang 1988).

Third, one might argue that the developmentalist state succeeded in Taiwan precisely because it responded to the *dependentistas'* critique of capitalist development in the periphery — by promoting land reform and income equality, by providing large educational investments that led to human capital formation and upward social mobility on a massive scale, and by regulating the activities of foreign capital. Finally, while state actions in Taiwan are usually viewed as promoting development, embarrassing policy failures, such as the attempts to promote an automobile industry, are easy to find as well (Arnold 1989, Huang 1990, Noble 1987). It seems that in the case of Taiwan as well as the other East Asian NICs (especially South Korea), the coherence and the efficacy of the state's developmental policies may have been exaggerated (Moon 1988, 1990). The strength and autonomy of the executive branch of the state have varied across time and issue areas. They seem to be declining in Taiwan relative to both the other branches of the state (the judiciary, the legislature, the bureaucracy) as well as relative to the civil society (T. Cheng 1989, 1990).

More broadly, statist arguments sometimes also run the risk of putting too many analytic eggs in the same basket; that is, of presenting the state as a *deus ex machina* in the drama of economic development. If the strength and autonomy of a state are in and of themselves such a decisive factor in determining the fate of economic development, then why was Hong Kong able to thrive with its laissez-faire economy? Alternatively, why did China — which has had a stronger and more autonomous state than Taiwan — develop less rapidly? Thus, it seems that the statist perspective at best provides only a partial explanation of the East Asian development phenomena (Clark & Chan 1990b).

A qualitative and historical analysis of Taiwan's developmental experience, therefore, implies the need to construct more sophisticated and theoretical perspectives on the processes of development. Moreover, the conclusion that all the political economy paradigms possess both insights and oversights in explaining Taiwan's development history is supported by quantitative modeling. Thus, we present an overall regression attempting to account for the annual rate of real (that is, adjusting for the effects of inflation) change in Taiwan's GNP during the period 1952–88, using variables that represent all four theoretical approaches.

Economic growth is usually taken as the central factor in development (even though strong arguments can be made that other factors, such as distributive justice, are important components of development too). Thus, we use the annual GNP growth rate as our dependent variable for modeling Taiwan's development record, and try to explain it with items representing the principal explanations of growth adduced by the four paradigms. Their respective central tenets are that the operation of a free market (both supply and demand) promotes economic growth for the developmentalists, that external dependency stunts or distorts economic growth for the *dependentistas*, that the pursuit of some national goals can hinder the realization of others for the tradeoff perspective, and that state guidance and entrepreneurship can enhance economic growth for the statists.

In all, ten explanatory variables were included in the regression equation. The supply of physical and human capital was measured by the investment rate (that is, the ratio of investment to GNP) and by the literacy rate (which was subjected to a logarithmic transformation because the impact of literacy on GNP growth levels off as it approaches 100%). Two direct indicators of economic demand were also used: the annual rate of real change in private consumption and in export trade. Since Taiwan has been highly dependent upon the U.S. market for much of its postwar history, we also included the rate of change of U.S. GNP as a more indirect measure of economic demand. In addition to the two export-related items, external dependency was measured by the level of foreign investment as a proportion of total investment and by a dummy variable for the era of U.S. combat involvement in the Vietnam War (1964–72). The role of the state in Taiwan's development history is represented by its fiscal (government spending) as well as monetary (money suppy) policies, both measured in terms of real rates of annual changes. Finally, to see whether a tradeoff between growth and security exists, defense burden is measured by the ratio of military spending to GNP.

The four paradigms for development studies imply overlapping as well as divergent hypotheses. All would agree that investment, consumption, and human capital formation should stimulate growth; and except possibly for the statist perspective, they would probably not question that defense burden should retard economic growth. The developmental and dependency approaches, however, clash directly over the impact of the externally-related items (that is, foreign capital, exports, U.S. growth, and the Vietnam era) upon economic growth and upon its internal determinants (that is, investment, consumption, and human capital). The former would expect this impact to be positive, whereas the latter would expect it to be negative. Finally, statists would expect government economic activities to promote growth, while the developmentalists would posit an opposite tendency.

Table 6.1 presents these regression results after adjustments have been made for autocorrelated errors in the time series data (that is, after we have controlled for the serial dependencies in these data). Three of the explanatory variables — defense burden, private consumption, and foreign investment — turned out to have a statistically insignificant impact upon economic growth and were, thus, dropped from the final regression equation. The other seven explanatory variables have highly significant (at the 0.03 level or better) independent and positive influences on GNP growth. In combination, they are able to explain 85% of the latter's variance.

These statistical results cut across the predictions of our competing paradigms. As all would expect, domestic investment and human capital formation promoted economic growth.

Table 6.1 Explaining GNP growth rate: autoregression results.

Independent variable	*B* coefficient	Standard error	*T* value	Significance
Rate of U.S. GNP Growth	0.679	0.115	5.903	0.000
Rate of export growth	0.059	0.019	3.116	0.006
Rate of money supply	0.086	0.022	4.002	0.001
Rate of government expenditure	0.254	0.076	3.617	0.002
Log of literacy rate	12.722	4.915	2.588	0.019
Rate of investment	0.055	0.023	2.331	0.032
Vietnam War	1.616	0.638	2.531	0.021
Constant	−55.726	22.057	−2.506	0.021

Adjusted R^2: 0.85
Standard error: 1.26
Durban–Watson: 1.85

Sources: see data sources cited in the Appendix.

Additionally, the Vietnam War provided a window of opportunity for Taiwan's economic takeoff. The strong and independent effects that both export expansion and U.S. GNP growth have had on the island's GNP changes show that Taiwan has in effect pursued a strategy of coattail growth, or what Cardoso (1973) has called "associated-dependent development." However, the positive outcome of this export-based growth strategy is certainly more congruent with developmentalist expectations than dependency arguments.

On the other hand, the strong and positive showing of the government's fiscal and monetary policies is more supportive of the statist than the developmentalist view. These results are the more remarkable because higher rates of government spending and money supply growth are normally considered to be inflationary. This, then, suggests the ironic conclusion that Taiwan's generally "conservative" economic policies have had "liberal" or stimulative effects.

The negative results are substantively important as well. First, the *dependentistas* can claim empirical confirmation to the extent that the right-wing KMT regime had followed their prescriptions about guarding against the economic and social distortions brought by foreign capital penetration. Foreign investment (as opposed to foreign aid) came to Taiwan relatively late and in manageable size and has, therefore, not played a determinative role in its developmental history. Second, the failure of private consumption to stimulate growth underlines the export-dependent nature of Taiwan's economy. While this challenges conventional dependency theory, it is consistent with the more sophisticated formulation of Gereffi & Wyman (1989) summarized above. Finally, the failure of defense burden to exert a drag on economic expansion provides further support for the descriptive data in Table 4.1 showing that Taiwan has not experienced a *direct* tradeoff between economic growth and military expenditures. Much of the possible indirect effects of defense burden on economic growth — such as through the former's influences on the investment rate, export competitiveness, and the government's fiscal and monetary policies — were explicitly controlled for by including these variables in the regression. Still, these null findings show that Taiwan has escaped an important tradeoff.

In short, the island's developmental experience clearly calls for a composite explanation that draws upon different aspects of the developmental, dependency, statist, and tradeoff traditions. Thus, all four paradigms offer some useful insights for explaining Taiwan's economic success. At the same time, each of them alone seems to be too deterministic or incomplete to be able to account fully for this phenomenon, thus suggesting the need for more inclusive and integrated theories (Chan *et al.* 1990, Clark 1987, 1989, Deyo 1987a, Gereffi & Wyman 1989, Haggard 1990, Winckler & Greenhalgh 1988). The developmental perspective is too unrealistic in assuming that the experience of the early Western industrializers would inevitably be replicated in the Third World, and in assuming that the structure of the global political economy is of little consequence in the latter's development. On the other hand, the dependency perspective emphasizes so much the structure of the external environment that it leaves relatively little analytic room for human volition, effort mobilization, and effective statecraft. In its orthodox form, dependency theory almost advocates an economic form of predestination, implying that short of a fundamental break with the capitalist world system the developing countries are locked into a perpetual position of weakness and backwardness. For its part, the tradeoff perspective points up possible problems in the process of development but says little about how they can be mitigated, as the clash between growth and security evidently was in Taiwan.

Replacing the market efficiency of the developmentalists with the argument of "politics in command," statists emphasize the need for a strong, autonomous state in guiding the development effort of the late-industrializing countries and in managing or minimizing the tradeoffs among alternative policy goals. Yet by being over-concerned with the power of the state in the domestic context, the statist perspective often misses the point that the dependent state is also very much a creature of its external environment. Without the legacy of Japanese colonialism, the Chinese civil war, and the U.S. patronage, the KMT state would have been very different. Like the developmental and the dependency perspectives, the statist perspective does not give sufficient recognition to fortuitous occurrences — such as the removal of the Japanese colonial regime resulting from Tokyo's defeat in World War II, the outbreak of the Korean War that led to the U.S. intervention in the Taiwan Strait, and the booming world economy of the 1960s and early 1970s when Taiwan was making its major export push — that turned out to be critical in the island's developmental history. A full account of Taiwan's success story has to include domestic and international structural conditions, policy choice and behavioral conduct, as well as facilitative timing and, in a few instances, pure luck.

We argue therefore that the theories discussed in this chapter do not necessarily constitute logical opposites; they can instead be seen to offer complementary but bimodal policy injunctions. From this perspective, the key to Taiwan's — as well as its other East Asian neighbors' (Japan, South Korea, Singapore) — economic success has been their eclecticism (Chan & Clark 1991). That is, these countries have eschewed a rigid adherence to any one particular theoretical convention or policy orthodoxy, while attending effectively at the same time to the seemingly divergent implications and lessons of several contending perspectives. Thus, Taiwan's political economy has been characterized by the *dual* traits of vigorous private enterprise *and* active state intervention, intense market competition *and* extensive central planning, energetic promotion of export expansion *and* systematic protection of key domestic industries, and eager solicitation of foreign technology and capital *and* conscious attempts to control and regulate external economic penetration. Accordingly, a developmental state can seek to combine important conclusions from competing scholarly or policy traditions that need not be logically incompatible. For example, it can choose to pursue an outward-looking policy of export expansion based on its comparative advantage in labor costs, while at the same time seeking import substitution in particular strategic sectors. Similarly, it can try to solicit certain foreign factors (capital, technology, markets) to facilitate indigenous industrialization, while attempting to keep out other foreign factors (ownership and managerial control) to avoid external domination.

The principal policy implication of this discussion is accordingly that, as indicated in Chapter 1, the hallmark of effective statecraft is to be able to dampen and skirt policy tradeoffs, to unpack and recombine seemingly divergent perspectives, and to attend to bimodal policy concerns. The primary theoretical implication is that we should perhaps eschew the temptation to search for universal generalizations that are ostensibly valid across space and time, and to render dichotomous verdicts (true or false) on the validity of contending perspectives which do not actually have to constitute logical opposites. Rather, we should search for middle-range theories with more limited generalizability, and identify those scope conditions that indicate under what circumstances one such theory may be more illuminating than another (Most & Starr 1989). Moreover, we should perhaps look for ways in which these theories can be reconciled and integrated in order to provide a more accurate comprehension of a complex reality.

Chapter 7

Competing Models and Partial Results

In the last chapter, both qualitative and quantitative analyses found that Taiwan's economic history offers partial support for particular aspects of the developmental, dependency, statist, and tradeoff perspectives. This history, however, fails to confirm fully the entire range of theoretical expectations derived from each of these prevailing paradigms of political economy. In this chapter, we undertake a series of more specific regression analyses to explore selective arguments presented by the contending models about the causes as well as the consequences of economic growth. We concentrate on the statistical determinants of such policy performance as GNP growth, export expansion, popular well-being, and income equity. Because we only study the historical experience of one country, our analysis cannot be generalized cross-nationally to infer either the necessity or the sufficiency of various conditions for the policy desiderata just mentioned. Thus, this study constitutes less of a formal test of the competing empirical models than an attempt to assess the extent to which the longitudinal data from Taiwan fit with some "stylized facts" gleaned from cross-national research in different settings.

Instead of one overall regression equation that combines the predictions of all the paradigms, such as the results presented in Table 6.1, in this chapter we seek to evaluate a series of less sweeping equations that try to capture the arguments of each theory. With the major exception of those dealing with the defense burden, these equations cover the period between 1952 and 1988. The data sources are reported in the Appendix. In a few instances, we interpolate the data in order to estimate missing values in the time series.

The results of our longitudinal analyses are reported in Tables 7.1 to 7.6. They include the adjusted R^2 which measures the combined impact of all the explanatory variables in each equation, and the B coefficients and their statistical significance. Because the nominal R^2 is reduced to take account of autocorrelation in the data series, an adjusted R^2 may become slightly negative when the initial relationship is very weak.

There are two types of variables included in this study. First, *rate* variables measure the annual percentage increase or decrease in an item. For example, real GNP growth was 10.3% in 1977 and 5.1% in 1985 (see Table A.1 in the Appendix). Incidentally, in order to control for the effects of inflation, all monetary variables have been converted to real 1981 New Taiwan dollars for this study. Second, *level* variables measure how much of something exists. For example, in 1976 real GNP per capita was NT\$69,964 and investment stood at 30.6% of GNP (see Tables A.1 and A.4 in the Appendix). A problem with many level variables is that they increase steadily over time. Thus, when two such items are correlated longitudinally, very strong positive relationships emerge which in many cases exaggerate the actual linkage between them. Consequently, almost all of our dependent variables are rate ones. The two exceptions are the income ratio between the richest and poorest fifths of the population and the number of labor disputes, because their values tend to fluctuate over time. The situation for explanatory variables is not so clearcut, though. In some instances, a theory focuses on level. For example, dependency theory argues that higher levels of external dependency produce poorer economic and social outcomes. In other instances, it is not entirely clear whether the level or rate measurement is more appropriate (for example, the stimulus that investment is presumed to give to economic growth). In such cases, we adopt an inductive stance by reporting the independent variable with the greater statistical power.

As a final methodological note, some of the empirical relationships suggested by the contending models may be curvilinear. For example, the impact of literacy on GNP growth is likely to diminish with increasing economic maturity. Similarly, per capita income (GNPPC) tends to have different effects on income distribution for countries at different stages of development. Therefore, we use the log values of some variables (as well as the square of this log value in the case of GNPPC) in order to capture such curvilinear relationships (see Chapter 4 for a discussion of the specification of such curvilinear relationships).

As discussed in Chapter 2, the liberal model of virtuous cycle presents a neoclassical interpretation of the causes of economic growth. It emphasizes the importance of capital formation and accumulation in promoting rapid economic modernization. It also stresses the contribution of human capital, physical infrastructure, and a stable social, economic, and political order that promotes business confidence. Moreover, it takes a dim view of governmental intervention in the marketplace, and advocates instead the virtues of free enterprise and market competition. Finally, this perspective advocates an outward-looking strategy of economic growth, paying particular attention to the pursuit of each country's comparative advantage in the international economic order.

The model of virtuous cycle also leads one to expect that rising per capita income, prolonged political stability, and gradual democratization have a positive impact on distributive equity. It recognizes that the impact of the former variables on social equity may level off over time and, in this sense, admits possible nonlinear statistical associations between them. Assuming, however, continuing improvements in per capita income, political stability, and regime liberalization, any evidence of retrogression in distributive equity would contradict the expectation of a virtuous cycle.

Our first regression seeks to explain real GNP growth (GNPRATE) by the internal supply of physical and human capital, the external demand for Taiwan's products, political stability, and the extent of state involvement in the economy. We employ the rate of capital formation (CAPFRATE), the rate of growth in communications and transportation facilities (COMTRSRT), and the log of literacy level (lnLIT) to reflect the kind of investment in physical and human capital emphasized by the developmentalists. In addition to these possible domestic determinants, the rate of change in Taiwan's exports (EXPRATE) is used to measure an important external source of stimulation for its economic growth. We also measure the government's budget as a percentage of GNP (GOVGNP) in order to examine the alleged negative impact of "big government" on rapid

Table 7.1 Time series analysis of developmentalism.

Equation	Y	X	B	T significance	Adjusted R^2
1	GNPRATE	CAPFRATE	0.045	0.167	
		lnLIT	14.788	0.007	
		COMTRSRT	0.161	0.167	
		lnLABDIS	−0.612	0.072	
		GOVGNP	−0.130	0.557	
		EXPRATE	0.110	0.001	
		constant	−58.345	0.009	0.534
2	EXPRATE	USRATE	2.443	0.045	
		FORINVRT	−0.014	0.251	
		CAPFRATE	0.181	0.438	
		lnLIT	−40.518	0.234	
		COMTRSRT	1.129	0.131	
		lnLABDIS	0.581	0.793	
		GOVGNP	0.861	0.572	
		constant	153.575	0.262	0.161
3	INCRATIO	lnGNPPC	−32.340	0.000	
		$lnGNPPC^2$	1.406	0.000	
		lnPRESS	0.403	0.130	
		lnLABDIS	0.088	0.024	
		constant	186.279	0.000	0.837

Sources: Advisory Commission on Intergovernmental Relations (1989), p. 2 for USRATE. For other variables, see sources cited in the Appendix.

economic expansion. Finally, we use the log value of the number of labor disputes (lnLABDIS) to indicate the level of political instability. We resort to this indirect measure of political instability because, as discussed in Chapter 3, the data for more direct measures (such as riots and demonstrations) are rather problematic due to their short temporal coverage and low variation over time.

The results of this analysis are reported as Equation 1 in Table 7.1. The developmental perspective receives substantial support from this equation. The adjusted R^2 is fairly high at 0.53. More importantly, the regression coefficients show that the rate of change in Taiwan's GNP (GNPRATE) has been positively and significantly affected by rising human capital (lnLIT), dampening political instability (lnLABDIS), and pursuing a strategy of export expansion (EXPRATE). The fact that the export rate turns out to be the most significant determinant demonstrates the heavy external orientation of Taiwan's economic growth. The rates of capital formation (CAPFRATE) and infrastructural development (COMTRSRT) have also made a contribution to the island's GNP growth, although these variables do not quite attain the customary levels of statistical significance. However, the size of Taiwan's government relative to its economy does not have a significant impact upon economic growth.

These results indicate that export performance has been a key to the island's economic health. Thus, our second regression equation examines whether export expansion has been influenced by the other variables of interest to developmentalists included in Equation 1, as well as by two market factors particularly tied to Taiwan's trade performance — the rate of growth of the U.S. economy (USRATE) and the rate of change in incoming foreign investment (FORINVRT). Equation 2 in Table 7.1 indicates that these explanatory variables have only a moderate impact on export performance (adjusted $R^2 = 0.16$). The health of the U.S. economy was the only variable to attain statistical significance at the 0.05 level, again underlining Taiwan's dependency upon the American market. Additionally, the growth of communications and transportation infrastructure (such as ports and highways) seemed to have contributed to the island's export competitiveness, although this variable is not as statistically significant.

Although we have already commented on the importance of the U.S. market for Taiwan's exports, it is rather remarkable that economic fluctuations in the United States have turned out to be much more influential than Taiwan's own domestic economic conditions in shaping its export success. This fact indicates just how tightly the island's economy has been integrated with the global economy (since, as we have seen in Equation 1, export performance has been such an important determinant of Taiwan's overall economic growth, and since the U.S. economy looms so large in the capitalist world system). It also indicates that the U.S. economy has served as a locomotive for Taiwan's export sector, which has in turn performed the same role for the rest of the island's economy. In combination, Equations 1 and 2 underscore Taiwan's pursuit of a coattail strategy of growth by hitching its economy to the pocketbook of U.S. consumers. To that extent, the characterization of "associated-dependent growth" used by some *dependentistas* to describe countries such as Brazil is also applicable to Taiwan. Although developmentalists are likely to argue that our results negate the dependency theory, recent refinements of this perspective (Gereffi & Wyman 1989) explicitly recognize that certain types of dependency situations can promote indigenous growth.

Finally, we examine the developmentalists' arguments about the chief determinants of income distribution. We focus on the ratio (INCRATIO) between the income share of the top (that is, the richest) 20% of the population and that of the bottom (that is, the poorest) 20%. A high value for INCRATIO indicates greater inequity, whereas a low value indicates less inequity. We consider the effects of economic affluence, political stability, and the level of democratization on this variable. A quadratic polynomial specification is used to assess the impact of GNP per capita (GNPPC) on INCRATIO. Cross-national research has previously reported that income distribution tends to become less equal during the transition stage from traditionalism to modernity (a period usually characterized by rapid socioeconomic change). This distribution, however, subsequently becomes more equal when a country attains more economic affluence and industrial maturity (Kuznets 1955). As in Equations 1 and 2, lnLABDIS is used to indicate the level of political instability of the island. Unfortunately, the assessments of political rights and civil liberties made by the Freedom House are limited in duration and variance. We therefore adopt a more indirect measure to reflect the overtime changes in Taiwan's political liberalization. Specifically, the KMT government has historically engaged in stringent regulation and censorship of the press, requiring news publishers to apply and compete for a relatively small number of government licenses. Accordingly, we use the number of periodicals published on the island (lnPRESS) as a measure of press freedom.

Turning to Equation 3 in Table 7.1, lnGNPPC and its square have been highly significant in shaping the over-time changes in Taiwan's income distribution. However, contrary to the cross-national norm, the regression signs for these variables indicate that there has been an initial decline in the island's income inequity (INCRATIO), and then a more recent rise in this inequity. Thus, instead of the customary inverted U-curve characterizing the over-time relationship between income inequity and GNP per capita, we observe in Taiwan's case a straight U-curve. That is, the typical expectation by the developmentalists is stood on its head. Historically, Taiwan's remarkable ability to reduce income inequity at the beginning of its industrialization drive can be attributed to its radical land reform in the early 1950s and the emphasis on labor-intensive exports which created nearly full employment after the mid 1960s. Conversely, the economic transformation toward more capital- and technology-intensive production during the 1980s has evidently increased income inequity (Fei *et al.* 1979, Greenhalgh 1988b).

More congruent with the developmentalist expectation, lnLABDIS has been positively and significantly associated with changes in income inequity, thus implying that political instability tends to undermine egalitarianism (dependency theorists, however, would reverse the causal interpretation, and argue that income inequity leads to labor disputes). Finally, in conformity with previous research (see the review in Chapter 2), the level of democracy has not apparently helped to reduce income inequity.

Dependency theorists, for their part, argue that the key determinants of economic growth and industrialization lie in the nature of a developing country's external relations with the capitalist world system. Specifically, a heavy reliance on foreign trade and capital would in their view produce economic stagnation and impair or distort indigenous industrialization. Moreover, a tendency to rely heavily on a few partners or primary products in one's export trade would result in the same deleterious outcomes.

To represent the classical dependency perspective, we emphasize three concepts related to international trade. They are the share of sugar and rice in Taiwan's total exports, the value of Taiwan's exports to the United States and Japan (its two biggest trade partners) as a percentage of its total exports, and the value of Taiwan's exports as a percentage of its GNP. These variables attempt to tap concerns with export concentration in agricultural products (AGRCON), export partner concentration (PART-CON), and total export dependency (EXPGNP). According to the traditional dependency formulation, a high value on each of these variables should undermine economic growth and income equity. In addition to these trade-related variables, we include the share of foreign investment in Taiwan's domestic capital formation (FORINV), in order to reflect the focus on foreign capital penetration on the part of more recent formulations of associated-dependent growth (Bornschier & Chase-Dunn 1985).

The regression results for the dependency arguments are reported in Table 7.2. As formulated in Equations 4 and 5 in this table, the dependency perspective fails to receive any support. None of the key variables emphasized by it is a statistically significant determinant of either economic growth or income equity. However, the dependency perspective can offer a couple of potential explanations for these null results. First, overall foreign investment in Taiwan has been much lower than in many other Third World countries, especially those in Latin America (Evans 1987). Second, the state in Taiwan has played a more effective role in managing foreign capital (Gold 1986, Haggard & Cheng 1987, Huang 1989). Therefore, these special considerations might well account for Taiwan's ability to dampen or deflect the expected ill effects of its external dependency (Clark 1989b, Gereffi & Wyman 1989, Haggard 1990).

Table 7.2 Time series analysis of the dependency perspective.

Equation	Y	X	B	T significance	Adjusted R^2
4	GNPRATE	AGRCON	0.028	0.581	
		PARTCON	0.126	0.292	
		EXPGNP	0.023	0.747	
		FORINV	0.438	0.158	
		constant	−0.607	0.915	0.014
5	INCRATIO	lnGNPPC	−32.347	0.001	
		lnGNPPC^2	1.428	0.001	
		AGRCON	−0.014	0.239	
		PARTCON	0.007	0.569	
		EXPGNP	−0.003	0.834	
		FORINV	0.010	0.667	
		constant	187.156	0.001	0.754

Sources: see note to Table 7.1.

Turning to the expected tradeoffs between the various policy desiderata, the adherents of the social disruption model contend that a high *rate* of economic growth could actually undermine distributive equity. First, the well-known inverted U-curve hypothesis (Kuznets 1955) suggests that income distribution becomes more unequal with the onset of industrialization — thus producing a widespread sense of relative deprivation. This distribution tends to improve only after a country achieves a certain threshold of collective affluence. Second, increasing social mobilization is a likely correlate of rapid socioeconomic change. It is apt to bring about rising demands for government service. These demands may overload the government, thereby resulting in its incapacity. In short, these views imply that rapid economic growth and social mobilization tend to be a source of socio-political instability and frustration as well as a hindrance to distributive equity. We employ the rate of increase in the percentage of population with at least a secondary education as an approximate measure of social mobilization (SECEDRT). The rate of proliferation in periodicals (PRESSRT) serves as a surrogate for the democratization process, and the log value of labor disputes (lnLABDIS) is used as an indicator of political instability.

The results of our time series analysis for the social disruption model are presented in Table 7.3. This model fails to receive any support in Equation 6, where neither GNPRATE nor SECEDRT offers a statistically significant explanation of income distribution.

Table 7.3 Time series analysis of the social disruption model.

Equation	Y	X	B	T significance	Adjusted R^2
6	INCRATIO	GNPRATE	0.000	0.986	
		SECEDRT	−0.003	0.471	
		constant	4.883	0.000	−0.114
7	lnLABDIS	GNPRATE	−0.034	0.479	
		SECEDRT	−0.005	0.869	
		PRESSRT	0.003	0.787	
		constant	8.254	0.000	−0.119

Sources: see note to Table 7.1.

Similarly, Equation 7 provides scant support for the social disruption model. The three independent variables included in that equation (GNPRATE, SECEDRT, and PRESSRT) have not had a major influence on the trend of political instability as indicated by the number of labor disputes. Therefore, the social disruption model fares quite poorly in our analysis.

The null findings in Table 7.3, however, are far from insignificant substantively. They provide evidence in support of the Taiwan success story of combining effectively "growth with equity" and "growth with stability." In contrast to the cross-national pattern of rapid growth and social mobilization undermining equity and stability, the longitudinal data from Taiwan show GNPRATE and SECEDRT to be statistically unrelated with the latter two variables in Equations 6 and 7 respectively. Therefore, this island has evidently avoided these negative effects of rapid growth.

Whereas the social disruption model emphasizes the deleterious consequences of rapid socioeconomic change, other analysts are more concerned with the undesirable effects of long-term sociopolitical stability, especially in liberal democracies. As noted earlier, the theory of distributional coalitions (Olson 1982) suggests that countries with extended political continuity and social tranquility are especially likely to accumulate strong interest groups whose power over national policy in turn exacts a cost in economic stagnation and social rigidity. We employ the rate of increase in Taiwan's civic organizations (ORGANRT) as an approximate measure of the growth of distributional coalitions over time. As before, the rate of increase in periodicals (PRESSRT) is used to reflect the island's democratization process. Additionally, lnLABDIS offers one of the more important indicators of distributive conflict between workers and capitalists. In Equation 8 (Table 7.4), we examine the individual effects of these three variables on the rate of Taiwan's GNP change (GNPRATE) while considering at the same time the effects of EXPRATE and CAPFRATE.

The results for Equation 8 are not encouraging for the argument that the democratization process and especially the formation of distributional coalitions tend to impair economic performance, once the export-driven nature of Taiwan's economy is taken into account. Neither lnLABDIS nor ORGANRT has

Table 7.4 Time series analysis of the negative spinoffs of stability.

Equation	Y	X	B	T significance	Adjusted R^2
8	GNPRATE	EXPRATE	0.115	0.002	
		CAPFRATE	0.038	0.292	
		ORGANRT	−0.019	0.909	
		PRESSRT	−0.052	0.266	
		lnLABDIS	−0.059	0.868	
		constant	7.350	0.019	0.249

Sources: see note to Table 7.1.

had any effect on growth. Similarly, the rate of increase in periodicals (our indicator of democratization) fails to reach statistical significance at the customary level. Only Taiwan's export rate (EXPRATE) turns out to be highly significant in this equation, thus reconfirming the importance of exports as an engine for the island's economic growth. As in our analysis of the social disruption model, the results in Table 7.4 give general support to the view that Taiwan has avoided some of the policy tradeoffs suggested by cross-national research — in this case, the negative spinoffs of political liberalization and stability.

The third kind of tradeoff considered here concerns the effects of military vigilance on economic growth. Thus, we examine the impact of defense spending upon two central components of economic growth in Taiwan — EXPRATE and CAPFRATE — in Equations 9 and 10 respectively. It turns out that the level of military expenditure as a percentage of GNP (MEGNP) provides a better prediction of export growth, whereas the rate of change in real defense spending (DEFRATE) is a more powerful predictor for the investment rate. In addition, the rate of change of the U.S. GNP (USRATE) is included as an explanatory variable in Equation 9, because of the dependence of Taiwan's export performance upon the American market. Finally, Equation 11 checks for any evidence of tradeoff between over-time changes in the government's defense and welfare expenditures by using DEFRATE and GNPRATE to explain WELBUDRT.

The results of these analyses of the possible tradeoffs resulting from military vigilance are reported in Table 7.5. Contrary to the

Table 7.5 Time series analysis of defense tradeoffs.

Equation	Y	X	B	T significance	Adjusted R^2
9	EXPRATE	USRATE	2.147	0.061	
		MEGNP	2.871	0.072	
		constant	−13.279	0.314	0.176
10	CAPFRATE	DEFRATE	−0.551	0.000	
		constant	15.657	0.000	0.416
11	WELBUDRT	GNPRATE	0.677	0.559	
		DEFRATE	0.018	0.950	
		constant	8.705	0.455	−0.118

Sources: see note to Table 7.1.

available cross-national evidence, Taiwan's defense burden as measured by MEGNP has not had a negative impact upon its export performance. In fact, Equation 9 shows that along with the U.S. economy, it has exercised a major positive influence in this regard. Nevertheless, even though Taiwan has apparently escaped this guns-versus-exports tradeoff, Equation 10 offers evidence that defense spending has tended to undermine investment; the adjusted R^2 for this equation is fairly strong at 0.42. There is, however, no evidence to support yet another type of tradeoff that has been widely discussed in the literature. That is, in Equation 11 the rates of change in the government's defense and welfare expenditures have been statistically unrelated. Even more surprisingly, economic growth has not had a statistically significant impact on WELBUDRT, suggesting the importance of political factors in promoting the rising level of governmental commitment to social welfare over time. Thus, with regard to the possible deleterious impact of defense spending on export competitiveness and government support for welfare programs, Taiwan's experience tends to contradict popular expectations. On the other hand, this island conforms to the cross-national norm that a heavy defense burden undermines capital formation (Chan 1988a, Davis & Chan 1990).

Although it is difficult to speculate what Taiwan's economic growth would have been in the absence of a heavy defense burden, the evidence produced by this study fails to indicate a significant negative relationship between these variables over time. While the rates of defense spending and total investment have been inversely related, capital formation has only had a marginal impact upon the island's economic growth — probably because, unlike most other developing countries, the overall rates of savings and investment have been very high in Taiwan. In contrast, export promotion has been a main determinant of the island's economic growth. However, instead of undermining export competitiveness, defense spending seemed to have contributed to it. This probably has been the result of the domination of the island's export industries by small-scale enterprises, whose comparative advantage focuses upon flexible production (Friedman 1988, Lam 1988, 1990). Thus, they do not suffer severely when defense-related industries absorb investment capital as well as human capital in the form of skilled managers, engineers, and scientists. In fact, the emphasis of Taiwan's defense policy upon procuring sophisticated weaponry may have provided some stimulus to the technological upgrading of the island's economy.

To what extent is the statist model supported by our time series analysis? In Equation 12, the rate of increase in government spending (SPENDRT) and the relative capacity of the state (TAX) are considered as possible determinants of Taiwan's economic growth in addition to the island's rates of capital formation and export expansion. We use the extent of government's direct taxation as an indication of its capacity to extract resources from society. Weaker governments tend to depend more on indirect taxes such as custom duties and license fees, which are easier to collect than direct taxes (Snider 1987). Public investment, which is strongly emphasized in statist formulations, has not been included in this regression because it is very highly correlated with overall government spending, thus creating the problem of multicollinearity.

In Equation 13, we turn our attention to popular well-being as reflected by the rate of change in the island's physical quality of life index (PQLIRATE). We try to account for its over-time improvement by examining the possible contributions by GNPRATE, TAX, and WELBUDRT. Rapid GNP growth is seen by developmentalists to contribute to greater popular well-being, while adherents to the social disruption and dependency perspectives tend to doubt that macroeconomic expansion will necessarily trickle down to enhance the living conditions of the masses. In the context of Equation 13, we use the percentage of government revenues derived from direct taxes (TAX) as an indication of how regressive its tax system is. Generally speaking, the more a government's revenues rely on direct as opposed to indirect taxes, the less unfavorable its tax system is toward the poor people — and, hence, the less adverse is this system in regard to popular well-being. Finally, we consider the rate of change in the government's budget for social welfare and social security (WELBUDRT) as a possible contributor to the over-time improvement in the island's PQLI score.

The regression results in Table 7.6 provide some support for statist arguments. In Equation 12, the rate of change in government spending has been positively and significantly associated with GNP growth, just as the rates of capital formation and export promotion have been. However, the over-time increases in direct taxation fail to have a major influence upon GNP growth as hypothesized by the statist model. In Equation 13, the rate of increase in the government's welfare expenditures has had a positive and significant impact upon the rate of improvement in the island's PQLI. According to this equation, this public support has been more important in

Table 7.6 Time series analysis of the statist model.

Equation	Y	X	B	T significance	Adjusted R^2
12	GNPRATE	EXPRATE	0.129	0.000	
		CAPFRATE	0.071	0.032	
		SPENDRT	0.113	0.029	
		TAX	0.079	0.215	
		constant	2.539	0.256	0.419
13	PQLIRATE	GNPRATE	−0.028	0.441	
		WELBUDRT	0.013	0.045	
		TAX	−0.053	0.002	
		constant	2.477	0.000	0.274

Sources: see note to Table 7.1.

promoting popular well-being than the growth in GNP — a finding that is more congruent with the emphasis on government policy by the statists than with the laissez-faire orientation toward the trickling down of economic and social benefits on the part of the developmentalists. However, changes in direct taxation actually turn out to be a significant negative factor for the PQLIRATE. We attribute this otherwise counterintuitive finding to the fact that the PQLI has a theoretical ceiling of 100; therefore, as a country approaches this limit, it becomes increasingly difficult to improve further its accomplishments on this dimension. The declining rate of improvement for this index coincides with the rising tendency for the government to rely on direct taxes as a source for its revenues.

In conclusion, social scientists routinely face alternative explanations of the same phenomenon. In this chapter, we have tried to explicate some of the major perspectives about the conditions and policies affecting economic growth, export promotion, popular well-being, and distributive equity. We have also tried to apply these perspectives to the historical experience of Taiwan, admittedly an unusual case whose policy performance has deviated substantially from cross-national norms.

As expected, we do indeed find much evidence in support of the view that Taiwan's policy performance has been rather unusual along a number of dimensions. This island has been able to skirt or lessen most if not all of the popularly expected policy tradeoffs in its pursuit of prosperity, security, stability, and equity. Thus, we found that its rapid economic growth has not undermined political stability and, until recently, income equity. Similarly, it has launched a successful economic takeoff and export drive, despite its comparatively heavy defense burden (especially in the 1950s and 1960s). Nor has the pursuit of "guns" (that is, national defense) undercut the government's support for "butter" (that is, social welfare); the rates of change in these two expenditure items have been statistically unrelated over time. Finally, even though the island's economy has been heavily dependent upon foreign markets and capital, it has apparently avoided the fate of economic stagnation, social deprivation, and political subjugation predicted by *dependentistas* of various stripes. The absence of a malign dependency impact, however, is not necessarily incompatible with some recent extensions or reformulations of the dependency perspective.

Consequently, the statistical evidence offered in this chapter supports the general case that Taiwan has so far successfully steered a course between the Scylla and Charybdis of policy dilemmas, thereby compiling a record of "most good things tending to go together." In part, this seems to be so because Taiwan has been successful in combining state and market. The regression analyses provide strong support for several central tenets of neoclassical views on economic performance, but they also demonstrate the importance of statist contributions to the "Taiwan miracle."

Perhaps unsurprisingly, we discover that none of the perspectives examined in this chapter is able to fully account for Taiwan's achievements in sustained economic growth, rapid export expansion, rising physical quality of life, and substantial equity in the size distribution of its income. Each perspective has some of its arguments fail to receive the necessary support from Taiwan's longitudinal data — even though, on balance, the developmental and statist perspectives have clearly fared much better than the others. Consequently, we are faced with a situation of "complete paradigms, partial results," whereby each model can at best only fruitfully capture particular aspects of the historical evolution of Taiwan's political economy.

It is not difficult to imagine the reasons for the lack of complete correspondence between the models and Taiwan's historical experience. First, as already mentioned, Taiwan is quite an atypical case in terms of its policy performance relative to that of its peers. Second, many of the "stylized facts" used to formulate theoretical arguments are based on cross-sectional aggregate analysis and are, therefore, unlikely to be equally valid when examined over time for a single case. Third, our quantitative measures often fail to capture fully the ideas discussed in the verbal formulations of various models, leading consequently to considerable slippage in the operationalization of concepts. Fourth, the models examined above are themselves rather loose formulations containing a great deal of nuance, indeterminateness, and indeed disagreement among their adherents. For example, they do not indicate clearly whether the various causal factors emphasized by them are necessary and/or sufficient, or just probabilistic in their effect in bringing about certain outcomes. Fifth, many of the causal relationships may be reciprocal in nature (such as when rising per capita income increases PQLI, and improving PQLI in turn creates the human capital to promote further development). Whereas we have used the appropriate methodology to investigate such mutual influence relationships elsewhere (Chan *et al.* 1990), we settled for a less rigorous approach here in order to demonstrate that although the general theoretical expectations of the various models may be divergent, selective aspects of these models may coexist empirically.

That is to say that the contending perspectives do not necessarily suggest logically opposite models of reality. In fact, empirical reality is often sufficiently complex to accommodate a variety of loose theoretical perspectives. Consequently, each of these perspectives reveals insights as well as oversights in its explanation of Taiwan's postwar history (for example, Chan & Clark 1991, Chan *et al.* 1990, Clark 1989b, Haggard 1990, Winckler & Greenhalgh 1988). This being the case, we can try to develop a more synthetic account of Taiwan's political economy on the basis of our understanding of the scope conditions and theoretical limitations of each model. We turn to this effort in the next chapter.

Chapter 8
Eclecticism Beyond Orthodoxies

In the previous chapters, we presented various "stylized facts" from cross-national research that show the difficulty of pursuing successfully and simultaneously the entire array of policy values such as growth, equity, stability, security, and democracy. Indeed, much of this research indicates that these values tend to impose hard tradeoffs on public officials and, therefore, present formidable policy constraints to the officials' decision-making processes. The question then arises as to why some national elites are evidently better able to skirt or postpone such constraints than others. To the extent that we have been persuasive in our argument, the reader would perhaps agree that Taiwan offers an example of relative national success in these regards in comparison with both its own past and the performances of other developing countries.

The four developmental perspectives, of course, have quite different views of what shoals must be safely navigated by a country undergoing modernization. Developmentalists see the principal danger from the distortions of free market due to state intervention and the obstacles posed by traditional values. *Dependentistas* argue that capitalist economic relations will almost inevitably undermine any Third World country's development project. For their part, advocates of the tradeoff perspective contend that the pursuit of some policy goals will tend to entail sacrificing others. Finally, statists propose that strong governmental leadership can help to avoid the reefs and roiling waters depicted by the other approaches. Thus, singly and collectively, these perspectives bring to mind the metaphor of Scylla and Charybdis.

Over the past 40 years, Taiwan has safely navigated between the threats of various Scyllas and Charybdises which have sunk the development hopes of many nations. Moreover, instead of sacrificing an appreciable amount of several desirable but seemingly incompatible goals, Taiwan made substantial (if not quite simultaneous) progress on almost all the major desiderata of development. Thus, if there were sacrifices, they appear to have been remarkably short-lived.

This raises three sets of questions: First, did Taiwan escape all the basic tradeoffs that arise in the developmental processes? Or did its authoritarian government constitute a tradeoff between democracy and the other policy values (implying, incidentally, that expanding democratization may well bring problems along some other dimensions)? Second, were Taiwan's undeniable successes primarily the result of policy decisions and elite activities? Or did they result from more deep-seated structural factors, such as the island's place in the global economy or the enduring influence of Confucian cultural norms? Third, to the extent that development resulted from behavioral instead of structural factors, was this primarily the result of government leadership and policy? Or did the activity of people in the private sector (businessmen, intellectuals, workers, and farmers) contribute more to the development project? Definitive answers to these questions are probably impossible; the first and the third are especially central to the basic ongoing debate in Taiwan's politics today (Ling & Myers 1990). Still, a review of the theoretical insights about Taiwan's development should be suggestive.

Each of the paradigms clearly can help explain the evolution of Taiwan's political economy. Developmentalism's touting of neoclassical economics is clearly justified by important contributions that the market and private entrepreneurship have made to the island's economic dynamism. Over time, the economy became increasingly depoliticized (Fei 1989); the island's export competitiveness in foreign markets has been the major engine of growth since the early 1960s; small-scale businesses that receive little direct help from the government have been the backbone of the export sector; the island's extremely high savings rate, which primarily reflects private economic activities, has undergirded the record of rapid industrialization and industrial upgrading; and "full employment" after the late 1960s meant that the labor market has generally worked to decrease income inequity.

In contrast, the applicability of the dependency and tradeoff approaches is more concerned with the question of "the dog that didn't bark." Specifically, why, given Taiwan's high degree of external dependency in both the economic and political realms, did not the island suffer from the distortions and underdevelopment posited by conventional dependency theory or even from the inability to pursue most developmental goals simultaneously as predicted by the tradeoff perspective? One partial answer focuses upon the special nature of the dependency bonds to which Taiwan was subjected. For example, Japan's colonialism was exploitative and repressive by any standard, but the economic needs of the metropole stimulated the Japanese to lay a base for integrated economic development; and in the postwar era, Taiwan's external linkages centered upon market dependency in the economic realm and political clientelism during the Cold War in terms of its power dependency — a combination which stimulated external subsidy and growing international competitiveness rather than exploitation and a distorted internal economy. A second answer points to historical idiosyncracies — Japan's defeat in World War II removed the blockage of colonialism and prevented the former overlords from perpetuating their advantages in neocolonialism; the outbreak of the Korean War probably prevented a Communist takeover; and Taiwan's export drive began when the world market was expanding rapidly, when the international product cycle was pushing many U.S. and Japanese industries toward offshore production, and when a liberal international trading order was maintained under U.S. hegemony (Gilpin 1987). A third answer would point to the authoritarian nature of the Kuomintang regime for most of its tenure on Taiwan as the reason that it was able to devise and implement a successful developmental strategy and to resist the opposition of the traditional elites to socio-economic change undermining their power, status, and wealth.

This brings us to the arguments of the statist perspective that government leadership and policies can stimulate economic growth and social transformation. Clearly, the regime has made several signal contributions to the island's development. Its monetary and fiscal policies have controlled inflation, the scourge of the KMT in the late 1940s, and provided countercyclical adjustment; its ability to negotiate with more powerful trading partners and to regulate foreign capital on the island was instrumental in maximizing Taiwan's economic potential; and the state's investment in education both developed human capital and helped to promote social and political change. More broadly, while not pursuing the extent of government intervention and industrial targeting that Japan did (Chu 1989), the state acted to create conducive environments for specific economic activities (for example, small-scale agricultural production, the beginnings of light industry behind protectionist walls, the export of labor-intensive products and, more recently, the upgrading to heavy industry and high-tech goods) in what in retrospect must be regarded as a well-chosen developmental sequence. Several of these state-guided economic transformations, such as the land reform program and the period of import-substitution industrialization, it should also be noted, involved blatant interference in the market and private property rights.

Taiwan's successful political economy, in short, can be summarized by three Fs — flexibility, foresight, and *fortuna*. First, the island's market-based economy encouraged flexibility as neoclassical doctrine would predict; and, more specifically, the small-scale nature of industrial enterprises with complex subcontracting ties created a comparative advantage in international trade in which flexible production was probably just as important as cheap labor. Political flexibility can also be seen in the regime's repeated willingness to sponsor structural transformations of the economy and, more recently, significant political reforms. This policy flexibility, in turn, rested upon a more fundamental flexibility — the willingness of the regime to expand the elite segments included within it (for example, economic technocrats, Islander businessmen, and electoral politicians). Second, foresight is evident in such divergent activities as state-led economic transformations, the pushing of intellectuals for political reform, the high savings and investment rates of local businessmen and households, the willingness of new landowners in the 1950s to avail themselves of the agricultural extension system to increase their productivity, and the continual upgrading of the educational system. Finally, despite social science's abhorrence of indeterminacy, historical idiosyncracies have certainly left their mark on Taiwan. In plain language, Taiwan's ability to achieve major policy values has been aided by good luck. The island's economic success, as noted above, has been conditioned by Japan's need for agricultural goods in the 1920s and the state of the global economy in the 1960s. In addition, without the fortunes of war, the KMT might be living only in the faded scrapbook pictures of a few emigres, and Islander entrepreneurs might be still excluded from the most lucrative business positions by their Japanese masters or reading Mao's little red book for political inspiration. Thus, it is easy to imagine alternative historical scenarios for Taiwan's development.

The fact that all four paradigms of political economy have some applicability to Taiwan implies that their insights should be combined. Since it is hard to generalize from the experience of just one country, it is probably impossible to advance a "grand theory" or synthesis. Rather, it seems more valuable to focus upon middle-range theories that suggest what contextual factors or scope conditions under which the postulates of developmentalism, *dependencia*, statism, and the tradeoff perspective might apply (Most & Starr 1989). In particular, the nature of a nation's political economy and the trajectory of its developmental history appear to be the result of three general sets of factors: (a) its structural position in the international system, (b) the policy capacity of its leadership, and (c) its historical legacies which also, obviously, shape current structural position and policy capabilities.

Clearly, a country's *structural position* in the international system matters for its elite's relative ability to diffuse or dampen the pressure to make policy tradeoffs. By structural position, we mean physical or symbolic status in the global economic division of labor, strategic balance of power, and patterns of political alignment. Structural position forms the centerpiece of dependency theory and is generally ignored by the other approaches. However, dependency theorists sometimes imply that only a country's economic position is important, and suggest that the distribution of the benefits of cross-national exchanges is determined by the actors' tangible assets. Thus, they assume that transfers between the strong and the weak will always hurt the latter.

The case of Taiwan, however, shows that this conventional

dependency assumption is not necessarily true; and, in fact, even recent extensions of this approach recognize that some types of external ties can promote development (Gereffi & Wyman 1989). A nation's structural position in the international system, then, can help or hinder the recruitment of foreign military protection, political support, economic aid, and market accessibility — which can introduce needed resources (money, technology, legitimacy) in short supply domestically. Thus, one obvious way to lessen the imperative of "satisficing" among competing policy demands is to solicit and attract foreign contributions to offset domestic shortfalls. A substantial part of the tradeoff literature, for example, suffers from the limitation of treating nation states as if they were isolated entities in the international system. The possibility of making cross-national transfers is overlooked (Bobrow & Chan 1987).

Naturally, foreign contributions (military alliance, economic subsidy, political endorsement) come with a price tag attached in terms of increases in external dependency and decreases in national autonomy. Thus, they present a double-edged sword. Much of the debate about the advantages and disadvantages of an outward-looking export-expansion strategy of economic development, in comparison with an inward-looking import-substitution strategy, between what we have called the developmental and dependency schools of thought has to do with the costs and benefits of introducing foreign inputs into one's domestic political economy.

How effectively a government can attract facilitative foreign factors and negotiate effectively for favorable terms of their entry has to do with its structural position in the international system. In this sense, Mexico enjoys a more advantageous position than Bolivia, and Nigeria is more strategically located than the Central African Republic. In particular, four aspects of structural position seem important. First (and most obvious) is the possession of economic resources, industrial capability, population, and human capital. Second, geographic location can be important because countries can benefit simply from being in a dynamic region or suffer from being too close to a major power (for example, Latin America has been much more subject to U.S. economic penetration and political pressure than East Asia). Third, the nature of external dependency is pertinent. For example, in the postwar world, political dependency can bring economic benefits since both the United States and the Soviet Union were willing to subsidize client states in order to protect their rival empires during the Cold War (Clark & Bahry 1983, Richardson 1978). Finally (and perhaps counterintuitively), small size may actually be an advantage. Small countries are generally forced to become much more dependent upon foreign trade than large ones. This both forces their economies to become more efficient via the logic of the market *and* stimulates governmental intervention to mitigate the "creative destruction" of market-induced changes — that is, to promote equity in the society. Katzenstein (1985) describes this pattern for the small states in Western Europe but it also seems to apply to the state-led development in East Asia.

In Taiwan's case, the first of these structural factors — the possession of resources — clearly has little explanatory value since the island was an economic and political basketcase in the early 1950s as its industrialization drive commenced. The fourth factor — the advantages of being a small open economy — came into play during and after the 1960s, but this was only after significant development had occurred. Thus, the specific nature of Taiwan's dependency upon the United States and its regional location are probably the most important structural factors that influenced its political economy.

The role of the United States was clearly important in shaping the policy space available to the KMT. After the outbreak of the Korean War, Washington saw Taiwan as an essential link in its containment policy in East Asia. It pumped massive sums of economic and military aid to the KMT regime, and backed its efforts to suppress all sources of possible opposition (including labor). Consequently, tangible as well as intangible U.S aid dampened the severity of domestic tradeoff while at the same time helping to secure the dominance of the KMT state over Taiwan's civil society.

Washington's generosity in providing massive aid to the faltering KMT state was in turn derived from Taiwan's geo-strategic location at the fringe of the Eurasian land mass. The United States was motivated to support and sustain the KMT state, because it wanted to deny the island to Beijing (which was perceived to be a client of Moscow). Thus, Taiwan was not so much important for any intrinsic value of its own as for its significance to other countries that were important to Washington. Besides China, Japan was important for the U.S. containment policy in Asia. Due to historical ties and geographic proximity, the fate of Taiwan was a matter of some concern for Tokyo. The fall of Taiwan would have raised grave doubts about Japan's security position and the reliability of U.S. defense commitments. While Taiwan might be militarily and politically expendable in Washington's global strategy of contest with international communism, Japan was not. In short, then, Taiwan's structural position as a forward post in the rimland of Eurasia, as a rival government of China, and as a former colony of Japan enhanced Washington's willingness to contribute to its well-being. Contrary to the claim of dependency theorists, Taiwan's status as a dependent client did not automatically lead to unfavorable resource transfer or weak bargaining power.

In fact, the KMT enjoyed substantial influence because of Taiwan's symbolic position in U.S. domestic politics. Following the outbreak of the Korean War and the onset of McCarthyism, U.S. politicians and officials were eager to support the KMT state on Taiwan. Few were willing to run the risk of being charged "soft on communism" after the bitter partisan debate about "who lost China" and the subsequent electoral backlash against the Democrats. Consequently, the United States was self-motivated to come to the aid and defense of Taiwan.

In addition, Taiwan's regional location has clearly provided economic stimulation as well. Capitalist East Asia has been the most dynamic economic region of the world during the postwar era. Taiwan has benefitted from this regional dynamism in two ways. First, it has been able to learn from the industrial and commercial precedent set by Japan and from the experience of its regional neighbors. Second, the northeast Asian area constitutes an integrated economy in which a product cycle works. That is, as industries decline in the regional leader, Japan, due to rising labor costs and standardized production techniques, they move offshore to less developed countries like Taiwan. This imitation by example and mutual economic stimulation have been described as a flying-geese formation, whereby the industrial latecomers follow the lead of their predecessors (Cumings 1984). More recently, however, these favorable conditions have been jeopardized. Waning Cold War sentiments, rising protectionist demands, and increasing direct commercial competition among the East Asian trading nations suggest that the regional economy may face increasing problems in the future (Moon 1989a).

However, structural conditions regarding factors such as economic size, strategic location, political alignment, and possession of vital natural resources do not always allow one to predict the outcomes of cross-national negotiations on resource transfers. Accordingly, despite their more favorable structural positions in the international system, Brazil and Saudi Arabia have not necessarily been able to arrange more favorable terms for resource transfers than, say, Singapore and South Korea. For Taiwan, its very poor physical endowment in the 1950s strongly implies that nonstructural factors have had an important impact upon its developmental history.

Surely, the fact that countries can experience upward as well as downward status mobility — in the case of Taiwan, in a relatively short period of time — suggests that structural conditions are hardly completely determinative of national achievements. To gain a fuller explanation of these achievements, one needs also to recognize the role of governmental *policy capacity*. This role essentially involves the skill and effort devoted to the development of a coherent and realistic national policy agenda, and the mobilization of domestic and foreign support for it. To use our favorite analogy, in the game of poker as in the game of international bargaining, success is dependent not only upon the hand dealt to one by nature and history (that is, one's structural position), but also on one's skill (that is, policy capacity) in playing this hand.

A weak country (in the sense of structural position) may be able to shape and influence the incentives of a strong country, so that the latter refrains from hostile actions and is self-motivated to make contributions to the former's well-being. In international negotiations, a weak country can often achieve policy outcomes that are more favorable to it than its actual bargaining power would imply (Keohane & Nye 1977). It can resort to the manipulation of the bilateral policy agenda, the weaving of multiple issue linkages, and the formation of transnational interest groups (for example, the China lobby in the United States) in order to offset its objectively weaker bargaining position. Indeed, one would infer that with regard to the more intangible aspects affecting the bargaining processes and shaping their outcomes — such as policy attention, effort mobilization, and unity of purpose — there tends to be an asymmetric advantage favoring the weaker country because, as Hirschman (1945) commented long ago, the stakes are likely higher for it than for the stronger country. Policy achievement, according to this perspective, then becomes a joint function of structural position, policy capacity and, as noted above, good luck.

In regard to the recruitment and regulation of cross-national transfers of resources, the principal challenge to the recipient government is of course to unbundle the package offered by the foreigners. The host officials would want to obtain the most favorable arrangement by enticing certain wanted foreign inputs (capital, technology, or military protection) while keeping out other unwanted foreign inputs (foreign ownership of native industries, control of national defense, or interference in local politics). In this sense, the Japanese government serves as an official doorman (Pempel 1978). It scrutinizes and regulates the admission of external factors into Japan, such as foreign investment, consumer goods, and technology imports. Naturally, an effective gatekeeper controls exit as well as entrance. Accordingly, governmental efforts regarding matters such as profit repatriation by foreign firms and export quotas for the domestically produced goods of these firms also reflect policy capacity.

Policy capacity not only helps to create and sustain conducive foreign linkages in order to lessen domestic tradeoffs (by encouraging foreign subsidies), but also contributes to the elite's ability to dampen and stave off competing societal demands for policy attention. In this sense, the statists are correct in pointing to the importance of a strong and autonomous state in guiding a country's developmental experience (although these analysts tend to focus on the domestic aspects of state capacity to the relative neglect of its foreign aspects).

Taiwan has certainly appeared successful in using its policy capacity to offset its inferior structural position, showing that a weak country may exploit its objective vulnerability and symbolic value in order to influence the incentives of a stronger country. This island can do little about the superior hand held by the

United States while dealing with Washington. It could, however, abet and shape American inclinations to use its power to Taiwan's advantages. The once influential China lobby promoted the KMT's interests in the hallways of Congress and the Pentagon, and ensured the provision of vital resources such as military protection, economic assistance, technology transfer, and preferential trade treatment. Just in terms of direct U.S. aid, Taiwan received about $5.6 billion between roughly 1950 and 1965, in comparison with $3.2 billion of military aid extended by Washington to all of Latin America and all of Africa during the period 1950–77 (Cumings 1984).

Of course, while foreign contributions may help to dampen the pressure on domestic policy tradeoffs, they also introduce foreign influence to one's decision processes. Taiwan's various critical policy initiatives (for example, land reform, currency liberalization, export drive) were only partly due to foresight. In addition, U.S. pressure played an important role. Therefore, the KMT state was in part nudged to undertake various measures that in retrospect turned out to be very important in its quest for growth with equity and stability. Ironically, it was the KMT state's very vulnerability — stemming from its devastating loss in the Chinese civil war and its severe dependency on the United States — that enabled foreign influences to tip the balance of domestic forces in favor of reform. While it was in a more secure position on the Mainland, the KMT showed little inclination to accept U.S. advice for critical reform. This also points to the importance of Taiwan's political symbolism to Washington, since the United States' enthusiasm for reform in Taiwan contrasted with its generally foot-dragging position about socioeconomic change elsewhere in the world, such as most of Latin America where Washington's interests were primarily economic.

Internally, as described in Chapters 5 and 6, the state proved quite successful in designing an overall economic strategy and in leading the island through several important transformations of basic economic structures. More reluctantly perhaps, the state also implemented gradual political relaxation and reform that finally culminated in major steps toward democratization in the late 1980s. This domestic policy success can be explained by the fact that Taiwan almost perfectly fits the three conditions postulated by Rueschemeyer & Evans (1985) as defining a developmental state: (a) a developmentalist ideology, *San Min Chu I*; (b) a capable bureaucracy, staffed by civil servants who originally came from the Mainland and those who were later recruited through highly competitive examinations; and (c) autonomy from the dominant classes. This last condition is especially important. For example, if the Nationalists had been beholden to the dominant economic classes, as many authoritarian regimes are, they never would have destroyed the rural gentry with land reform and probably would not have threatened the protected profits of local businessmen by moving from import substitution to an export-oriented economy.

The very evident policy success and capacity of the regime in Taiwan, hence, calls attention to the nature of the regime which Zeigler (1988) has called "state corporatism" (Cumings uses the more cumbersome term "bureaucratic-authoritarian industrializing regime" or BAIR). It merits this appellation because, at least until quite recently, the state essentially stood above society and enforced a political and social compact upon the nation. This compact included the right of the Mainlander-dominated state to set general economic policy and to seek to upgrade the economy along market-conforming lines; the encouragement of Islanders to pursue economic activities with little government restraint as long as they did not challenge the institutions of the national government — which resulted in the Islanders being the major beneficiaries of the "economic miracle;" and the suppression of independent labor movements (see below) which was nevertheless offset by other policies benefitting the workers and farmers (for example, land reform, education, and the discouragement of large-scale corporations) due to the elite's view of itself as protecting the people from Islander landlords and capitalists. This enforced social compact is also notable for what it has not included — the state's using its monopoly power to "milk" society, as occurred in the "crony capitalism" of the Philippines under Ferdinand Marcos, for instance. Rather, the Mainlander-dominated regime has been willing to permit Islanders to garner the greatest profits from rapid growth, to expand the elite segments included in the regime, and to sponsor continual socioeconomic transformation (Amsden 1985, Chu 1989, Clark 1989b, Gold 1986, Haggard 1990, Pang 1990, Wade 1990, Zeigler 1988).

In short, the state has clearly played a key role in Taiwan's economic development. In terms of the three types of state roles summarized in Figure 2.7, it has certainly had a leading part in economic management. While its leadership in industrial targeting has usually been indirect and informal with the exception of the activities of public corporations (Chu 1989, Lam 1990), it has appeared to be quite successful in devising macroeconomic (fiscal and monetary) policies, constructing infrastructure, regulating MNCs, providing a conducive environment for entrepreneurship, and promoting (at least indirectly) social equity and welfare.

The state has also been given credit (and with more than a little justification, blame) for maintaining political order and for controlling both the dominant and subordinate interest groups — thus helping to explain the absence of expected tradeoffs, such as the ones that rapid growth would create political instability and that prolonged stability would unleash forces leading to economic stagnation and social rigidity. In addition, the authoritarian power of the state might also have helped it to manage huge defense expenditures without evidently impairing economic performance or popular welfare. In contrast, economic austerity programs intended to dampen inflation and consumption often come unglued in Argentina, Brazil, and Mexico because the government is unable to impose the costs of adjustment on all social elements, particularly organized labor. Similarly, when faced with competing demands for more public spending on "guns" as well as "butter," Western liberal democracies customarily have a difficult time saying no to either. They are reluctant to bite the bullet and, as a result, tend to succumb to tendencies of fiscal extravagance and monetary excess. By trying to get a quart out of a pint pot (through deficit financing), they in effect transform the tradeoff between alternative public expenditures to that between current government consumption on the one hand, and future economic growth and stability on the other hand.

Finally, the staunchly anticommunist Kuomintang would certainly not appear to be much of a candidate for the role advocated by many dependency theorists — that of destroying capitalism and implementing a planned economy. Yet, in less radical ways, Taiwan's government has taken important steps along this line. The land reform destroyed the power of the rural gentry; popular education permitted massive upward socioeconomic mobility for much of the population; and the regime appears to have manipulated rather than fawned upon foreign capital.

We do not mean to imply that the success and flexibility of Taiwan's political economy should be entirely attributed to conscientious policy choice and a deliberate eclectic inclination. A significant part of this flexibility has in fact been due to *historical legacies*. One central set of legacies is the timing and sequence of social, economic, and political change in a nation. Thus, it appears that a policy capacity to control the speed and sequence of sociopolitical transformation helps to deflect or contain the deleterious feedback due to the pursuit of multiple policy desiderata. Effective statecraft calls for the government to stay ahead of the revolution of rising expectations by the masses, and yet to pace the process of modernization in such a way as not to overload its policy capacity (Huntington 1968). As Lipset (1963) has remarked in regard to a country's prospect for achieving liberal democracy, the timing and sequence of various historical challenges to governmental authority is critical. To the extent that the onset of these challenges is temporally separated, officials can focus on them one at a time (and thus avoid the danger of being overwhelmed by them simultaneously). Moreover, the successful resolution of each historical crisis enhances the government's credibility and legitimacy, thus putting it in a better position to deal with the next policy challenge.

In Taiwan's case, timing and sequence were important in several respects. First, learning from its disastrous experience on the Mainland, the KMT had the foresight to undertake a series of basic land reforms on the island as one of its first priorities in the late 1940s and early 1950s. These reforms laid the groundwork for the island's subsequent system of equitable distribution of income, and removed two of the common causes for social unrest and political instability cross-nationally (namely, the peasants' thirst for land and the people's sense of relative deprivation as a result of an unequal distribution of income). It gave the KMT state a degree of popular support and legitimacy in Taiwan's countryside that it did not enjoy on the Mainland. Second, the land reform program undermined the power of the landlord class and, as a consequence, defused another potential source of challenge to the KMT state. Moreover, by paying the landlords with bonds and shares of manufacturing and transportation enterprises for their land, the KMT converted them into future industrialists and in the process also removed a traditional rural source of opposition to economic modernization. Thus, for example, Taiwan does not have the equivalent of the so-called sugar bloc that is a bastion of conservative economic and political force in the Philippines. Finally, the land reform program increased the peasants' productive incentives, and through a variety of measures (particularly the enforced rice-for-fertilizer barter arrangement) the KMT state was able to extract the rural surplus and transfer it for urban and industrial purposes. In short, then, the Land-to-the-Tiller program seems crucial for Taiwan's subsequent achievement of distributive equity, political stability, and economic growth.

The timing of incoming foreign capital was also important in what Deyo calls "linkage sequencing." The massive U.S. economic and military aid, prompted by the outbreak of the Korean War, came at the most opportune time for the KMT. Taiwan's economy was at that time suffering from rampant inflation and a crushing defense burden. The U.S. aid, both directly and indirectly (by interposing the Seventh Fleet in the Taiwan Strait and thereby preventing a Communist invasion of the island), was critical for stabilizing prices and morale. In contrast to the inflow of official aid, the appearance of foreign private investment came to the island relatively late. Multinational corporations had been deterred by the political uncertainty due to the lingering Chinese civil war from investing in the island. When they did start to invest in the late 1960s (after the termination of official U.S. aid), the local businesses had already developed sufficient market presence and production experience to resist the common tendency of denationalization elsewhere in the Third World. Moreover, by then the KMT state was directly operating those large-scale enterprises (such as steel and energy) that have historically attracted foreign investors. It was also able to undertake careful approval and stringent regulation of the foreign direct investment, thereby serving the role of an official doorman mentioned earlier. Finally, much of the foreign direct investment going to Taiwan has come from the overseas Chinese community and, as such, has not raised the same sort of political overtone that foreign direct investment has customarily engendered in Third World countries.

In Taiwan, political reform has followed social and economic reform. Concerns with the looming presence of the People's Liberation Army across the Taiwan Strait had provided official justification for and mass acquiescence to a brand of "soft authoritarianism." Until the mid 1980s the KMT state had a practical monopoly of power and severely restricted the people's civil liberties and political rights. The KMT state, however, did ensure social order and political continuity, and in this sense provided a stable business environment for the island's economic growth to take place. The democratization process, defined to mean partisan politics and pluralistic competition among various interest groups, has been only unfolding tentatively in the past few years, after the island has undergone its most rapid period of economic growth.

Another set of important historical legacies concerns several dualistic features of Taiwan's society and political economy. That certain aspects of a dual political economy can have positive benefits is somewhat ironic, since dependency theory sees a dual economy (in the form of the exclusion of most of the population from the modern sector) as the primary distortion of dependent development. More specifically, the island has a dual economy featuring a select group of large industrial conglomerates at one tier, and many small and medium enterprises at another tier. The large corporations are naturally concentrated in the capital-intensive sectors, while the smaller firms tend to be involved in labor-intensive production. While there are several large-scale private firms, such as Formosa Plastics, many of the corporations in the former category are state enterprises. They have served the useful function of preventing the denationalization of the economy by preempting heavy industries, such as steel, that are usually dominated by foreign corporations. However, they have been charged with being inefficient, thereby raising the costs of key inputs for many parts of the private sector.

Fairly small companies have been the more dynamic sector of Taiwan's economy, and have been at the forefront of its highly successful export drive. Because of their smaller size and the absence of a rigid corporate structure (many of these businesses are family-owned and -operated), they are more adept in responding to changing commercial conditions. Indeed, as in the case of other East Asian trading nations such as Japan, this adaptability has been a key ingredient of Taiwan's successful export expansion. In contrast to the typical Western reliance on Fordism — with its emphasis on capturing economies of scale by making long production runs using standardized parts — the East Asians have stressed commercial adaptability (Friedman 1988, Lam 1990, Morawetz 1981). They tend to derive their competitive edge from timely adjustment to changing consumer tastes, product innovation and upgrading to overcome quantitative restrictions on their exports, and continuous cultivation of customer loyalty by paying attention to matters such as prompt delivery, attractive packaging, and follow-up service.

One should also mention that in contrast to other national economies that are dominated more by a small number of industrial giants, Taiwan's many small and medium companies help to distribute privation during times of economic hardship, and therefore serve a useful purpose as shock-absorbers. At the same time, however, the very existence and vigor of the small and medium companies (often serving as subcontractors for the larger firms) testify to the operation of industrial trickle down, and contribute to the island's comparatively egalitarian social system. Yet another implication of the relatively decentralized nature of Taiwan's economy (in comparison to, say, South Korea's which is more dominated by the *chaebol*) is that the government gains greater leverage over the business sector.

The government's leverage relative to various domestic actors had been enhanced by several other dualist aspects of Taiwan's society and politics. One notices on this island the combination of war trauma as well as ruling party continuity, both of which are featured prominently in Olson's (1982) theory of distributional coalitions. Taiwan was returned to Chinese rule after the Japanese defeat in World War II. The KMT regime was in turn transplanted to Taiwan as a result of its defeat in the Chinese civil war on the Mainland. This regime owed little to the vested interests on Taiwan and, consequently, was able to launch various socioeconomic reforms (principally the land reform) that it was unable and unwilling to undertake on the Mainland. These reforms helped to unblock social incentives and productive resources that were previously stifled. They therefore laid the foundation for the island's subsequent economic growth, income equity, and relative political stability.

Yet, while war or revolutionary trauma made possible crucial socioeconomic reforms, Taiwan did not suffer from chronic regime instability or leadership turnover — whether as a result of coups d'etat or electoral cycling. Instead, as in several other East Asian countries, this island features the long-term rule of a dominant party, namely, the KMT. Thus, it has been in a better position to develop policy consensus and personnel continuity that are important to promote long-term planning and a stable outlook in the management of a political economy. The liabilities associated with a constantly changing and even contradictory policy agenda due to electoral stalemate or partisan rotation have generally been avoided. In comparison with the rampant pluralism of interest groups' influence upon the U.S. government and the policy drift that it can induce (Lowi 1979), East Asian states certainly appear to be "strong and autonomous."

The ability of the KMT state to achieve and sustain this dominant position relative to the civilian society, in turn, has its historical origins in both the long-standing "benevolent" (and many times "malevolent") paternalism of Chinese rule on the Mainland which influenced the Kuomintang, and the period of Japanese colonialism which left many marks on Taiwan's society. One enduring legacy of the colonial period was, of course, the administrative system which suppressed and stunted the formation of organized interests by the island's native entrepreneurs, workers, and peasants. The authoritarian *sotokufu* laid the foundation for the subsequent strong and autonomous KMT state. The latter inherited a ubiquitous police force and bureaucratic apparatus from the Japanese, when the island was returned to Chinese rule after World War II.

Two other dualistic aspects of Taiwan's political economy have to do with the traditional bifurcation of the island's political and economic elite along the lines of their provincial origins, and with the division of labor between the politicians and the bureaucrats. The former arrangement has turned a potential source of political instability on the island into an important reason for cooperation between the public and private sectors. Political power, especially as reflected by the control of the military and secret police, has historically gone to the Mainlander officials, while the large private enterprises have traditionally been in the hands of

Islander businessmen. This informal pact eschews a monopoly of power and wealth by either group, and has thus far produced symbiotic coexistence and mutual adjustment by the Mainlander and Islander communities. Indeed, as discussed in Chapter 5, this policy accommodation and the gradual broadening of the KMT ruling elite to include new Islander elements represent considerable policy foresight.

Concomitantly, as Johnson (1981) has noticed for all the capitalist East Asian countries, there is a tendency in Taiwan for separating the functions of reigning from ruling. While the KMT stalwarts have continued to control the levers of political and military power, they have generally left the administration of Taiwan's political economy to the technocrats. This separation of politics from economics facilitates administrative latitude. It enables decisions to be undertaken on the basis of technical merit rather than political orthodoxy. Yet, this administrative flexibility and technical emphasis are sustained in the context of ruling-party continuity.

The observation concerning the separation of reigning and ruling should not be construed to imply some neutral or even aloof stance assumed by Taiwan's developmental state. The pact of domination between the KMT stalwarts and Islander business-men has definitely excluded organized labor (Deyo 1989). As in the case of several other capitalist East Asian countries, public spending in Taiwan has featured rather low levels of social overhead (for example, unemployment benefits, retirement pensions, workers' compensation). Indeed, and as has been commented on by many observers, much of the initial comparative advantage of the East Asian trading nations (including Taiwan) derived from their cheap, pliable, and relatively skilled workforce. Therefore, the island's industrial flexibility as well as its fiscal conservatism and monetary stability have been to a substantial extent due to the exploitation and suppression of the workers. Taiwan's previous ability to engage in competitive export pricing, to attract foreign direct investment, to absorb external economic shocks, and to practice fiscal balance can all be largely traced to the political weakness of its organized labor. The regime's policy space in the management of these matters has been less constrained by the demands of organized labor. Put in another way, the KMT state has had much more political room to execute policies intended to balance the desiderata of both economic growth and stability than the developed liberal democracies.

The weakness of Taiwan's organized labor is offset to some extent by a paternalistic management. Workers are often compensated less in strict wage terms than in fringe benefits (for example, cafeteria, dormitory) subsidized by the company, in relative job security, and in the tradition of year-end bonuses which constitutes a flexible form of employee profit-sharing. Consequently, Taiwan has not experienced widespread labor unrest despite its relatively low level of government expenditures for social overhead. Additionally, as mentioned earlier, labor peace is facilitated by the fact that many medium and small companies on the island are operated by family members.

In contrast to most developing countries, however, Taiwan's political economy has largely escaped one deleterious dualism, namely, the gap between the rural and urban sectors which has been one of the chief sources of income disparity elsewhere. Partly because of its small size, there has been (especially in the 1960s and 1970s) considerable seasonal migration of the labor force between farm work and factory work. The urban employees (especially young females) often send the bulk of their earnings to parents in the countryside, which serves to absorb the urban unemployed during economic recession. Given the decentralized structure of Taiwan's economy, much of the cottage industry has also found its way to the countryside, thus providing rural employment opportunities when there is a lull in agricultural work. These considerations suggest that Taiwan has largely avoided the economic and social biases stemming from a small industrial enclave surrounded by a large rural hinterland (Ho 1979).

The most important historical legacy undergirding Taiwan's successful political economy may well be its Confucian culture, which is widely seen as promoting both economic dynamism and political stability in East Asia (Hofheinz & Calder 1982, Pye with Pye 1985). In fact, Tai (1989) specifically argues that Confucianism encompasses an affective culture which can present an alternative basis for development to the Western cultural traditions of individualism, efficiency, and rationality. This affective culture has proved an important stimulus to economic innovation and entrepreneurship in several important ways. First, loyalty to the family as a kinship unit stimulates efforts to increase collective wealth and defer consumption for future benefits. Second, Confucian values emphasize education, hard work, and investment. Third, the affective culture encourages a paternalistic management style and a reliance on personalized business networks that form a distinctive East Asian commercial environment. While such practices contravene conventional Western management theory, they are increasingly seen as a key ingredient in the East Asian success story (Chang 1985, Fei 1986, Greenhalgh 1984, 1988a, Harrell 1985, Hofstede & Bond 1988, Lam 1988, Numazaki 1986, Prestowitz 1988, Silin 1976, Tai 1989, Winckler 1987, Wong 1986, 1988a, 1988b, Wu 1985).

Confucian culture is also widely credited with promoting stability in regime-society relations (Hofheinz & Calder 1982, Pye with Pye 1985, Zeigler 1988). First, the respect for authority and government in Confucian society undoubtedly contributed to the acceptance of KMT rule through the early 1980s. Second, the emphasis on consensus and mediation in decision-making has probably facilitated the mutual acceptance of the social pact between the Mainlander-dominated government and Islander business community, despite the fact that business–government relations are usually described as "cool" and "distant" (Chu 1989; Pang 1990). Third, the willingness of the political elites to forego maximizing their own material benefits, as noted above, might also be explained by the Confucian value system, which gives the highest status to scholar-bureaucrats in contrast to money-grubbing businessmen.

Confucian culture has also been related, however, to a less salubrious recent change in Taiwan and several other East Asian nations — the growing acrimony in political conflict between regime and opposition. Traditional government in China was based on personalistic ties and the normative assumption that the state ruled for the moral benefit of the nation. Thus, there was little precedent for democratic competition among parties and interest groups and, in particular, political debate was conducted in highly moralistic terms (Moody 1988, Pye with Pye 1985). This Confucian tradition, then, can explain why the KMT and DPP have trouble accepting each other's legitimacy (Myers 1987).

This also points out that Taiwan's experience with Confucian culture contrasts sharply with that of 19th-century China where a conservative Confucian bureaucracy stifled political and economic change, giving rise to the received wisdom until lately that Confucian culture inhibits development (Weber 1951). More broadly, it seems that Confucian culture bears an ambiguous relationship to development, because its implications for developmental activities are clearly contradictory. Its secularism, advocacy of a merit-based bureaucracy committed to national betterment, emphasis on individual contributions to collective (especially family) accumulation, and commitment to social mobility based on achievement criteria are all seen as conducive for development. On the other hand, the low status of entrepreneurs, emphasis on ritual and order, and distrust of specialized expertise all create pressures for reactionary politics and stagnant economies. Moreover, other important aspects of Confucianism, such as familism, respect for hierarchy and authority, and reliance on past precedents to determine and justify social values, are certainly central tenets of traditionalism.

Wong (1986) takes this line of reasoning a step farther in his study of the impact of Confucian culture upon Hong Kong's economy. In essence, he asks what characteristics of an economy and polity would determine whether Confucian culture would help or hinder development. The major factors in Hong Kong's political economy which he sees as making Confucianism facilitative — (a) a "refugee" ethic disrupting the traditional institutions of social and political control, (b) a government independent of dominant social classes, and (c) a small and urbanized nation — would all seem to apply to Taiwan under the KMT. Thus, even the impact of Taiwan's cultural heritage may reflect *fortuna* in the sense that it was determined by the fortuitous outcomes of World War II and the Chinese civil war.

Thus, Taiwan's pursuit of various policy desiderata has been helped by favorable structural position, policy foresight and flexibility, and simply good luck. Its developmental history reflects a sequence of mutually reinforcing stages: (1) a preoccupation with military security and political control; (2) the big push to launch industrialization through export expansion; (3) concerted efforts to translate the fruits of economic growth into higher qualities of life (first quantitatively, and then qualitatively); and (4) the initiation of political liberalization and democratization. In the economic sphere, Taiwan also passed through a series of stages, moving it along the product cycle of ever higher value-added activities: (1) land reform and increased rural productivity, (2) the "easy" stage of import-substitution industrialization, (3) low-cost labor-intensive exports, (4) heavy industrialization, and (5) high-technology production.

These stages can overlap temporally, and might not have been always planned in advance. They were sometimes precipitated by unexpected events. For example, the succes of import substitution forced the government to make further strategic economic choices; and the rise of a middle class increased pressure for political reform (Cheng & Haggard 1991, Tien 1989). However, political and economic adaptability to changing circumstances (as discussed in Chapter 5) contributed each time to role graduation.

The sequence of Taiwan's recent political history differs from the normal pattern suggested by Leonard Binder and his associates (1971). They conceptualized political development as the successful surmounting of five crises: (a) identity, (b) legitimacy, (c) penetration, (d) participation, and (e) distribution. While their formulation does not imply that these crises have to be solved in any specific order, it does suggest that the successful resolution of the earlier crises will make it easier to tackle the later ones. In Taiwan, however, the Kuomintang's first priority was *penetration*. Its economic success made *distribution* relatively easy and facilitated significant *legitimacy*. However, moving to the next stage of *participation* has led to a questioning of Taiwan's *identity* by the Democratic Progressive Party — that is, are its residents Chinese or Taiwanese (Cheng & Haggard 1991)? Thus, this island's experience suggests both that the developmental processes may be quite variegated and that even successful sequences are not assured of ultimate stability.

From the preceding discussion of a country's structural position and policy capacity, we see that the developmentalist, dependency, statist, and tradeoff perspectives do not really offer logically opposite descriptions of reality or prescriptions for policy conduct. Rather, they present views on different faces or aspects of interrelated policy issues. Thus, for example, the developmentalists advocate an outward-looking strategy of export expansion because they see this approach as maximizing a country's comparative advantage, thus enabling it to exploit particularly favorable niches offered by the structure of global division of economic labor. In contrast, the *dependentistas* argue that due to the discrepant assets held by different countries, this structure of global economy tends to be biased in favor of the developed countries' bargaining leverage and to the relative detriment of the developing countries' interests. It seems that both of these arguments can be quite compatible with a posture of active pursuit of foreign markets and resources based on one's evolving comparative advantage, as well as guarded vigilance to protect the domestic political economy against unwanted foreign intrusion.

Indeed, we would argue that much of the recent social, economic, and political accomplishments of the East Asian capitalist countries, including Taiwan, can be traced to their effective combination of the bimodal injunctions embodied in the various models of political economy. They have thus encouraged private entrepreneurship while at the same time insisting on governmental economic tutelage. Vigorous market competition has accompanied active statist intervention, and private firms have coexisted and indeed developed a symbiotic relationship with public enterprises. Similarly, while pursuing a policy of active commercial expansion abroad, these countries have not necessarily eschewed the option of import substitution and indeed protectionism (most notably in the agricultural sector) as a matter of doctrinaire principle. As another example, efforts to recruit various foreign contributions (capital, technology, arms imports) go hand in hand with other efforts to regulate and contain the influence of their providers (for example, various requirements regarding domestic contents, export quotas, joint ownership, and technology transfer).

Accordingly, this pragmatic flexibility — eclecticism, if you will — seems to be a hallmark of Taiwan's and the other capitalist East Asian countries' (Japan, South Korea, Singapore) economic success. A reluctance to be boxed in by any given orthodoxy, and a concomitant sensitivity to the received wisdom presented by competing paradigms offer an important insight to the policy capacity of their elites. In this light, the inability of our earlier qualitative and quantitative analysis to validate fully the contentions of one or another perspective does not necessarily imply some "failure" on the part of these formulations. In fact, our results suggest that each has a kernel of truth. Thus, the particular features suggested by these rival perspectives can coexist in the same political economy (or apply to it at different periods of its developmental experience). Indeed, as we have argued, an ability to bridge and synthesize these perspectives and to address their competing concerns serves a country better in adapting to a rapidly evolving and uncertain world than a rigid adherence to any one orthodoxy.

Despite its accomplishments to date, however, Taiwan faces considerable challenge to sustain its success story. This challenge stems in part from the imperative of industrial adjustment in order to maintain the island's commercial edge in foreign exports. Taiwan can no longer claim a comparative advantage in cheap labor; countries with even lower wage costs (the Philippines, Thailand, and China) have turned to export promotion as a means of financing their domestic growth. Concomitantly, the rising exchange value of the Taiwan currency and protectionist measures in the United States and Western Europe threaten to derail the island's export drive. Taiwan is therefore undergoing a period of economic transformation whereby its manufacturers strive to upgrade their exports from labor-intensive to capital- and knowledge-intensive products.

Concomitantly, mass employment and economic structure are shifting from the relatively high-productivity sector of manufacturing to the relatively low-productivity sector of service. These trends raise the ominous prospect of eventual industrial hollowing-out, a process that has been abetted by the rising value of the New Taiwan dollar. Rising currency value makes Taiwan's exports less competitive and investment in foreign production sites more attractive, developments that have been further compounded by mounting protectionism abroad. However, as foreign direct investment moves an increasing share of domestic production to overseas plants, it redistributes practical production experience from one's own workers to foreign nationals. As well, traditional management–labor relations and subcontracting networks are disrupted, with serious implications for the workers' incentives, the management's decision flexibility, and the transmission of technical knowledge and economic profits throughout society. Thus, Taiwan might be following Japan's footsteps in this respect as well; in its turn, Japan might be repeating the

American and British precedents of gradual deindustrialization through export of capital and technology for overseas production (Yoon 1990).

Another challenge facing Taiwan heralds the arrival to some extent of a "post-material" generation. Having successfully met most basic human needs, the government is faced with the task of confronting other aspects of quality of life that have become a casualty of rapid economic growth and social transformation. Examples include the island's very serious problems of air and water pollution, traffic congestion, inadequate social welfare system, and rising incidence of crime. Additionally, "easy money" has fueled speculative investment in the stock market and real estate. The resultant inflation has put affordable housing beyond the reach of most young people, and threatens to undermine the previous achievement of a comparatively egalitarian society.

Finally, the island faces the challenge of political adjustment. On the one hand, the KMT state is undergoing a period of democratic transition, learning to share power with other political and social groups. This democratization process has brought considerable stress and schism within the KMT between its so-called conservative and liberal wings. It has also aroused concerns about social order and political stability in the wake of increasingly frequent and fractious partisan confrontations in governmental fora and in the streets. On the other hand, the KMT state is groping for some acceptable status in the international system and modus vivendi with China. Neither Taiwan independence nor reunification with China according to Beijing's terms is currently acceptable to the ruling elite.

More theoretically, these challenges suggest that the relative applicability of the four theoretical traditions to Taiwan may be stood on their head. For the last four decades, developmentalism and statism have probably best described the island's political economy, while the warnings of the dependency and tradeoff perspectives seemed to be missing the mark. Now, however, the island is being challenged in precisely the way the latter two approaches would predict, while the former two's confidence in, respectively, the market and the state seems more questionable. Despite neoclassical faith in the market, Taiwan's export-based economy is being threatened by both the operation (that is, competition from the next wave NICs) and the distortion (that is, rising protectionism in the developed world) of international markets. Moreover, the economy's enforced movement away from labor-intensive production endangers the system of small-scale enterprises on which the island's flexible-production strategy has been based. In terms of the state, perceptions of growing political instability and governmental paralysis in policy-making call to mind Huntington's (1968) argument about the necessity for political order and Olson's (1982) warning about the danger of distributional coalitions. Whereas the government's defense burden has declined over time, popular pressure for it to increase public support for social welfare, environmental protection, and political accountability has mounted precipitously. The very process of democratization and liberalization undermines the strength and autonomy of the state relative to society. Thus, it remains to be seen whether flexibility, foresight, and *fortuna* will continue to sustain Taiwan's policy achievement in the last decade of the 20th century.

Appendix

Table A.1 Indicators of economic growth.

Year	GNP per capita			Real GNP growth rate (%)	Real Indl growth rate (%)	Agriculture % of NDP	Industry % of NDP
	Real 1981 NT$	Current NT$	Current US$				
1952	17155	2019	153	12.0	—	36.0	18.0
1953	18160	2602	176	9.3	25.4	38.3	17.7
1954	19214	2759	177	9.5	5.7	31.7	22.2
1955	20014	3162	203	8.1	12.9	32.9	21.1
1956	20377	3502	141	5.5	3.6	31.6	22.4
1957	21188	3959	160	7.3	12.6	31.8	23.9
1958	21870	4282	173	6.6	8.5	31.1	24.0
1959	22812	4782	131	7.8	11.9	30.5	25.7
1960	23524	5601	154	6.5	14.2	32.9	24.9
1961	24356	6078	152	6.8	15.6	31.6	25.0
1962	25508	6498	162	7.9	8.0	29.4	25.7
1963	27089	7137	178	9.4	9.2	26.8	28.1
1964	29549	8113	202	12.3	21.1	28.3	28.9
1965	31892	8697	217	11.0	16.3	27.4	28.6
1966	33826	9480	236	9.0	15.6	26.3	28.8
1967	36495	10685	266	10.6	16.7	23.9	30.8
1968	38887	12151	302	9.1	22.3	22.1	32.5
1969	41460	13783	344	9.1	19.9	18.9	34.6
1970	45198	15544	388	11.3	20.1	18.0	34.5
1971	50050	17730	442	13.0	23.6	14.9	36.7
1972	55708	20885	522	13.4	21.2	14.2	40.3
1973	61668	26596	696	12.8	16.2	14.1	43.8
1974	61262	34974	920	1.2	−4.5	14.5	41.2
1975	62797	36642	964	4.4	9.5	14.9	39.1
1976	69964	43033	1132	13.7	23.3	13.4	42.7
1977	75604	49449	1301	10.3	13.3	12.5	43.4
1978	84610	58282	1575	14.0	22.5	11.3	44.9
1979	90005	69115	1920	8.5	6.4	10.4	45.1

Appendix

Table A.1 Contd.

Year	GNP per capita			Real GNP growth rate (%)	Real Indl growth rate (%)	Agriculture % of NDP	Industry % of NDP
	Real 1981 NT$	Current NT$	Current US$				
1980	94580	84398	2344	7.1	6.8	9.2	44.7
1981	98179	98179	2675	5.7	3.5	8.7	44.4
1982	99687	103090	2650	3.4	−0.9	9.2	42.7
1983	105893	111558	2782	8.0	12.7	8.8	43.4
1984	115356	122479	3093	10.6	11.8	7.6	45.2
1985	119606	127210	3196	5.1	2.7	6.9	44.9
1986	132019	145392	3841	11.7	13.9	6.5	46.8
1987	146111	161726	5083	11.9	10.7	6.3	47.5
1988	155168	173137	6055	7.3	4.3	6.1	46.2

Sources: see note on pp. 178–80.

Table A.2 Export performance and domestic consumption.

Year	Exports as % of GNP	Real export growth rate (%)	Industrial content of exports (%)	Trade balance (current million US$)	Real growth private consumption (%)	Real growth government consumption (%)
1952	8.5	—	8.1	−71	16.7	9.3
1953	8.6	11.0	8.4	−64	8.6	5.0
1954	5.8	−27.0	10.6	−118	9.9	14.7
1955	6.4	20.1	10.4	−74	5.4	8.8
1956	8.5	40.6	17.0	−76	1.8	15.9
1957	9.2	15.3	12.6	−64	6.3	6.8
1958	8.6	0.3	14.0	−70	8.0	7.0
1959	11.0	38.1	23.6	−74	4.9	7.9
1960	9.5	−8.0	32.3	−133	4.2	1.5
1961	11.2	24.9	40.9	−127	7.5	3.9
1962	11.3	9.5	50.5	−86	8.3	9.1
1963	15.2	47.0	41.1	−30	6.6	4.1
1964	17.0	25.4	42.5	5	13.8	6.2
1965	16.0	4.3	46.0	−106	9.8	5.4
1966	17.0	16.0	55.1	−86	6.4	7.8
1967	17.6	14.4	61.6	−165	9.6	9.9
1968	18.6	15.4	68.4	−114	9.4	8.9
1969	21.4	25.0	74.0	−164	7.8	10.5
1970	26.2	36.5	78.6	−43	8.2	8.2

Table A.2 Contd.

Year	Exports as % of GNP	Real export growth rate (%)	Industrial content of exports (%)	Trade balance (current million US$)	Real growth private consumption (%)	Real growth government consumption (%)
1971	31.3	35.0	80.9	216	9.2	5.2
1972	37.8	37.0	83.3	474	10.9	5.1
1973	41.6	24.2	84.6	691	12.2	6.7
1974	38.9	−5.4	84.5	−1327	5.1	−9.1
1975	34.4	−7.8	83.6	−643	6.5	13.8
1976	44.1	45.9	87.6	567	8.3	10.4
1977	43.1	7.8	87.5	850	7.4	11.8
1978	47.4	25.2	89.2	1660	9.2	7.0
1979	48.4	10.9	90.5	1329	10.7	8.2
1980	47.8	5.8	90.8	78	5.3	7.8
1981	47.0	4.0	92.2	1411	3.7	3.4
1982	45.8	0.7	92.4	3316	4.8	6.6
1983	48.5	14.2	93.1	4836	6.0	4.4
1984	52.1	18.9	93.9	8497	8.7	6.8
1985	50.2	1.3	93.8	10624	5.1	5.7
1986	53.5	18.8	93.5	15684	6.4	4.0
1987	53.9	12.6	93.9	18655	10.2	7.4
1988	50.5	0.6	94.5	10929	12.6	8.2

Sources: see note on pp. 178–80.

Table A.3 Prices and employment.

Year	Wholesale price growth (%)	Consumer price growth (%)	Money supply growth (%)	Unemployment rate (%)	Total employment (1,000s)	Real manufacturing wage growth (%)
1952	—	—	—	4.6	2929	—
1953	8.8	18.8	—	4.4	2964	—
1954	2.4	1.7	—	4.2	3026	10.8
1955	14.1	9.9	—	4.0	3108	1.5
1956	12.7	10.5	—	3.8	3149	3.2
1957	7.2	7.5	—	3.9	3229	1.6
1958	1.4	1.3	—	4.0	3340	4.3
1959	10.3	10.6	—	4.0	3422	−2.4
1960	14.1	18.4	—	4.1	3473	−1.6
1961	3.2	7.8	—	4.3	3505	12.7

Table A.3 Contd.

Year	Wholesale price growth (%)	Consumer price growth (%)	Money supply growth (%)	Unemployment rate (%)	Total employment (1,000s)	Real manufacturing wage growth (%)
1962	3.0	2.3	5.0	4.3	3541	2.9
1963	6.5	2.2	28.1	4.5	3592	1.6
1964	2.5	-0.2	35.0	4.5	3658	3.7
1965	-4.7	-0.1	15.9	3.4	3763	7.8
1966	1.5	2.0	12.2	3.1	3856	4.4
1967	2.5	3.4	30.1	2.3	4050	8.6
1968	3.0	7.9	11.5	1.8	4225	2.6
1969	-0.3	5.0	15.6	1.9	4390	-3.7
1970	2.7	3.6	15.0	1.7	4576	5.2
1971	0.0	2.8	30.6	1.7	4738	13.6
1972	4.4	3.0	34.1	1.5	4948	4.2
1973	22.9	8.2	50.4	1.3	5327	1.1
1974	40.6	47.5	10.5	1.5	5486	-9.0
1975	-5.1	5.2	28.8	2.5	5521	14.6
1976	2.8	2.5	25.1	1.8	5669	11.9
1977	2.8	7.0	33.6	1.8	5980	13.1
1978	3.5	5.8	37.0	1.7	6228	5.8
1979	13.8	9.8	7.7	1.3	6424	8.6
1980	21.5	19.0	22.7	1.3	6547	5.5
1981	7.6	16.3	13.8	1.4	6672	5.9
1982	-0.2	3.0	14.6	2.2	6811	6.0
1983	-1.2	1.4	18.4	2.8	7070	4.4
1984	0.5	0.0	9.3	2.5	7308	14.6
1985	-2.6	-0.2	12.2	3.0	7428	-2.0
1986	-3.3	0.7	51.4	2.7	7733	6.3
1987	-3.3	0.5	37.8	2.0	8022	9.2
1988	-1.6	1.3	24.4	1.7	8108	9.8

Sources: see note on pp. 178–80.

Table A.4 Savings and capital formation.

Year	Savings % of GNP	Investment % of GDP	Rediscount rate (%)	Foreign reserves (billion current US$)
1952	9.2	15.3	—	—
1953	8.9	14.1	—	—
1954	7.7	16.0	—	—
1955	9.0	13.3	—	—
1956	9.2	16.1	—	—
1957	10.6	15.8	—	—
1958	9.9	16.6	—	—
1959	10.3	18.8	—	—
1960	12.7	20.2	—	—
1961	12.8	20.0	14.40	0.1
1962	12.4	17.8	12.96	0.1
1963	17.1	18.3	11.52	0.2
1964	19.6	18.7	11.52	0.2
1965	19.6	22.7	11.52	0.2
1966	21.5	21.2	11.52	0.3
1967	22.5	24.6	10.80	0.3
1968	22.1	25.1	11.88	0.3
1969	23.8	24.5	10.80	0.4
1970	25.5	25.5	9.80	0.5
1971	28.8	26.2	9.25	0.6
1972	32.1	25.6	8.50	1.0
1973	34.6	29.1	10.75	1.0
1974	31.7	39.2	12.00	1.1
1975	26.9	30.4	10.75	1.1
1976	32.5	30.6	9.50	1.5
1977	32.9	28.1	8.25	1.3
1978	34.9	28.2	8.25	1.4
1979	34.5	32.9	11.80	1.4
1980	33.0	33.8	11.00	2.2
1981	32.0	29.9	11.75	7.2
1982	30.4	24.8	7.75	8.5
1983	32.1	22.7	7.25	11.9
1984	33.7	21.2	6.75	15.7
1985	33.5	17.6	5.25	22.6
1986	37.8	16.0	4.50	46.3
1987	38.5*	19.7	4.50	76.7
1988	34.9*	24.0	4.50	79.0

* There was a slight change in the definition of savings from earlier years (the two indices based on these definitions differed by 1–3% during the 1980s). The earlier definition was used for 1952–1987 because the later one would have included U.S. aid in domestic savings.
Savings: see note on pp. 178–80.

Table A.5 Distribution of personal income by household.

Year	Lowest fifth	Second fifth	Third fifth	Fourth fifth	Highest fifth	Ratio top/ bottom fifth	Gini coefficient
1953	3.0	8.3	9.1	18.2	61.4	20.47	—
1961	4.5	9.7	14.0	19.8	52.0	11.56	—
1964	7.71	12.57	16.62	27.03	41.07	5.33	0.321
1966	7.90	12.45	16.19	22.01	41.45	5.25	0.323
1968	7.84	12.22	16.25	22.32	41.37	5.28	0.326
1970	8.44	13.27	17.09	22.51	38.69	4.58	0.294
1972	8.60	13.25	17.06	22.48	38.61	4.49	0.291
1974	8.84	13.49	16.99	22.05	38.63	4.37	0.287
1976	8.91	13.64	17.48	22.71	37.26	4.18	0.280
1978	8.89	13.71	17.53	22.70	37.17	4.18	0.287
1979	8.64	13.68	17.48	22.68	37.52	4.34	0.285
1980	8.82	13.90	17.70	22.78	36.80	4.17	0.277
1981	8.80	13.76	17.62	22.78	37.04	4.21	0.281
1982	8.69	13.80	17.56	22.68	37.27	4.29	0.283
1983	8.61	13.64	17.47	22.73	37.55	4.36	0.287
1984	8.49	13.69	17.62	22.84	37.36	4.40	0.287
1985	8.37	13.59	17.52	22.88	37.64	4.50	0.290
1986	8.30	13.51	17.38	22.65	38.16	4.60	0.296
1987	8.11	13.50	17.53	22.82	38.04	4.69	0.299
1988	—	—	—	—	—	4.85	0.303

Sources: see note on pp. 178–80.

Table A.6 Rural–urban inequality

Year	Town households' income as % of city households	Village households' income as % of city households	Farm households' income as % of nonfarm households
1964	—	—	96.6
1966	—	—	92.1
1968	—	—	71.2
1970	—	—	67.1
1971	—	—	71.7
1972	—	—	75.6
1973	—	—	76.9
1974	—	—	77.8
1975	—	—	75.4
1976	81.7	70.2	82.1

Table A.6 Contd.

Year	Town households' income as % of city households	Village households' income as % of city households	Farm households' income as % of nonfarm households
1977	79.8	70.6	78.1
1978	83.1	72.0	79.0
1979	85.3	71.1	79.7
1980	84.1	70.3	81.6
1981	83.0	68.5	78.5
1982	82.3	69.7	81.0
1983	80.6	70.3	80.0
1984	82.8	68.9	80.0
1985	82.4	70.1	81.4
1986	82.9	69.9	83.3
1987	84.0	67.1	83.1
1988	80.4	67.4	80.8

Sources: see note on pp. 178–80.

Table A.7 Ownership of agricultural land

Year	Full owner (%)	Part owner (%)	Tenant (%)
1952	38	26	36
1953	55	24	21
1954	57	24	19
1955	59	23	18
1956	60	23	17
1957	60	23	17
1958	61	23	16
1959	62	23	15
1960	64	22	14
1961	65	21	14
1962	65	21	14
1963	66	21	13
1964	67	20	13
1965	67	20	13
1966	67	20	13
1967	67	21	12
1968	68	20	12
1969	80	11	9
1970	77	13	10

Table A.7 Contd.

Year	Full owner (%)	Part owner (%)	Tenant (%)
1971	78	12	10
1972	78	12	10
1973	79	12	9
1974	80	11	9
1975	82	9	9
1976	82	9	9
1977	82	9	9
1978	83	9	8
1979	85	7	8
1980	82	11	7
1981	84	9	7
1982	87	7	6
1983	83	11	6
1984	82	12	6
1985	82	12	6
1986	83	12	5
1987	83	12	5
1988	85	11	4

Sources: see note on pp. 178–80.

Table A.8 Physical quality of life.

Year	Literacy rate (% over age 6)	Infant mortality (per 1,000 live births)	Life expectancy	PQLI
1950	56.0	35.16	55.57	63
1951	56.8	34.47	56.15	64
1952	57.9	44.71	60.29	66
1953	58.5	43.68	62.04	68
1954	60.3	39.90	63.55	70
1955	62.1	44.79	64.36	71
1956	62.9	41.55	64.27	72
1957	67.7	45.85	64.42	73
1958	69.1	41.00	65.95	75

Table A.8 Contd.

Year	Literacy rate (% over age 6)	Infant mortality (per 1,000 live births)	Life expectancy	PQLI
1959	71.1	39.11	65.84	76
1960	72.9	35.99	65.74	77
1961	74.1	33.97	66.25	78
1962	75.2	31.41	66.35	79
1963	76.4	28.51	66.68	80
1964	77.6	25.94	67.24	81
1965	76.9	24.11	67.89	82
1966	76.9	21.69	67.37	82
1967	80.6	22.57	67.47	83
1968	83.6	20.71	67.04	84
1969	84.7	19.14	68.24	86
1970	85.3	16.85	68.81	87
1971	86.0	15.51	69.01	87
1972	86.7	14.02	70.08	89
1973	86.2	14.08	70.23	89
1974	86.7	12.94	70.37	89
1975	87.1	12.57	70.81	90
1976	87.9	10.60	71.10	90
1977	88.3	11.47	71.63	91
1978	88.8	9.91	71.62	91
1979	89.3	9.55	71.81	92
1980	89.7	9.83	71.94	92
1981	90.1	8.86	72.09	92
1982	90.4	8.08	72.26	93
1983	90.9	7.64	72.39	93
1984	91.2	6.86	73.03	94
1985	91.6	6.78	73.22	94
1986	92.0	6.29	73.33	94
1987	92.2	5.08	73.61	95
1988	92.6	5.34	73.51	95

Sources: see note on pp. 178–80.

Table A.9 Standard of living.

Year	Calorie intake per day	Protein intake per day (grams)	Household spending on food, beverages, tobacco (%)	Employed with workers' insurance (%)	Communic-able disease rate (per 100,000 people)	% Population with: Elec-tricity	Tap water
1952	2078.2	49.0	62.0	6.7	14.1	—	29
1953	2283.0	53.4	60.3	9.1	20.9	—	28
1954	2176.4	51.9	60.7	9.2	12.7	—	28
1955	2247.2	53.2	59.9	10.0	11.4	—	28
1956	2262.0	53.9	60.3	11.9	16.5	—	27
1957	2369.4	56.8	59.2	13.6	26.3	—	27
1958	2358.6	56.9	59.2	13.8	22.7	—	29
1959	2338.9	56.6	59.1	14.3	22.3	—	29
1960	2390.0	57.1	61.0	15.2	11.5	73	30
1961	2430.3	60.3	58.8	15.3	6.5	75	31
1962	2317.1	57.8	57.8	15.5	8.3	77	31
1963	2325.5	58.8	56.3	15.3	6.5	80	33
1964	2363.8	59.5	56.1	15.5	6.5	83	37
1965	2410.6	61.2	55.9	16.8	8.0	86	38
1966	2432.8	62.3	55.4	17.6	7.6	89	39
1967	2503.9	64.5	54.3	17.8	8.2	92	39
1968	2545.0	64.9	53.6	18.3	6.3	94	41
1969	2638.7	69.1	52.1	19.2	4.3	95	37
1970	2661.7	72.2	50.9	20.5	2.1	96	39
1971	2673.7	72.4	49.9	21.8	1.6	97	41
1972	2737.5	74.6	49.5	23.1	1.1	98	44
1973	2753.7	73.7	49.0	25.9	1.3	98	46
1974	2780.0	74.2	51.0	26.3	1.0	99	49
1975	2721.7	74.7	51.0	28.4	0.8	99	50
1976	2770.5	75.9	49.1	30.5	1.0	99	54
1977	2804.6	76.6	48.0	31.5	0.7	99	58
1978	2822.1	77.0	47.1	33.8	0.5	99	62
1979	2845.1	78.7	43.7	35.7	0.5	99	64
1980	2811.8	78.2	41.4	38.9	1.0	99	67
1981	2728.6	75.3	40.7	41.8	0.5	99	70
1982	2749.2	76.6	40.0	43.4	1.4	99	72
1983	2721.3	77.0	39.3	47.1	1.7	99	75
1984	2810.9	80.2	37.7	50.6	1.1	99	76
1985	2874.2	83.3	36.4	55.9	2.1	99	78
1986	2969.1	85.1	35.8	62.4	0.9	99	79
1987	2999.5	88.4	34.5	69.1	1.2	99	80
1988	3017.2	89.5	32.4	82.1	1.2	99	82

Sources: see note on pp. 178–80.

Table A.10 Housing and home quality.

Year	% Homes self-owned	People per family	Average space (*ping**)	% Homes with				
				Refrigerator	Washing machine	Air conditioning	Color TV	Video-recorder
1961	—	5.57	—	—	—	—	—	—
1976	67.4	5.19	23	74	39	4	23	0
1977	68.0	5.08	23	81	47	5	35	0
1978	69.6	4.99	24	86	54	9	47	0
1979	71.6	4.86	25	90	60	12	59	1
1980	73.5	4.76	26	92	65	14	69	1
1981	73.3	4.66	27	94	69	16	78	4
1982	74.2	4.58	28	94	71	17	83	6
1983	74.9	4.52	29	95	74	20	88	9
1984	76.0	4.48	30	96	75	23	90	14
1985	77.3	4.42	30	97	78	24	92	21
1986	77.6	4.33	31	97	79	25	94	27
1987	78.6	4.24	32	97	81	29	96	38
1988	77.8	4.14	32	98	84	34	97	51

* One *ping* equals approximately 36 square feet.
Sources: see note on pp. 178–80.

Table A.11 Social mobilization.

Year	Real Expds per Prm Std (1981 NT$)	% Population with secondary education	% Primary graduates to Junior high school	College students as % population	Mail items per capita per year	Telephone subscribers per 100 population	Real transport/ communications growth
1952	3296	10.2	34.9	0.12	7.7	0.30	—
1953	2904	10.4	36.5	0.14	9.6	0.32	18.4
1954	3468	10.9	39.7	0.16	11.6	0.34	14.9
1955	2962	11.3	43.9	0.20	13.8	0.37	16.2
1956	3671	11.3	47.8	0.24	16.8	0.40	7.5
1957	2729	12.5	49.3	0.26	23.2	0.42	11.3
1958	2784	13.0	51.1	0.28	30.8	0.46	9.3
1959	3225	13.5	51.8	0.29	34.6	0.50	7.0
1960	3045	14.3	52.2	0.32	33.0	0.52	4.1
1961	3366	14.9	53.8	0.34	27.8	0.59	7.1
1962	3501	15.7	55.1	0.38	29.6	0.63	1.5
1963	3689	16.7	54.1	0.44	31.2	0.67	6.1

Table A.11 Contd.

Year	Real Expds per Prm Std (1981 NT$)	% Population with secondary education	% Primary graduates to Junior high school	College students as % population	Mail items per capita per year	Telephone subscribers per 100 population	Real transport/ communications growth
1964	4057	17.6	55.6	0.52	32.3	0.72	17.5
1965	4470	17.5	58.2	0.68	29.8	0.78	10.5
1966	3668	18.3	59.0	0.87	28.0	0.87	9.7
1967	3815	21.1	63.7	1.04	29.1	1.02	9.7
1968	4781	22.1	74.2*	1.18	32.0	1.22	14.8
1969	4981	28.0†	75.5	1.29	34.6	1.42	12.2
1970	7217	30.2	78.6	1.39	37.5	1.70	14.5
1971	6992	31.6	80.8	1.48	41.6	2.05	15.5
1972	7503	32.9	83.3	1.64	45.4	2.50	12.4
1973	7861	32.2	83.7	1.74	48.6	3.13	16.1
1974	10153	33.9	88.0	1.78	52.5	3.78	9.3
1975	11179	35.4	89.5	1.79	49.5	4.79	10.3
1976	12665	37.5	90.4	1.81	43.7	5.97	16.2
1977	12022	39.1	93.6	1.84	43.9	7.11	13.6
1978	13002	41.0	94.1	1.84	46.0	8.74	10.3
1979	14790	42.6	95.6	1.88	49.1	10.61	6.9
1980	16728	44.0	96.1	1.92	51.6	13.00	5.8
1981	18353	45.8	96.8	1.98	56.0	15.49	7.8
1982	19377	47.2	98.0	2.04	59.0	17.44	5.0
1983	18927	48.4	98.0	2.11	61.7	19.25	8.1
1984	24385	49.6	98.7	2.16	64.5	20.70	6.9
1985	24552	50.8	98.7	2.22	68.2	21.89	3.3
1986	23477	52.0	99.0	2.28	73.7	23.27	4.6
1987	24714	53.1	99.5	2.36	73.1	24.89	9.5
1988	20224	54.3	99.1	2.49	77.4	26.72	8.9

* Change in definition from those enrolled in graduating class to actual graduates.
† Affected by including military personnel in population statistics.
Sources: see note on pp. 178–80.

Table A.12 Civic organizations and publications.

Year	Number of civic organizations	Civic organizations' membership as % of population aged 15–64	Number of newspapers	Number of periodicals
1952	2560	29.4	30	245
1953	3823	27.0	32	299
1954	3381	28.6	32	331
1955	3569	30.8	34	378
1956	3654	32.4	31	505
1957	4194	34.1	30	576
1958	4324	36.8	29	675
1959	4395	35.6	29	666
1960	4664	35.9	30	676
1961	4973	40.3	31	686
1962	5217	39.4	31	555
1963	5230	39.1	31	730
1964	5310	38.7	31	758
1965	5226	37.1	31	820
1966	5289	35.0	31	953
1967	5296	34.8	31	1081
1968	5433	34.5	31	1228
1969	5597	30.9	31	1322
1970	5818	37.6	31	1404
1971	5980	37.8	31	1534
1972	6173	37.7	31	1370
1973	6462	38.1	31	1528
1974	6705	38.2	31	1398
1975	6891	32.6	31	1316
1976	7189	35.2	31	1459
1977	7476	37.3	31	1556
1978	7787	38.7	31	1485
1979	8080	41.3	31	1772
1980	8327	39.8	31	1982
1981	8740	42.0	31	2244
1982	9060	45.7	31	2331
1983	9800	45.8	31	2543
1984	10096	49.7	31	2661
1985	10482	51.2	31	2849
1986	10625	52.1	31	3023
1987	11306	63.8	31	3353
1988	12605	69.4	124	3748

Sources: see note on pp. 178–80.

Table A.13 Indicators of political stability.

Year	Political demonstrations, strikes, and riots	Deaths from political violence	Political executions	Government sanctions	Executive adjustments
1948–52	10	19	247	33	4
1953–7	5	4732	70	12	4
1958–62	1	125	1	21	3
1963–7	0	470	0	8	3
1968	0	0	0	2	0
1969	0	0	1	5	1
1970	0	2	2	8	0
1971	4	0	1	7	0
1972	4	0	0	2	0
1973	1	1	0	1	0
1974	0	0	0	2	0
1975	0	0	0	1	0
1976	0	0	0	1	1
1977	1	0	0	1	1

Sources: see note on pp. 178–80.

Table A.14 Indicators of social stability.

Year	Number of labor disputes	Number of workers involved	Emigration as % of population	Crimes per 10,000 population
1956	35	837	—	—
1961	30	1109	0.27	34.7
1962	64	3581	0.37	34.0
1963	20	542	0.37	45.4
1964	7	42	0.46	37.9
1965	15	140	0.37	38.6
1966	3	101	0.44	35.9
1967	6	396	0.53	27.1
1968	30	716	0.58	27.7
1969	92	1135	0.59	27.4
1970	92	900	0.67	26.6
1971	157	2254	0.75	24.3
1972	217	2667	1.54	24.4
1973	262	27430	1.36	24.9

Table A.14 Contd.

Year	Number of labor disputes	Number of workers involved	Emigration as % of population	Crimes per 10,000 population
1974	494	17319	1.93	26.6
1975	458	16647	1.02	28.6
1976	371	12512	0.93	26.9
1977	380	3858	1.30	28.7
1978	506	3955	1.31	28.7
1979	503	11383	1.04	30.3
1980	626	6244	0.90	29.7
1981	891	6951	0.63	28.5
1982	1153	9129	0.73	24.4
1983	921	11989	0.93	27.7
1984	907	8805	1.20	27.6
1985	1443	15086	1.72	31.7
1986	1485	10837	1.59	48.1
1987	1609	15404	2.08	45.7
1988	1314	23449	1.98	44.6

Sources: see note on pp. 178–80.

Table A.15 Indices of political and civil rights, in scales on which 1 represents full freedom and 7 maximum authoritarian controls.

Year	Political rights index	Civil rights index
1973	6	5
1974	6	5
1975	6	5
1976	5	5
1977	5	5
1978	5	5
1979	5	5
1980	5	5
1981	5	5
1982	5	5
1983	5	5
1984	5	5
1985	5	5
1986	5	5
1987	5	4
1988	5	3

Sources: see note on pp. 178–80.

Table A.16 Indicators of electoral competition for Provincial Assembly.

Year	% of candidates elected	KMT % of vote	KMT % of seats
1951	39.3	—	78
1954	51.8	69	84
1957	55.9	68	80
1960	57.9	65	80
1963	54.0	68	82
1968	55.0	76	85
1972	60.3	69	80
1977	61.6	66	73
1981	38.7	70	77
1985	48.7	70	77
1989	49.0	62	70

Sources: see note on pp. 178–80.

Table A.17 Foreign financial and trade dependence.

Year	U.S. aid as % of GDCF	Foreign investment as % of GDCF	Net flows foreign capital (% of GDCF)	% Exports to U.S. and Japan	Sugar and rice as % of total exports
1952	45.5	0.5	40.0	56.1	74.1
1953	41.0	1.6	36.9	49.8	77.8
1954	37.9	0.9	52.2	56.2	65.8
1955	53.8	1.8	32.5	63.9	73.2
1956	29.2	1.6	42.8	42.8	66.3
1957	22.8	0.6	33.2	38.7	74.5
1958	37.3	0.8	40.9	48.1	68.7
1959	36.2	0.4	45.6	50.1	55.5
1960	31.8	4.5	37.5	49.2	47.1
1961	33.8	4.1	36.6	50.9	33.7
1962	20.2	1.5	30.8	48.3	23.7
1963	20.5	4.5	7.0	48.0	36.2
1964	9.7	4.2	−4.2	49.5	34.2
1965	10.1	6.5	14.0	51.9	22.2
1966	5.8	4.4	−1.0	45.6	15.4
1967	2.6	6.4	9.2	44.1	9.2
1968	0.6	8.4	12.4	51.5	7.6
1969	—	9.1	3.4	53.0	5.0
1970	—	9.6	0.9	52.7	3.2

Table A.17 Contd.

Year	U.S. aid as % of GDCF	Foreign investment as % of GDCF	Net flows foreign capital (% of GDCF)	% Exports to U.S. and Japan	Sugar and rice as % of total exports
1971	—	9.4	−9.2	53.6	3.3
1972	—	6.3	−24.4	54.5	2.9
1973	—	7.9	−18.2	55.8	2.3
1974	—	3.3	19.8	51.1	5.4
1975	—	2.5	12.7	47.4	5.0
1976	—	2.5	−4.7	50.6	1.9
1977	—	2.7	−15.2	50.8	1.6
1978	—	2.8	−22.0	51.9	1.0
1979	—	3.0	−3.5	49.1	1.1
1980	—	3.3	3.9	45.1	1.5
1981	—	2.7	−5.0	47.0	0.7
1982	—	3.2	−20.8	50.1	0.7
1983	—	3.5	−39.7	55.0	0.6
1984	—	4.6	−58.5	59.3	0.2
1985	—	6.6	−90.9	59.4	0.1
1986	—	6.5	−131.9	59.1	0.1
1987	—	7.4	−99.3*	57.1	0.1
1988	—	4.2	−49.5*	53.2	0.1

* There was a slight change in the definition of net capital flows from earlier years (the two indices based on these definitions differed by 3–7% during 1980–6). The earlier definition was used for 1952–87 because the later one excludes U.S. aid.
Sources: see note on pp. 178–80.

Table A.18 Military spending and personnel

Year	Military spending as % of GNP	Military personnel per 1,000 population
1961	9.5	50.4
1962	9.4	47.9
1963	9.6	44.3
1964	9.5	47.6
1965	7.7	40.3
1966	11.6	40.7
1967	10.7	39.9
1968	10.5	37.7
1969	10.4	38.8

Table A.18 Contd.

Year	Military spending as % of GNP	Military personnel per 1,000 population
1970	10.6	35.8
1971	10.0	36.2
1972	8.8	36.2
1973	8.1	32.5
1974	6.8	31.2
1975	7.3	31.3
1976	6.8	28.9
1977	7.4	27.4
1978	7.5	27.5
1979	6.7	26.8
1980	6.6	26.1
1981	6.5	25.4
1982	7.8	24.8
1983	8.0	24.2
1984	6.6	24.7
1985	7.6	22.8
1986	7.0	20.0
1987	4.6	18.5

Sources: see note on pp. 178–80.

Table A.19 State economic involvement.

Year	State % of industrial production	State % of manufacturing production	State % of investment	Government budget as % of GNP	Tax burden as % of personal income	Government employees as % of workforce
1952	56.6	56.2	55.7	—	—	—
1953	55.9	55.9	43.4	—	—	—
1954	52.7	49.7	36.3	21.3	—	—
1955	51.1	48.7	47.6	21.8	—	—
1956	50.0	48.3	48.4	22.0	—	—
1957	51.3	48.7	54.3	22.2	—	—
1958	50.0	47.2	62.6	23.8	—	—
1959	48.7	45.2	53.1	— *	—	—
1960	47.9	43.8	45.3	19.5	—	—
1961	48.2	45.3	41.8	20.1	14.5	—
1962	46.2	42.3	46.8	20.0	15.4	6.1
1963	44.8	40.6	36.0	18.9	14.6	6.2
1964	43.7	38.9	34.4	18.1	15.2	6.2

Table A.19 Contd.

Year	State % of industrial production	State % of manufacturing production	State % of investment	Government budget as % of GNP	Tax burden as % of personal income	Government employees as % of workforce
1965	41.3	36.8	31.3	19.9	15.7	6.3
1966	38.2	33.3	34.6	18.9	16.2	6.4
1967	34.7	28.8	37.5	21.1	16.4	6.3
1968	31.1	24.7	36.6	19.5	18.2	6.3
1969	29.4	22.7	41.8	21.3	19.9	6.3
1970	27.7	20.6	40.1	21.7	18.6	6.3
1971	22.9	15.3	40.4	20.8	17.8	6.4
1972	21.3	14.0	39.3	20.1	18.3	6.3
1973	21.1	13.8	34.7	19.5	19.0	6.2
1974	21.9	14.1	38.1	16.4	19.0	6.4
1975	22.1	14.2	57.7	21.6	20.1	6.6
1976	22.5	15.2	53.3	21.4	20.2	6.6
1977	22.8	15.8	50.7	23.4	20.0	6.4
1978	21.5	14.9	45.0	22.9	21.1	6.3
1979	21.2	14.7	39.4	21.3	21.9	6.3
1980	20.9	14.5	48.5	23.2	21.1	6.4
1981	20.0	13.5	49.4	24.6	20.4	6.6
1982	20.1	13.3	53.6	26.2	19.2	6.7
1983	19.8	13.0	48.9	24.0	19.1	6.6
1984	18.8	12.2	42.8	22.5	18.5	6.5
1985	18.8	12.0	46.7	23.2	17.6	6.6
1986	17.5	10.7	44.4	22.5	16.2	6.5
1987	17.3	10.5	40.9	22.9	17.9	6.3
1988	18.1	11.1	34.6	24.0	19.8	6.4

* No data provided because the government switched the definition of the fiscal year.
Sources: see note on pp. 178–80.

Table A.20 Government professionalism and budget policies.

Year	Percent government employees		Percent budget on social welfare	Direct taxes as % of all taxes	Real government spending growth
	Passed civil service exam	College education			
1952	—	—	—	—	—
1953	—	—	—	—	—
1954	—	—	6.0	24.4	—
1955	—	—	6.7	28.0	10.9
1956	—	—	7.0	24.2	6.2
1957	—	—	6.1	23.4	8.5
1958	—	—	6.9	22.8	14.4
1959	—	—	— *	— *	— *
1960	—	—	6.9	22.1	— *
1961	—	—	6.5	24.0	10.1
1962	10.8	—	7.2	21.6	7.3
1963	12.4	—	7.6	20.9	3.2
1964	13.8	—	8.1	22.5	7.8
1965	14.6	—	7.6	22.1	22.0
1966	15.5	—	4.7	20.4	3.6
1967	16.4	—	7.2	19.5	23.4
1968	18.7	—	7.8	21.4	0.6
1969	20.9	—	8.9	23.2	19.3
1970	23.2	—	9.6	23.6	13.5
1971	24.2	—	10.4	25.4	8.3
1972	25.8	38.2	12.7	26.3	9.8
1973	27.6	37.6	10.8	26.2	9.1
1974	30.1	43.3	10.8	26.6	−15.0
1975	31.6	45.8	10.0	28.3	35.4
1976	32.6	50.8	11.3	29.6	14.4
1977	33.0	53.8	10.6	31.0	20.7
1978	33.9	55.5	10.8	30.8	11.9
1979	34.9	56.7	11.4	32.1	0.7
1980	35.5	58.0	11.1	32.6	16.7
1981	37.8	—	11.8	35.2	11.9
1982	38.6	—	14.5	38.0	10.2
1983	38.6	—	15.2	37.8	−1.0
1984	40.8	—	15.7	36.8	3.4
1985	43.4	—	15.7	37.9	8.4
1986	44.5	—	15.6	38.9	8.4
1987	45.0	—	15.5	41.3	4.1
1988	45.3	—	17.5	45.1	12.7

* No data provided because the government switched the definition of the fiscal year.
Sources: see note on pp. 178–80.

Appendix sources

C. Chang (1989). Table A.14: p. 23 for number of labor disputes and workers involved, 1956.

Council for Economic Planning and Development (1987). Table A.4: p. 56 for savings as a percentage of GNP, 1952–86. Table A.5: p. 61 for income distribution, 1964. Table A.17: p. 55 for net capital flows into Taiwan as a percentage of total investment, 1952–86.

Council for Economic Planning and Development (1989a). Table A.6: p. 9 for farm households' income as a percentage of nonfarm households. Table A.9: p. 12 for percentage of population receiving tap water and electricity.

Council for Economic Planning and Development (1989b). p. 26 for current and real GNP in constant 1981 prices whose ratio was used to convert other data series reported in current NT dollars to real NT dollars; p. 208 for total trade in both NT and US dollars whose ratio was used to convert other data series reported in US dollars to NT dollars. Table A.1: p. 2 for the real growth of GNP and industrial production, 1953–88; p. 26 for growth of real GNP, 1952; p. 29 for nominal and real GNP per capita; p. 41 for agricultural and industrial production as a percentage of net domestic product. Table A.2: p. 26 for nominal GNP; p. 45 for the real growth of private and government consumption; p. 208 for nominal exports and trade balance; p. 213 for the industrial composition of exports. Table A.3: p. 2 for the growth of wholesale prices, consumer prices, and money supply; p. 13 for the number of people in the labor force and actually employed; p. 18 for nominal monthly earnings in manufacturing, 1975–88. Table A.4: p. 43 for investment as a percentage of GDP; p. 56 for savings as a percentage of GNP, 1987–8; p. 145 for the rediscount rate. Table A.5: pp. 61–2 for income distribution, 1966–87. Table A.7: p. 65 for agricultural population by land tenure. Table A.8: p. 4 for percentage of women in population; p. 7 for literacy rate. Table A.9: p. 13 for total number of employed people; p. 300 for communicable disease rate per 100,000 people; p. 301 for daily consumption of calories and proteins; p. 305 for number of people with labor and farmer insurance. Table A.11: p. 2 for the real growth of transportation and communications; p. 7 for percentage of population over the age of 6 with secondary education; p. 140 for mail per capita; p. 143 for telephone subscribers per 100 people; p. 286 for college students as a percentage of total population; p. 290 for percentage of primary school graduates going to junior high school; p. 292 for nominal expenditures per student in primary school. Table A.12: p. 9 for population aged 15–64; p. 293 for number of newspapers and periodicals; p. 303 for number of civic organizations and their members. Table A.17: p. 42 for nominal total investment; p. 55 for net capital flows into Taiwan as a percentage of total investment, 1987–8; p. 222 for percentage of exports to the United States and

Japan; p. 227 for rice and sugar as a percentage of total exports; p. 268 for foreign investment in current US dollars. Table A.19: p. 26 for nominal GNP; p. 47 for the state's (government and public corporations) percentage of total investment; p. 89 for the state's percentage of industrial and manufacturing production; p. 171 for nominal government expenditures. Table A. 20: p. 171 for nominal government expenditures; p. 172 for social welfare spending as a percentage of budget; p. 178 for direct taxes as a percentage of all taxes.

Directorate-General of Budget, Accounting, and Statistics (1989). Table A.5: p. 49 for income distribution, 1988 and for the Gini coefficients. Table A.6: p. 49 for the income of town and village households as a percentage of city households. Table A.8: p. 155 for life expectancy, 1961–88; p. 159 for infant mortality rate, 1961–88. Table A.9: p. 51 for food, beverages, and tobacco as percentage of household consumption expenditures, 1961–88. Table A.10: p. 21 for average persons per family; p. 202 for percentage of self-owned homes; p. 203 for average space per household; p. 204 for percentage of homes with specific types of equipment. Table A.14: p. 22 for emigration rate; pp. 96–7 for the number of labor disputes and the workers involved, 1961–88; p. 222 for crime rate. Table A.16: p. 274 for percentage of candidates elected to Provincial Assembly. Table A.19: p. 58 for tax burden as a percentage of personal income; p. 83 for government employees as a percentage of all employed. Table A.20: p. 83 for percentage of government employees who passed civil service examination.

Directorate-General of Budget, Accounting, and Statistics (1985). Table A9: pp. 146–7 for food, beverages, and tobacco as a percentage of household consumption expenditures, 1952–60.

Directorate-General of Budget, Accounting, and Statistics (1988). Table A.4: p. 191 for foreign reserves, 1961–87.

Galenson (1979b). Table A.3: p. 415 for real manufacturing wage growth, 1954–74.

Gastil (various years). Table A.15: for Taiwan's scores on indices of political rights and civil liberties.

Jiang (1990). Table A.16: p. 46 for KMT's share of Provincial Assembly seats, 1989.

Kuo (1983). Table A.5: p. 96 for income distribution, 1953 and 1961.

Ling & Myers (1990). Table A.16: p. 376 for KMT's share of Provincial Assembly votes, 1989.

Lu (1984). Table A.20: p. 147 for government employees with a college education.

Lui (1989). Table A.16: p. 14 for KMT's share of Provincial Assembly votes and seats, 1950–85.

Morris (1979). Table A.8: p. 45 for the formula for computing PQLI from the three component indices; and p. 168 for the PQLI scores during 1950–76.

Scott (1979). Table A.17: p. 370 for U.S. aid as a percentage of gross
    investment.
Sorich (1990). Table A.4: p. 69 for foreign reserves, 1988.
Taylor & Jodice (1983). Table A.13: pp. 24, 31 and 35 for protest
    demonstrations, political strikes, and riots; p. 48 for deaths from
    political violence; p. 65 for the imposition of government sanctions;
    p. 73 for political executions; p. 98 for executive adjustments.
United States Arms Control and Disarmament Agency (various years).
    Table A.18: for the data on military spending and personnel.

Bibliography

Adelman, I. & C. T. Morris 1973. *Economic growth and social equity in developing countries*. Stanford, Calif.: Stanford University Press.

Advisory Commission on Intergovernmental Relations 1989. *Significant features of fiscal federalism, 1989 edn.*, Vol. 1. Washington, D.C.: Advisory Commission on Intergovernmental Relations.

Ahluwalia, M. S. 1974. Income inequality: some dimensions of the problem. In *Redistribution with Growth*, H. Chenery, M. Ahluwalia, C. L. G. Bell, J. H. Duloy & R. Jolly (eds.), 3–37, London: Oxford University Press.

Ahluwalia, M. S. 1976a. Inequality, poverty and development. *Journal of Development Economics* 3, 307–42.

Ahluwalia, M. S. 1976b. Income distribution and development: some stylized facts. *American Economic Review* 66, 128–35.

Alam, M. S. 1989. *Governments and markets in economic development strategies: lessons from Korea, Taiwan, and Japan*. New York: Praeger.

Alcock, N. & G. Kohler 1979. Structural violence at the world level: diachronic findings. *Journal of Peace Research* 16, 255–63.

Aldrich, J., R. Duvall & J. Weldes, no date. The cost of national security: spending for defense and spending for welfare in the United States, 1948–1983. Manuscript.

Almond G. A. and G. B. Powell, Jr. 1966. *Comparative politics: a developmental approach*. Boston: Little, Brown.

Amin, S. 1974. *Accumulation on a world scale: a critique of the theory of underdevelopment*. New York: Monthly Review Press.

Amsden, A. H. 1979. Taiwan's economic history: a case of etatism and a challenge to dependency theory. *Modern China* 5, 341–79.

Amsden, A. H. 1985. The state and Taiwan's economic development. In *Bringing the state back in*, P. B. Evans, D. Rueschemeyer & T. Skocpol (eds.), 78–104. New York: Cambridge University Press.

Amsden, A. H. 1989. *Asia's next giant: South Korea and late industrialization*. New York: Oxford University Press.

Anschuler, L. R. 1976. Satellization and stagnation in Latin America. *International Studies Quarterly* 20, 39–82.

Appleton, S. 1976. The social and political impact of education on Taiwan. *Asian Survey* 16, 703–20.

Apter, D. E. 1965. *The politics of modernization.* Chicago: University of Chicago Press.

Arnold, W. 1989. Bureaucratic politics, state capacity, and Taiwan's automobile industrial policy. *Modern China* 15, 178–214.

Arrow, K. J. 1951. *Social choice and individual values.* New York: Wiley.

Balassa, B. 1981. *The newly industrializing countries in the world economy.* New York: Pergamon.

Baldwin, D. A. 1985. *Economic statecraft.* Princeton, N.J.: Princeton University Press.

Baran, P. A. & P. M. Sweezy 1966. *Monopoly capital: an essay on the American economic and social order.* New York: Monthly Review Press.

Barclay, G. W. 1954. *Colonial development and population in Taiwan.* Princeton, N.J.: Princeton University Press.

Barrett, R. E. 1988. Autonomy and diversity in the American state on Taiwan. In *Contending approaches to the political economy of Taiwan,* E. A. Winckler & S. Greenhalgh (eds.), 121–37. Armonk, N.Y.: Sharpe.

Barrett, R. E. & M. K. Whyte 1982. Dependency theory and Taiwan: analysis of a deviant case. *American Journal of Sociology* 87, 1064–89.

Bedeski, R. E. 1981. *State-building in modern China: the Kuomintang in the prewar period.* Berkeley: Institute of East Asian Studies, University of California.

Bendix, R. 1964. *Nation-building and citizenship: studies of our changing social order.* Berkeley: University of California Press.

Benjamin, R. W. & J. H. Kautsky 1968. Communism and economic development. *American Political Science Review* 62, 110–23.

Benoit, E. 1973. *Defense and economic growth in developing countries.* Lexington, Mass.: Heath.

Benoit, E. 1978. Growth and defense in developing countries. *Economic Development and Cultural Change* 26, 271–80.

Berger, P. L. & H. H. M. Hsiao (eds.) 1988. *In search of an East Asian development model.* New Brunswick, N.J.: Transaction Books.

Biersteker, T. J. 1978. *Distortion or development? Contending perspectives on the multinational corporation.* Cambridge, Mass.: MIT Press.

Binder, L., J. S. Coleman, J. LaPalombara, L. W. Pye, S. Verba & M. Weiner 1971. *Crises and sequences in political development.* Princeton, N.J.: Princeton University Press.

Bobrow, D. B. 1990. Eating your cake and having it too: the Japanese case. Paper presented at the annual meeting of the International Studies Association, Washington, D.C.

Bobrow, D. B. & S. Chan 1986. Assets, liabilities, and strategic conduct: status management by Japan, Taiwan, and South Korea. *Pacific Focus* 1, 23–55.

Bobrow, D. B. & S. Chan 1987. Understanding anomalous successes: Japan, Taiwan, and South Korea. In *New Directions in the*

Comparative Study of Foreign Policy, C. F. Hermann, C. W. Kegley, Jr. & J. N. Rosenau (eds.), 111–30. Boston: Allen & Unwin.

Bollen, K. A. 1980. Issues in the comparative measurement of political democracy. *American Sociological Review* 45, 370–90.

Bollen, K. A. and B. D. Grandjean 1981. The Dimension(s) of democracy: further issues in the measurement and effects of political democracy. *American Sociological Review* 46, 651–9.

Bollen, K. A. & R. Jackman 1985. Political democracy and the size distribution of income. *American Sociological Review* 50, 438–57.

Bornschier, V. & T. H. Ballmer-Cao 1979. Income inequality: a cross-national study of the relationships between MNC-penetration, dimensions of the power structure and income distribution. *American Sociological Review* 44, 487–506.

Bornschier, V. & C. Chase-Dunn 1985. *Transnational corporations and underdevelopment*. New York: Praeger.

Bornschier, V., C. Chase-Dunn & R. Rubinson 1978. Cross-national evidence of the effects of foreign investment and aid on economic growth and inequality: a survey of findings and a reanalysis. *American Journal of Sociology* 84, 651–83.

Botjer, G. F. 1979. *A short history of Nationalist China, 1919–1949*. New York: Putnam.

Bradford, C. I. Jr. & W. H. Branson (eds.) 1987. *Trade and structural change in Pacific Asia*. Chicago: University of Chicago Press.

Bradshaw, Y. & Z. Tshandu 1990. Foreign capital penetration, state intervention, and development in sub-Saharan Africa. *International Studies Quarterly* 34, 229–51.

Cappelen, A., N. P. Gleditsch & O. Bjerkholt. 1984. Military spending and economic growth in the OECD countries. *Journal of Peace Research* 21, 361–73.

Cardoso, F. H. 1973. Associated dependent development: theoretical and practical implications. In *Authoritarian Brazil: Origins, Policy, and Future*, A. Stepan (ed.), 149–72. New Haven, Conn.: Yale University Press.

Cardoso, F. H. & E. Faletto 1979. *Dependency and development in Latin America*. Berkeley: University of California Press.

Chan, S. 1984. Mirror, mirror on the wall . . .: are the freer countries more pacific? *Journal of Conflict Resolution* 28, 617–48.

Chan, S. 1985. The impact of defense spending on economic performance: a survey of evidence and problems. *ORBIS* 29, 403–34.

Chan, S. 1987a. Growth with equity: a test of Olson's theory for the Asian Pacific-rim countries. *Journal of Peace Research* 24, 133–49.

Chan, S. 1987b. The mouse that roared: Taiwan's management of trade relations with the U.S. *Comparative Political Studies* 20, 251–92.

Chan, S. 1987c. Comparative performances of East Asian and Latin American NICs. *Pacific Focus* 2, 35–56.

Chan, S. 1987–8. Overachievers and underachievers: a cross-national comparison of some policy performances. *Korean Journal of International Studies* 19, 103–19.

Chan, S. 1988a. Defense burden and economic growth: unravelling the Taiwanese 'Enigma'. *American Political Science Review* 82, 913–20.

Chan, S. 1988b. Developing strength from weakness: the state in Taiwan. *Journal of Developing Societies* 4, 38–51.

Chan, S. 1989a. Income inequality among LDCs: a comparative analysis of alternative perspectives. *International Studies Quarterly* 33, 45–65.

Chan, S. 1989b. Income inequality and war trauma: a cross-national analysis. *Western Political Quarterly* 42, 263–81.

Chan, S. 1990a. The differential impact of the Cultural Revolution on Chinese provincial industrial growth: some evidence on Olson's theory of distributional coalitions. *Pacific Focus* 5, 61–79.

Chan, S. 1990b. *East Asian dynamism: growth, order, and security in the Pacific region.* Boulder, Col.: Westview.

Chan, S. & C. Clark 1991. Economic growth and popular well-being in Taiwan: a time series examination of some preliminary hypotheses. *Western Political Quarterly* 44, forthcoming.

Chan, S., C. Clark & D. R. Davis 1990. State entrepreneurship, foreign investment, export expansion, and economic growth: Granger causality in Taiwan's development. *Journal of Conflict Resolution* 34, 102–29.

Chang, C. H. 1989. A study on the labor market in Taiwan. In *1989 Joint Conference on the Industrial Policies of the Republic of China and the Republic of Korea*, 11–31. Taipei: Chung-hua Institution for Economic Research.

Chang, D. W. W. 1989. Political development in Taiwan: the Sun Yat-sen model for national reconstruction. *Issues and Studies* 25:5, 11–32.

Chang, H. Y. & R. Myers 1963. Japanese colonial development policy in Taiwan. *Journal of Asian Studies* 22, 433–49.

Chang, P. H. 1986. Evolution of Taiwan's political leadership after Chiang Ching-kuo. *AEI Foreign Policy and Defense Review* 6, 12–18.

Chang, S. K. C. 1985. American and Chinese managers in U.S. companies in Taiwan: a comparison. *California Management Review* 27, 144–56.

Chase-Dunn, C. 1975. The effects of international economic dependence on development and inequality: a cross-national study. *American Sociological Review* 40, 720–38.

Chase-Dunn, C. 1981. Interstate system and capitalist world-economy: one logic or two? *International Studies Quarterly* 25, 19–42.

Chase-Dunn, C. 1983. Inequality, structural mobility, and dependency reversal in the capitalist world economy. In *North/South relations: studies of dependency reversal*, C. F. Doran, G. Modelski & C. Clark (eds.), 73–95. New York: Praeger.

Chen, E. I. T. 1972. Formosan political movements under Japanese colonial rule, 1914–1937. *Journal of Asian Studies* 31, 477–97.

Chen, I. H. & W. C. Wu 1989. New way for ROC diplomacy. *Free China Journal* 6 (Oct. 16), 5.

Chen, I. H. & W. C. Wu 1990. Lively debate on key issues. *Free China Review* 40:9, 48–53.

Chen, T. E. 1981. The educational system: a commentary. In *Contemporary Republic of China: The Taiwan Experience, 1950–1980*, J. C. Hsiung (ed.), 65–77. New York: Praeger.

Chenery, H. 1979. *Structural change and development policy*. New York: Oxford University Press.

Chenery, H. & M. Syrquin. 1975. *Patterns of development 1950–70*. London: Oxford University Press.

Cheng, C. Y. (ed.) 1989. *Sun Yat-sen's doctrine in the modern world*. Boulder, Col.: Westview.

Cheng, T. J. 1987. The rise and limits of the East Asian NICs. *Pacific Focus* 2, 51–75.

Cheng, T. J. 1989. Democratizing the quasi-Leninist regime in Taiwan. *World Politics* 41, 471–99.

Cheng, T. J. 1990. Is the dog barking? The middle class and democratic movements in the East Asian NICs. *International Studies Notes* 15, 10–16.

Cheng, T. J. & S. Haggard 1987. *Newly industrializing Asia in transition: policy reform and American response*. Berkeley: Institute of International Studies, University of California.

Cheng, T. J. & S. Haggard (eds.) 1991. *Political change in Taiwan*. Boulder, Col.: Rienner.

Chira, S. 1988. In Taiwan: change sweeps out taboos. *New York Times* May 4, 1.

Choi, K. 1983. *Theories of comparative economic growth*. Ames: Iowa State University Press.

Chou, Y. & A. J. Nathan 1987. Democratizing transition in Taiwan. *Asian Survey* 27, 277–99.

Chu, S. 1963. Liu Ming-ch'uan and the modernization of Taiwan. *Journal of Asian Studies* 23, 37–53.

Chu, Y. H. 1989. State structure and economic adjustment of the East Asian newly industrializing countries. *International Organization* 43, 647–72.

Chu, Y. P. 1988. Taiwan's trade surplus, U.S. responses, and adjustment policies. *Issues and Studies* 24:11, 83–100.

Chu, Y. P. & T. W. Tsaur 1984. Growth, stability, and income distribution in Taiwan. Paper presented at the annual meeting of the Western Social Science Association, San Diego.

Clark, C. 1987. The Taiwan exception: implications for contending political economy paradigms. *International Studies Quarterly* 31, 327–56.

Clark, C. 1989a. External shocks and instability in Taiwan: the dog that didn't bark. In *Markets, politics, and change in the global economy*, W. Avery & D. Rapkin (eds), 173–97. Boulder, Col.: Rienner.

Clark, C. 1989b. *Taiwan's development: implications for contending political economy paradigms*. Westport, Conn.: Greenwood.

Clark, C. 1991. The limits of America as a "predatory hegemon": the case of U.S. trade with Taiwan. Paper presented at the Hendricks Symposium on American Trade Policy in A Changed World Political Economy, University of Nebraska.

Clark, C. & D. Bahry 1983. Dependent development: a socialist variant. *International Studies Quarterly* 27, 271–93.

Clark, C. & S. Chan 1990a. China and Taiwan: a security paradox. Paper presented at the annual meeting of the American Association of Chinese Studies, Fullerton, California.

Clark, C. & S. Chan (eds.) 1990b. *The East Asian development model: looking beyond the stereotypes*. Special Issue of *International Studies Notes* 15.

Cline, R. S. 1980. *World power trends and U.S. foreign policy for the 1980s*. Boulder, Col.: Westview.

Clough, R. N. 1978. *Island China*. Cambridge, Mass.: Harvard University Press.

Coble, P. M. 1980. *The Shanghai capitalists and the Nationalist government, 1927–1937*. Cambridge, Mass.: Harvard University Press.

Cole, A. B. 1967. The political roles of Taiwanese entrepreneurs. *Asian Survey* 7, 645–54.

Copper, J. F. 1988. *A quiet revolution: political development in the Republic of China*. Washington, D.C.: Ethics and Public Policy Center.

Copper, J. F. 1989. Taiwan: a nation in transition. *Current History* 88, 173–6 and 198–9.

Copper, J. F. 1990. *Taiwan: nation-state or province?* Boulder, Col.: Westview.

Copper, J. F. with G. P. Chen 1984. *Taiwan's elections: political development and democratization in the Republic of China*. Baltimore: School of Law, University of Maryland.

Council for Economic Planning and Development 1987. *Taiwan statistical data book, 1987*. Taipei: Council for Economic Planning and Development.

Council for Economic Planning and Development 1989a. *Social welfare indicators, Republic of China, 1989*. Taipei: Manpower Planning Department, Council for Economic Planning and Development.

Council for Economic Planning and Development 1989b. *Taiwan statistical data book, 1989*. Taipei: Council for Economic Planning and Development.

Crane, G. T. 1982. The Taiwanese ascent: system, state, and movement in the world economy. In *Ascent and Decline in the World System*, E. Friedman (ed.), 93–113. Beverly Hills: Sage.

Crozier, B. 1976. *The man who lost China: the first full biography of Chiang Kai-shek*. New York: Scribner's.

Cumings, B. 1984. The origins and development of the northeast Asian political economy: industrial sectors, product cycles, and political consequences. *International Organization* 38, 1–40.

Cutright, P. 1967. Inequality: a cross-national analysis. *American Sociological Review* 32, 562–78.

Dabelko, D. & J. M. McCormick 1977. Opportunity costs of defense: some cross-national evidence. *Journal of Peace Research* 14, 145–54.

Dabelko, D. & J. M. McCormick 1984. Response to Lyttkens and Vedovato. *Journal of Peace Research* 21, 395–7.

Davis, D. R. & S. Chan 1990. The security-welfare relationship: longitudinal evidence from Taiwan. *Journal of Peace Research* 27, 87–100.

Deger, S. & R. Smith 1983. Military expenditure and growth in less developed countries. *Journal of Conflict Resolution* 27, 335–53.

de Janvry, A. 1981. *The agrarian question and reformism in Latin America*. Baltimore: Johns Hopkins University Press.

Deutsch, K. W. 1961. Social mobilization and political development. *American Political Science Review* 55, 493–514.

Deyo, F. C. 1987a. Coalitions, institutions, and linkage sequencing — toward a strategic capacity model of East Asian development. In *The political economy of the new Asian industrialism*, F. C. Deyo (ed.), 227–47. Ithaca, N.Y.: Cornell University Press.

Deyo, F. C. (ed.) 1987b. *The political economy of the new Asian industrialism*. Ithaca, N.Y.: Cornell University Press.

Deyo, F. C. 1989. *Beneath the miracle: labor subordination in the new Asian industrialism*. Berkeley: University of California Press.

Directorate-General of Budget, Accounting, and Statistics 1985. *National income in Taiwan area, the Republic of China: national accounts for 1951–1983 and preliminary estimates for 1984*. Taipei: Directorate-General of Budget, Accounting, and Statistics.

Directorate-General of Budget, Accounting, and Statistics 1988. *Statistical yearbook of the Republic of China, 1988*. Taipei: Directorate-General of Budget, Accounting, and Statistics.

Directorate-General of Budget, Accounting, and Statistics 1989. *Social indicators in Taiwan area of the Republic of China, 1988*. Taipei: Directorate-General of Budget, Accounting, and Statistics.

Dixon, W. J. & B. E. Moon 1986. The military burden and basic human needs. *Journal of Conflict Resolution* 30, 660–84.

Dixon, W. J. & B. E. Moon 1989. Domestic political conflict and basic needs outcomes. *Comparative Political Studies* 22, 178–98.

Domes, J. 1981. Political differentiation in Taiwan: group formation within the ruling party and the opposition circles, 1979–80. *Asian Survey* 21, 1011–28.

Domes, J. 1989. The 13th Party Congress of the Kuomintang: towards political competition? *China Quarterly* 118, 345–59.

Domke, W. K., R. C. Eichenberg & C. M. Kelleher 1983. The illusion of choice: defense and welfare in advanced industrial democracies, 1948–1978. *American Political Science Review* 77, 19–35.

Doran, C. F. 1983. Structuring the concept of dependency reversal. In *North/South relations: studies in dependency reversal*, C. F. Doran, G. Modelski & C. Clark (eds.), 1–27. New York: Praeger.

Dos Santos, T. 1970. The structure of dependence. *American Economic Review* 60, 231–6.

Dreyer, J. T. 1990. Taiwan in 1989: democratization and economic

growth. *Asian Survey* 30, 52–8.
Durdin, T. 1975. Chiang Ching-kuo and Taiwan: a profile. *ORBIS* 18, 1023–42.
Duvall, R. D. & J. R. Freeman 1981. The state and dependent capitalism. *International Studies Quarterly* 25, 99–118.
Duvall, R. D. & J. R. Freeman 1983. The techno-bureaucratic elite and the entrepreneurial state in dependent industrialization. *American Political Science Review* 77, 569–87.

Eastman, L. E. 1974. *The abortive revolution: China under nationalist rule, 1927–1937.* Cambridge, Mass.: Harvard University Press.
Eastman, L. E. 1984. *Seeds of destruction: nationalist China in war and revolution, 1937–1949.* Cambridge, Mass.: Harvard University Press.
Eckstein, H. 1975. Case study and theory in political science. In *Handbook of political science*, F. I. Greenstein and N. W. Polsby (eds.), Vol. 7, 79–138. Reading, Mass.: Addison-Wesley.
Eisenstadt, S. N. 1966. *Modernization, protest, and change.* Englewood Cliffs, N.J.: Prentice-Hall.
Eisenstadt, S. N. 1973. *Tradition, change, and modernity.* New York: Wiley.
Emmanuel, A. 1972. *Unequal exchange: a study of the imperialism of trade.* New York: Monthly Review Press.
Encarnation. D. J. 1989. *Dislodging multinationals: India's strategy in comparative perspective.* Ithaca, N.Y.: Cornell University Press.
Evans, P. B. 1979. *Dependent development: the alliance of multinational, state, and local capital in Brazil.* Princeton, N.J.: Princeton University Press.
Evans, P. B. 1985. Transnational linkages and the economic role of the state: an analysis of developing and industrialized nations in the post-World War II period. In *Bringing the state back in*, P. B. Evans, D. Rueschemeyer & T. Skocpol (eds.), 192–226. New York: Cambridge University Press.
Evans, P. B. 1987. Class, state, and dependence in East Asia: lessons for Latin Americanists. In *The political economy of the new Asian industrialism*, F. C. Deyo (ed.), 203–26. Ithaca, N.Y.: Cornell University Press.
Evans, P. B. & M. Timberlake 1980. Dependence, inequality, and the growth of the tertiary: a comparative analysis of less developed countries. *American Sociological Review* 45, 531–52.
Evans, P. B., D. Rueschemeyer & T. Skocpol (eds.) 1985. *Bringing the state back in.* New York: Cambridge University Press.

Fei, J. C. H. 1986. Economic development and traditional Chinese cultural values. *Journal of Chinese Studies* 3, 109–24.
Fei, J. C. H. 1989. The modernization of the political economy of ROC in a historical perspective. Paper presented at the 18th Sino-American Conference on Mainland China, Stanford University.
Fei, J. C. H., G. Ranis & S. W. Y. Kuo 1979. *Growth with equity: the*

Taiwan case. New York: Oxford University Press.

Feldman, H., M. Y. M. Kau & I. J. Kim (eds.) 1988. *Taiwan in a time of transition*. New York: Paragon House.

Fields, K. J. 1989. Public finance, private business: financing of business groups in Taiwan. Paper presented at the annual meeting of the American Political Science Association, Atlanta.

Finkle, J. L. & R. W. Gable (eds.) 1971. *Political development and social change*. New York: Wiley.

Frank, A. G. 1969. *Capitalism and underdevelopment in Latin America*. New York: Monthly Review Press.

Frederiksen, P. C. & R. E. Looney 1983. Defense expenditures and economic growth in developing countries. *Armed Forces and Society* 9, 633–45.

Free China Journal 1990. New National Assembly. 7 (Nov. 8), 2

Freeman, J. R. 1982. State entrepreneurship and dependent development. *American Journal of Political Science* 26, 90–112.

Freeman, J. R. 1989. *Democracy and markets: the politics of mixed economies*. Ithaca, N.Y.: Cornell University Press.

Freeman, J. R. & R. D. Duvall 1984. International economic relations and the entrepreneurial state. *Economic Development and Cultural Change* 32, 373–400.

Friedman, D. 1988. *The misunderstood miracle: industrial development and political change in Japan*. Ithaca, N.Y.: Cornell University Press.

Friedman, M. & R. Friedman 1980. *Free to choose*. New York: Harcourt, Brace & Jovanovich.

Galenson, W. (ed.) 1979a. *Economic growth and structural change in Taiwan: the postwar experience of the Republic of China*. Ithaca, N.Y.: Cornell University Press.

Galenson, W. 1979b. The labor force, wages, and living standards. In *Economic growth and structural change in Taiwan: the postwar experience of the Republic of China*, W. Galenson (ed.), 384–447. Ithaca, N.Y.: Cornell University Press.

Gallin, B. 1966. *Hsin Hsing, Taiwan: a Chinese village in change*. Berkeley: University of California Press.

Gallin, B. & R. S. Gallin 1982. Socioeconomic life in rural Taiwan: twenty years of development and change. *Modern China* 8, 205–46.

Galtung, J. 1971. A structural theory of imperialism. *Journal of Peace Research* 8, 81–117.

Gastil, R. D. various years. The comparative survey of freedom. *Freedom At Issue* (Jan./Feb.).

Gates, H. 1979. Dependency and the part-time proletariat in Taiwan. *Modern China* 5, 381–407.

Gates, H. 1981. Ethnicity and social class. In *The anthropology of Taiwanese society*, E. M. Ahern & H. Gates (eds.), 241–81. Stanford, Calif.: Stanford University Press.

Gates, H. 1987. *Chinese working-class lives: getting by in Taiwan*. Ithaca, N.Y.: Cornell University Press.

George, A. L. 1979. Case studies and theory development: the method of structured, focused comparison. In *Diplomacy: new approaches in history, theory, and policy*, P. G. Lauren (ed.), 43–68. New York: Free Press.

Gereffi, G. 1983. *The pharmaceutical industry and dependency in the Third World*. Princeton, N.J.: Princeton University Press.

Gereffi, G. & D. Wyman 1989. Determinants of development strategies in Latin America and East Asia. In *Pacific dynamics: the international politics of industrial change*, S. Haggard & C. I. Moon (eds.), 23–52. Boulder, Col.: Westview.

Gerschenkron, A. 1962. *Economic backwardness in historical perspective: a book of essays*. Cambridge, Mass.: Harvard University Press.

Gillespie, J. V. & B. A. Nesvold (eds.) 1971. *Macro-quantitative analyses: conflict, development, and democratization*. Beverly Hills, Calif.: Sage.

Gilpin, R. 1987. *The political economy of international relations*. Princeton, N.J.: Princeton University Press.

Gleditsch, N. P., O. Bjerkholt & A. Cappelen 1988. Military R&D and economic growth in industrialized market economies. In *Peace research: achievements and challenges*, P. Wallerstein (ed.), 198–215. Boulder, Col.: Westview.

Gold, T. B. 1986. *State and society in the Taiwan miracle*. Armonk, N.Y.: Sharpe.

Gold, T. B. 1987. The status quo is not static: Mainland–Taiwan relations. *Asian Survey* 27, 300–15.

Gold, T. B. 1988a. Colonial origins of Taiwanese capitalism, In *Contending approaches to the political economy of Taiwan*, E. A. Winckler & S. Greenhalgh (eds.), 101–17. Armonk, N.Y.: Sharpe.

Gold, T. B. 1988b. Entrepreneurs, multinationals, and the state. In *Contending approaches to the political economy of Taiwan*, E. A. Winckler & S. Greenhalgh (eds.), 175–205. Armonk, N.Y.: Sharpe.

Gold, T. B. 1989. Taiwan in 1988: the transition to a post-Chiang world. In *China Briefing, 1989*, A. J. Kane (ed.), 87–108. Boulder, Col.: Westview.

Goldsmith, A. A. 1986. Democracy, political stability, and economic growth in developing countries: some evidence on Olson's theory on distributional coalitions. *Comparative Political Studies* 18, 517–31.

Goldstein, J. S. 1985. Basic human needs: the plateau curve. *World Development* 13, 595–609.

Gray, V. & D. Lowery 1988. Interest group politics and economic growth in the U.S. states. *American Political Science Review* 82, 109–31.

Greenhalgh, S. 1984. Networks and their nodes: urban society in Taiwan. *China Quarterly* 99, 529–52.

Greenhalgh, S. 1988a. Families and networks in Taiwan's economic development. In *Contending approaches to the political economy of Taiwan*, E. A. Winckler & S. Greenhalgh (eds.), 224–45. Armonk, N.Y.: Sharpe.

Greenhalgh, S. 1988b. Supranational processes of income distribution. In *Contending approaches to the political economy of Taiwan*, E. A. Winckler & S. Greenhalgh (eds.), 67–100. Armonk, N.Y.: Sharpe.

Gregor, A. J. with M. H. Chang & A. B. Zimmerman 1981. *Ideology and development: Sun Yat-sen and the economic history of Taiwan*. Berkeley: Institute of East Asia Studies, University of California.

Gurr, T. R. 1970. *Why men rebel*. Princeton, N.J.: Princeton University Press.

Hagen, E. E. 1975. *The economics of development*, 2nd edn. Homewood, Ill.: Richard D. Irwin.

Haggard, S. 1986. The newly industrializing countries in the international system. *World Politics* 38, 340–70.

Haggard, S. 1990. *Pathways from periphery: the politics of growth in the newly industrializing countries*. Ithaca, N.Y.: Cornell University Press.

Haggard, S. & T. J. Cheng 1987. State and foreign capital in the East Asian NICs. In *The political economy of the new Asian industrialism*, F. C. Deyo (ed.), 84–135. Ithaca, N.Y.: Cornell University Press.

Haggard, S. & T. J. Cheng 1989. The new bilateralism: the East Asian NICs in American foreign economic policy. In *Pacific dynamics: the international politics of industrial change*, S. Haggard & C. I. Moon (eds.), 305–29. Boulder, Col.: Westview.

Hamilton, C. 1983. Capitalist industrialisation in East Asia's Four Little Tigers. *Journal of Contemporary Asia* 13, 35–73.

Harrell, S. 1985. Why do the Chinese work so hard? Reflections on an entrepreneurial ethic. *Modern China* 11, 203–26.

Harrison, S. S. 1988. Taiwan after Chiang Ching-kuo. *Foreign Affairs* 66, 790–808.

Hewitt, C. 1977. The effect of political democracy and social democracy on equality in industrial societies: a cross-national comparison. *American Sociological Review* 42, 450–64.

Hickey, D. V. V. 1988. America's two-point policy and the future of Taiwan. *Asian Survey* 28, 881–96.

Hirschman, A. O. 1945. *National power and the structure of foreign trade*. Berkeley: University of California Press.

Ho, S. P. S. 1978. *Economic development in Taiwan, 1860–1970*. New Haven, Conn.: Yale University Press.

Ho, S. P. S. 1979. Decentralized industrialization and rural development: evidence from Taiwan. *Economic Development and Cultural Change* 28, 77–96.

Ho, S. P. S. 1987. Economics, economic bureaucracy, and Taiwan's economic development. *Pacific Affairs* 60, 226–47.

Ho, S. Y. 1990. The Repubic of China policy toward the United States, 1979–89. In *Foreign policy of the Republic of China on Taiwan: an unorthodox approach*, S. Wang (ed.), 29–44. New York: Praeger.

Ho, Y. M. 1980. The production structure of the manufacturing sector and its distribution implications: the case of Taiwan. *Economic Development and Cultural Change* 28, 321–43.

Hofheinz, R., Jr. & K. E. Calder 1982. *The Eastasia edge*. New York: Basic Books.

Hofstede, G. & M. H. Bond 1988. The Confucius connection: from cultural roots to economic growth. *Organizational Dynamics* 16, 4–21.

Hoole, F. W. & C. Huang 1989. The global conflict process. *Journal of Conflict Resolution* 33, 142–63.

Hoyt, E. P. 1989. *The rise of the Chinese Republic: from the last Emperor to Deng Xiaoping*. New York: McGraw-Hill.

Hsiao, H. H. M. 1988. An East Asian development model: empirical explorations. In *In search of an East Asian development model*, P. L. Berger & H. H. M. Hsiao (eds.), 12–23. New Brunswick, N.J.: Transaction Books.

Hsiao, H. H. M. 1989. Development, class transformation, social movements, and the changing state–society relations in Taiwan. Paper presented at the 18th Sino-American Conference on Mainland China, Stanford University.

Hsiao, H. H. M. 1990. Changing theoretical explanations of Taiwan's development experience: an examination. *International Journal of Comparative Sociology* 31, forthcoming.

Hsieh, C. M. 1964. *Taiwan — Ilha Formosa: a geography in perspective*. Washington, D.C.: Butterworth.

Hsiung, J. C. (ed.) 1981. *Contemporary Republic of China: the Taiwan experience, 1950–1980*. New York: Praeger.

Huang, C. 1989. The state and foreign investment: the cases of Taiwan and Singapore. *Comparative Political Studies* 22, 93–121.

Huang, C. 1990. Joint ventures between state enterprises and multinational corporations in Taiwan. *International Studies Notes* 15, 35–40.

Huang, P. H. 1984. Modernization of education in the Republic of China since 1949. In *Chinese Modernization*, Y. M. Shaw (ed.), 171–91. San Francisco: Chinese Materials Center Publications.

Huang, S. M. 1981. *Agricultural degradation: changing community systems in rural Taiwan*. Lanham, Md.: University Press of America.

Huntington, S. P. 1968. *Political order in changing societies*. New Haven, Conn.: Yale University Press.

Ignatius, A. 1990. Coming home. *Wall Street Journal* Aug. 2, A1 and A8.

Inkeles, A. 1983. *Exploring individual modernity*. New York: Columbia University Press.

Jackman, R. W. 1975. *Politics and social equality: a comparative analysis*. New York: Wiley.

Jackman, R. W. 1982. Dependence on foreign investment and economic growth in the Third World. *World Politics* 34, 175–96.

Jacoby, N. H. 1966. *U.S. aid to Taiwan: a study of foreign aid, self-help, and development*. New York: Praeger.

Jiang, J. P. L. 1990. Post-election analysis: rise of a two-party system. *Free China Review* 40: 2, 44–7.

Johnson, C. 1962. *Peasant nationalism and communist power: the emergence of revolutionary China, 1937–1945*. Stanford, Calif.: Stanford University Press.
Johnson, C. 1981. Introduction — The Taiwan model. In *Contemporary Republic of China: the Taiwan experience, 1950–1980*, J. C. Hsiung (ed.), 9–18. New York: Praeger.
Johnson, C. 1982. *MITI and the Japanese miracle: the growth of industrial policy, 1925–1975*. Stanford, Calif.: Stanford University Press.
Johnson, E. L., F. Fligel, J. L. Woods & M. C. Chu 1987. *The agricultural technology system of Taiwan*. Urbana: Office of International Agriculture, University of Illinois.
Jones, L. P. & E. S. Mason 1982. The role of economic factors in determining the size and structure of the public-enterprise sector in less-developed countries with mixed economies. In *Public enterprise in less-developed countries*, L. P. Jones (ed.), 17–47. New York: Cambridge University Press.
Jones, L. P. & J. Sakong 1980. *Government, business, and entrepreneurship in economic development: the Korean case*. Cambridge, Mass.: Harvard University Press.

Kahn, H. 1984. The Confucian ethic and economic growth. In *The gap between the rich and poor*, M. A. Seligson (ed.), 78–80. Boulder, Col.: Westview.
Katzenstein, P. J. (ed.) 1978. *Between power and plenty: foreign economic policies of advanced industrial states*. Madison: University of Wisconsin Press.
Katzenstein, P. J. 1985. *Small states in world markets: industrial policy in Europe*. Ithaca, N.Y.: Cornell University Press.
Kau, M. Y. M. 1988. Beijing's campaign for unification. In *Taiwan in a time of transition*. In H. Feldman, M. Y. M. Kau & I. J. Kim (eds.), 175–200. New York: Paragon House.
Kaufman, R. R., H. I. Chernotsky & D. S. Geller 1975. A preliminary test of the theory of dependency. *Comparative Politics* 7, 303–31.
Keohane, R. O. & J. S. Nye 1977. *Power and interdependence: World politics in transition*. Boston: Little, Brown.
Kerr, G. H. 1965. *Formosa betrayed*. Boston: Houghton Mifflin.
Kerr, G. H. 1974. *Formosa: licensed revolution and the home rule movement, 1895–1945*. Honolulu: University Press of Hawaii.
Knapp, R. G. (ed.) 1980. *China's island frontier*. Honolulu: University Press of Hawaii.
Koen, R. Y. 1974. *The China lobby in American politics*. New York: Octagon.
Kohler, G. & N. Alcock 1976. An empirical table of structural violence, *Journal of Peace Research* 13, 343–56.
Kohli, A., M. F. Altfeld, S. Lotfian & R. Mardan 1984. Inequality in the Third World: an assessment of competing explanations. *Comparative Political Studies* 17, 283–318.

Krasner, S. D. 1978. _Defending the national interest: raw materials investments and U.S. foreign policy_. Princeton, N.J.: Princeton University Press.

Kublin, H. 1973. Taiwan's Japanese interlude: 1895–1945. In _Taiwan in modern times_, P. K. T. Sih (ed.), 317–35. New York: St. John's University Press.

Kugler, J. 1983. Use of residuals: an option to measure concepts. _Political Methodology_ 9, 103–20.

Kugler, J. & M. Arbetman 1989. Exploring the 'Phoenix Factor' with the collective goods perspective. _Journal of Conflict Resolution_ 33, 84–112.

Kugler, J. & W. Domke 1986. Comparing the strength of nations. _Comparative Political Studies_ 19, 39–69.

Kuhn, T. S. 1970. _The structure of scientific revolutions_. Chicago: University of Chicago Press.

Kuo, S. W. Y. 1983. _The Taiwan economy in transition_. Boulder, Col.: Westview.

Kuo, S. W. Y. & J. C. H. Fei 1985. Causes and roles of export expansion in the Republic of China. In _Foreign trade and investment: economic development in the newly industrializing Asian countries_, W. Galenson (ed.), 54–84. Madison, University of Wisconsin Press.

Kuo, S. W. Y., G. Ranis & J. C. H. Fei 1981. _The Taiwan success story: rapid growth with improved income distribution in the republic of China_. Boulder, Col.: Westview.

Kuo, T. Y. 1973. The internal development and modernization of Taiwan, 1683–1891. In _Taiwan in modern times_, P. K. T. Sih (ed.), 171–240. New York: St. John's University Press.

Kuznets, P. W. 1988. An East Asian model of economic development: Japan, Taiwan, and South Korea. _Economic Development and Cultural Change_ 36, S11–S43.

Kuznets, S. 1955. Economic growth and income inequality. _American Economic Review_ 45, 1–28.

Kuznets, S. 1963. Quantitative aspects of the economic growth of nations VIII: the distribution of income by size. _Economic Development and Cultural Change_ 11, 1–80.

Kuznets, S. 1976. _Modern economic growth: rate, structure and spread_. New Haven, Conn.: Yale University Press.

Lake, D. A. 1988. _Power, protection and free trade: international sources of U.S. commercial strategy, 1887–1939_. Ithaca, N.J.: Cornell University Press.

Lam, D. K. K. 1988. Guerrilla capitalism: export oriented firms and the economic miracle in Taiwan (1973–1987). Paper presented at the annual meeting of the American Association for Chinese Studies, Stanford University.

Lam, D. K. K. 1990. Independent economic sectors and economic growth in Hong Kong and Taiwan. _International Studies Notes_ 15, 28–34.

Lee, T. B. 1988. Quasi-diplomatic relations of the Republic of China: their development and status in international law. *Issues and Studies* 24: 7, 104–17.

Lee, T. H. 1971. *Intersectoral capital flows in the economic development of Taiwan, 1895–1960*. Ithaca, N.Y.: Cornell University Press.

Leontief, W. & F. Duchin 1983. *Military spending: facts and figures, worldwide implications and future outlook*. Oxford: Oxford University Press.

Lerman, A. J. 1977. National elites and local politicians in Taiwan. *American Political Science Review* 71, 1406–22.

Lerman, A. J. 1978. *Taiwan's politics: the provincial assemblyman's world*. Washington, D.C.: University Press of America.

Lerner, D. 1958. *The passing of traditional society: modernizing the Middle East*. New York: Free Press.

Levy, M. Jr. 1952. *The structure of society*. Princeton, N.J.: Princeton University Press.

Levy, M. Jr. 1953–4. Contrasting factors in the modernization of China and Japan. *Economic Development and Cultural Change* 2, 161–97.

Levy, M. Jr. 1986. Modernization exhumed. *Journal of Developing Societies* 2, 1–11.

Lewis, W. A. 1955. *The theory of economic growth*. Homewood, Ill.: Richard D. Irwin.

Li, K. T. 1988. *The evolution of policy behind Taiwan's development success*. New Haven, Conn.: Yale University Press.

Li, W. L. 1984. Social development in the Republic of China, 1949–1981. In *China: seventy years after the Hsin Hai Revolution*, H. Chiu & S. C. Leng (eds.), 478–99. Charlottesville: University of Virginia Press.

Li, W. L. 1986. Entrepreneurial roles and societal development in Taiwan. *Journal of Chinese Studies* 3, 77–96.

Liang, K. S. & C. H. Liang 1988. Development policy formation and future policy priorities in the Republic of China. *Economic Development and Cultural Change* 36, S67–S101.

Lichbach, M. I. 1989. An evaluation of 'Does economic inequality breed political conflict?' studies. *World Politics* 41, 431–70.

Lim, D. 1983. Another look at growth and defense in less developed countries. *Economic Development and Cultural Change* 31, 377–84.

Lin, C. Y. 1973. *Industrialization in Taiwan, 1946–1972: trade and import substitution policies for developing countries*. New York: Praeger.

Linder, S. B. 1986. *The Pacific century: economic and political consequences of Asian-Pacific dynamism*. Stanford, Calif.: Stanford University Press.

Ling, T. A. & R. H. Myers 1990. Winds of democracy: the 1989 Taiwan elections. *Asian Survey* 30, 360–79.

Lipset, S. M. 1959. Some social requisites of democracy: economic development and political legitimacy. *American Political Science Review* 53, 69–105.

Lipset, S. M. 1963. *Political man: the social bases of politics.* Garden City, N.Y.: Doubleday.

Little, I. M. D. 1979. An economic reconnaissance. In *Economic growth and structural change in Taiwan: the postwar experience of the Republic of China*, W. Galenson (ed.), 448–507. Ithaca, N.Y.: Cornell University Press.

Liu, A. P. L. 1987. *Phoenix and the lame lion: modernization in Taiwan and Mainland China, 1950–1980.* Stanford, Calif.: Hoover Institution Press.

Liu, P. 1990. The decline and fall of the Taiwan exchange. *Free China Review* 40: 9, 58–63.

Lockwood, W. W. (ed.) 1965. *The state and economic enterprises in Japan.* Princeton, N.J.: Princeton University Press.

Lowi, T. J. 1979. *The end of liberalism: the second republic of the United States*, 2nd edn. New York: Norton.

Lu, A. Y. L. 1984. Political development in the Republic of China on Taiwan. In *Chinese Modernization*, Y. M. Shaw (ed.), 139–54. San Francisco: Chinese Materials Center Publications.

Lu, A. Y. L. 1985. Future democratic developments in the Republic of China on Taiwan. *Asian Survey* 25, 1075–95.

Lu, A. Y. L. 1989. Political modernization and future prospects of the ROC polity. Paper presented at the 18th Sino-American Conference on Mainland China, Stanford University.

Lui, F. L. 1989. Ballot power. *Free China Review* 39: 12, 9–15.

Lundberg, E. 1979. Fiscal and monetary policies. In *Economic growth and structural change in Taiwan: the postwar experience of the Republic of China*, W. Galenson (ed.), 261–307. Ithaca, N.Y.: Cornell University Press.

Lyttkens, C. H. & C. Vedovato 1984. Opportunity costs of defence: a comment on Dabelko and McCormick. *Journal of Peace Research* 21, 389–94.

Mahler, V. A. 1980. *Dependency approaches to international political economy.* New York: Columbia University Press.

Mancall, M. (ed.) 1964. *Formosa today.* New York: Praeger.

Maoz, Z. 1989. Joining the Club of Nations: political development and international conflict, 1816–1976. *International Studies Quarterly* 33, 199–231.

Maoz, Z. & N. Abdolali 1989. Regime types and international conflict, 1816–1976. *Journal of Conflict Resolution* 33, 3–35.

March, J. G. & H. A. Simon 1958. *Organizations.* New York: Wiley.

McClelland, D. 1961. *The achieving society.* New York: Van Nostrand.

McElderry, A. 1986. Confucian capitalism? Corporate values in Republican banking. *Modern China* 12, 401–16.

McGowan, P. J. & D. L. Smith 1978. Economic dependency in Black Africa: an analysis of competing theories. *International Organization* 32, 179–235.

McGregor, J. 1990. Bitter wrangling seen in Taipei after presidential vote. *Asian Wall Street Journal Weekly* Mar. 19, 1 and 12.

Melman, S. 1972. Ten propositions on the war economy. *American Economic Review* 62, 312–18.

Mendel, D. 1970. *The politics of Formosan nationalism.* Berkeley: University of California Press.

Metzger, T. A. 1987. Developmental criteria and indigenously conceptualized options: a normative approach to China's modernization in recent times. *Issues and Studies* 23: 2, 19–81.

Midlarsky, M. I. 1982. Scarcity and inequality: prologue to the onset of mass revolution. *Journal of Conflict Resolution* 26, 3–38.

Midlarsky, M. I. 1988. Rulers and the ruled: patterned inequality and the onset of mass political violence. *American Political Science Review* 82, 491–509.

Midlarsky, M. I. & K. Roberts 1985. Class, state, and revolution in Central America: Nicaragua and El Salvador compared. *Journal of Conflict Resolution* 29, 163–93.

Miller, N. R. 1983. Pluralism and social choice. *American Political Science Review* 77, 734–47.

Ministry of Finance 1988. *Monthly statistics of exports and imports: Taiwan Area, the Republic of China, October 1988.* Taipei: Ministry of Finance.

Mintz, A. 1989. 'Guns' Versus 'Butter': a disaggregated analysis. *American Political Science Review* 83, 1285–93.

Moody, P. R., Jr. 1988. *Political opposition in post-Confucian society.* New York: Praeger.

Moon, B. E. & W. J. Dixon 1985. Politics, the state, and basic human needs: a cross-national study. *American Journal of Political Science* 29, 661–94.

Moon, C. I. 1988. The demise of a developmentalist state? Neoconservative reforms and political consequences in South Korea. *Journal of Developing Societies* 4, 67–84.

Moon, C. I. 1989a. Conclusion: a dissenting view on the Pacific future. In *Pacific dynamics: the international politics of industrial change*, S. Haggard & C. I. Moon (eds.), 359–74. Boulder, Col.: Westview.

Moon C. I. with the assistance of C. H. Chang 1989b. Trade friction and industrial adjustment: the textiles and apparel in the Pacific basin. In *Pacific Dynamics: the international politics of industrial change*, S. Haggard and C. I. Moon (eds.), 185–207. Boulder, Col.: Westview.

Moon, C. I. 1990. Beyond statism: rethinking the political economy of growth in South Korea. *International Studies Notes* 15, 24–7.

Moran, T. H. 1974. *Multinational corporations and the politics of dependence: copper in Chile.* Princeton, N.J.: Princeton University Press.

Morawetz, D. 1981. *Why the Emperor's clothes are not made in Colombia.* London: Oxford University Press.

Morris, M. D. 1979. *Measuring the conditions of the world's poor: the physical quality of life index.* New York: Pergamon.

Most, B. A. & H. Starr 1989. *Inquiry, logic and international politics.*

Columbia: University of South Carolina Press.

Moulder, F. V. 1977. *Japan, China, and the modern world economy: toward a reinterpretation of East Asian development, ca. 1600 to ca. 1918.* London: Cambridge University Press.

Mueller, D. C. (ed.) 1983. *The political economy of growth.* New Haven, Conn.: Yale University Press.

Muller, E. N. 1985. Income inequality, regime repressiveness, and political violence. *American Sociological Review* 51, 47–61.

Muller, E. N. 1986. Income inequality and political violence: the effect of influential cases. *American Sociological Review* 51, 441–5.

Muller, E. N. 1988. Democracy, economic development, and income inequality. *American Sociological Review* 53, 50–68.

Muller, E. N. & M. A. Seligson 1987. Inequality and insurgency. *American Political Science Review* 81, 425–51.

Murray, B. 1990. Tiananmen: the view from Taipei. *Asian Survey* 30, 348–59.

Myers, R. H. 1972a. Taiwan under Ch'ing imperial rule, 1684–1895: the traditional economy. *Journal of the Institute of Chinese Studies of the Chinese University of Hong Kong* 5, 373–409.

Myers, R. H. 1972b. Taiwan under Ch'ing imperial rule, 1684–1895: the traditional society. *Journal of the Institute of Chinese Studies of the Chinese University of Hong Kong* 5: 413–51.

Myers, R. H. 1984. The economic transformation of the Republic of China on Taiwan. *China Quarterly* 99, 500–28.

Myers, R. H. 1987. Political theory and recent political developments in the Republic of China. *Asian Survey* 27, 1003–22.

Myrdal, G. 1968. *Asian drama: an inquiry into the poverty of nations.* New York: Pantheon.

Myrdal, G. 1971. *Economic theory and underdeveloped regions.* New York: Harper & Row.

Neubauer, D. E. 1967. Some conditions of democracy. *American Political Science Review* 61, 1002–9.

Nisbet, R. 1987. *The making of modern society.* New York: New York University Press.

Noble, G. W. 1987. Contending forces in Taiwan's economic policy-making: the case of Hua Tung heavy trucks. *Asian Survey* 27, 683–704.

Numazaki, I. 1986. Networks of Taiwanese big business: a preliminary analysis. *Modern China* 12, 487–534.

O'Donnell, G. 1973. *Modernization and bureaucratic authoritarianism: studies in South American politics.* Berkeley: University of California Press.

Olson, M., Jr. 1963. Rapid growth as a destabilizing force. *Journal of Economic History* 23, 529–52.

Olson, M., Jr. 1982. *The rise and fall of nations: economic growth, stagflation and social rigidities.* New Haven, Conn.: Yale University

Press.

Organski, A. F. K. & J. Kugler 1978. Predicting the outcomes of international wars. *Comparative Political Studies* 11, 141–80.

Pang, C. K. 1990. The state and socioeconomic development in Taiwan since 1949. *Issues and Studies* 26:5 11–36.

Parsons, T. 1964. *The social system*. New York: Free Press.

Pempel, T. J. 1978. Japanese foreign economic policy: the domestic bases for international behavior. In *Between power and plenty: foreign economic policies of advanced industrial states*, P. Katzenstein (ed.), 139–90. Madison: University of Wisconsin Press.

Pepper, S. 1978. *Civil war in China: the political struggle, 1945–1949*. Berkeley: University of California Press.

Petras, J. 1979. *Class perspectives on imperialism and social class in the Third World*. New York: Monthly Review Press.

Piore, M. J. & C. F. Sable 1984. *The second industrial divide: possibilities for prosperity*. New York: Basic Books.

Popper, F. J. 1971. Internal war as a stimulant of political development. *Comparative Political Studies* 3, 413–23.

Portes A. & J. Walton 1981. *Labor, class, and the international system*. New York: Academic Press.

Prebisch, R. 1950. *The economic development of Latin America and its principal problems*. New York: Free Press.

Prestowicz, C. V. 1988. *Trading places: how we allowed Japan to take the lead*. New York: Basic Books.

Prosterman, R. L. & J. M. Riedinger 1987. *Land reform and democratic development*. Baltimore: Johns Hopkins University Press.

Pye, L. W. 1966. *Aspects of political development*. Boston: Little, Brown.

Pye, L. W. with M. W. Pye 1985. *Asian power and politics: the cultural dimensions of authority*. Cambridge, Mass.: Harvard University Press.

Rangarajan, L. N. 1978. *Commodity conflict: the political economy of international commodity negotiations*. Ithaca, N.Y.: Cornell University Press.

Ranis, G. 1979. Industrial development. In *Economic growth and structural change in Taiwan: the postwar experience of the Republic of China*, W. Galenson (ed.), 206–62. Ithaca, N.Y.: Cornell University Press.

Ranis, G. & C. Schive 1985. Direct foreign investment in Taiwan's development. In *Foreign trade and investment: economic development in the newly industrializing Asian countries*, W. Galenson (ed.), 85–137. Madison: University of Wisconsin Press.

Rasler, K. A. & W. R. Thompson 1988. Defense burdens, capital formation, and economic growth: the systemic leader case. *Journal of Conflict Resolution* 32, 61–86.

Ray, J. L. 1981. Dependence, political compliance, and economic performance: Latin America and Eastern Europe. In *The political economy of foreign policy behavior*, C. W. Kegley & P. McGowan (eds.), 111–36. Beverly Hills, Calif.: Sage.

Richardson, N. R. 1976. Political compliance and U.S. trade dominance. *American Political Science Review* 70, 1098–1109.

Richardson, N. R. 1978. *Foreign policy and economic dependence.* Austin: University of Texas Press.

Richardson, N. R. & C. W. Kegley, Jr. 1980. Trade dependence and foreign policy compliance: a longitudinal analysis. *International Studies Quarterly* 24, 191–222.

Riggs, F. W. 1972. *Formosa under Chinese Nationalist rule.* New York: Octagon.

Rosenberg N. & L. E. Birdzell, Jr. 1986. *How the West grew rich: the economic transformation of the industrial world.* New York: Basic Books.

Rostow, W. W. 1965. Guerrilla warfare in the underdeveloped areas. In *World perspectives on international politics*, W. C. Clemens, Jr. (ed.), 231–8. Boston: Little, Brown.

Rostow, W. W. 1960. *The stages of economic growth: a non-communist manifesto.* Cambridge: Cambridge University Press.

Rothschild, K. W. 1973. Military expenditure, exports and growth. *Kyklos* 26, 804–14.

Rubinson, R. 1976. The world-economy and the distribution of income within states: a cross-national study. *American Sociological Review* 41, 638–59.

Rubinson, R. & D. Quinlan 1977. Democracy and social inequality. *American Sociological Review* 42, 611–23.

Rueschemeyer, D. & P. B. Evans 1985. The state and economic transformation: toward an analysis of the conditions underlying effective intervention. In *Bringing the state back in*, P. B. Evans, D. Rueschemeyer & T. Skocpol (eds.), 44–77. New York: Cambridge University Press.

Rummel, R. J. 1963. Dimensions of conflict behavior within and between nations. *General Systems Yearbook* 8, 1–50.

Rummel, R. J. 1983. Libertarianism and international violence. *Journal of Conflict Resolution* 27, 27–72.

Rummel, R. J. 1985. Libertarian propositions on violence within and between nations: a test against published research results. *Journal of Conflict Resolution* 29, 419–55.

Rummel, R. J. 1987. On Vincent's view of freedom and international conflict. *International Studies Quarterly* 31, 113–17.

Russett, B. M. 1964. Inequality and instability: the relation of land tenure to politics. *World Politics* 16, 442–54.

Russett, B. M. 1970. *What price vigilance? the burdens of national defense.* New Haven, Conn.: Yale University Press.

Russett, B. M. 1978. The marginal utility of income transfers to the Third World. *International Organization* 32, 913–28.

Russett, B. M. 1982. Defense expenditures and national well-being. *American Political Science Review* 76, 767–77.

Russett, B. M. 1983. Prosperity and peace. *International Studies*

Quarterly 27, 381–7.

Russett, B. M. 1987. Economic downturn as a cause of international conflict. In *Peace, Defence, and Economic Analysis*, C. Schmidt & F. Blackaby (eds.), 185–205. New York: St. Martin's Press.

Schive, C. 1987. Trade patterns and trends of Taiwan. In *Trade and structural change in Pacific Asia*, C. I. Bradford, Jr. & W. H. Branson (eds.), 307–31. Chicago: University of Chicago Press.

Schive, C. 1989. An economy in transition. *Free China Review* 39: 4, 4–9.

Schive, C. 1990. *The foreign factor: the multinational corporation's contribution to the economic modernization of the Republic of China*. Stanford, Calif.: Hoover Institution Press.

Schumpeter, J. A. 1950. *Capitalism, socialism, and democracy*, 3rd edn. New York: Harper & Row.

Scott, M. 1979. Foreign trade. In *Economic growth and structural change in Taiwan: the postwar experience of the Republic of China*, W. Galenson (ed.), 308–83. Ithaca, N.Y.: Cornell University Press.

Seagrave, S. 1985. *The Soong dynasty*. New York: Harper & Row.

Seymour, J. D. 1988. Taiwan in 1987: a year of political bombshells. *Asian Survey* 28, 71–7

Seymour, J. D. 1989. Taiwan in 1988: no more bandits. *Asian Survey* 29, 54–63.

Shack, D. C. 1989. Socioeconomic mobility and the urban poor in Taiwan. *Modern China* 15, 346–73.

Shaw, Y. M. 1985. Taiwan: a view from Taipei. *Foreign Affairs* 63, 1050–63.

Sheridan, J. E. 1975. *China in disintegration: the Republican era in Chinese history 1912–1949*. New York: Free Press.

Sih, P. K. T. (ed.) 1970. *The strenuous decade: China's nation-building efforts, 1927–1937*. New York: St. John's University Press.

Silin, R. H. 1976. *Leadership and values: the organization of large-scale Taiwanese enterprises*. Cambridge, Mass.: Harvard University Press.

Simon, D. F. 1988. External incorporation and internal reform. In *Contending approaches to the political economy of Taiwan*, E. A. Winckler & S. Greenhalgh (eds.), 138–50. Armonk, N.Y.: Sharpe.

Simon, D. F. 1986. Taiwan's political economy and the evolving links between the PRC, Hong Kong, and Taiwan. *AEI Foreign Policy and Defense Review* 6, 42–51.

Sivard, R. L. 1985. *World military and social expenditures: 1985*. Washington, D.C.: World Priorities.

Skocpol, T. 1979. *States and social revolutions*. Cambridge: Cambridge University Press.

Small, M. & J. D. Singer 1976. The war-proneness of democratic regimes, 1816–1965. *Jerusalem Journal of International Relations* 1, 49–69.

Smith, R. P. 1977. Military expenditure and capitalism. *Cambridge Journal of Economics* 1, 61–76.

Smith, R. P. 1980. Military expenditure and investment in OECD countries, 1954–1973. *Journal of Comparative Economics* 4, 19–32.

Smith, T. 1985. Requiem or new agenda for Third World studies? *World Politics* 37, 532–61.

Snider, L. W. 1987. Identifying the elements of state power. *Comparative Political Studies* 20, 314–56.

Song, S. F. 1990. ROC wealth distribution story. *Free China Journal* 7 (Oct. 8), 5.

Sorich, R. 1990. Cruel economic ironies. *Free China Review* 40: 4, 68–9.

Starr, H., F. W. Hoole, J. A. Hart & J. R. Freeman 1984. The relationship between defense spending and inflation. *Journal of Conflict Resolution* 26, 103–22.

Stohl, M. 1980. The nexus of civil and international conflict. In *Handbook of political conflict*, T. R. Gurr (ed.), 297–330. New York: Free Press.

Strouse, J. C. & R. P. Claude 1976. Empirical comparative rights research: some preliminary tests of development hypotheses. In *Comparative human rights*, R. P. Claude (ed.), 51–67. Baltimore: Johns Hopkins University Press.

Sutter, R. G. 1988. *Taiwan: entering the 21st century*. Lanham, Md.: University Press of America.

Szymanski, A. 1973. Military spending and economic stagnation. *American Journal of Sociology* 79, 1–14.

Tai, H. C. 1970. The Kuomintang and modernization in Taiwan. In *Authoritarian politics in modern society: the dynamics of established one-party systems*, S. P. Huntington & C. H. Moore (eds.), 406–36. New York: Basic Books.

Tai, H. C. 1989. The oriental alternative: a hypothesis on East Asian culture and economy. *Issues and Studies* 25, 10–36.

Tanter, R. 1966. Dimensions of conflict behavior within and between nations, 1958–60. *Journal of Conflict Resolution* 10, 41–64.

Taylor, C. L. & D. A. Jodice 1983. *World handbook of political and social indicators*, 3rd edn. New Haven, Conn.: Yale University Press.

Thorbecke, E. 1979. Agricultural development. In *Economic growth and structural change in Taiwan: the postwar experience of the Republic of China*, W. Galenson (ed.), 132–205. Ithaca, N.Y.: Cornell University Press.

Tien, H. M. 1972. *Government and politics in Kuomintang China, 1927–1937*. Stanford, Calif.: Stanford University Press.

Tien, H. M. 1989. *The great transition: political and social change in the Republic of China*. Stanford, Calif.: Hoover Institution Press.

Tilly, C. (ed.) 1975. *The formation of national states in Western Europe*. Princeton, N.J.: Princeton University Press.

Tilly, C. 1978. *From mobilization to revolution*. Reading, Mass.: Addison-Welsey.

Tilly, C. 1984. *Big structures, large processes, huge comparisons*. New York: Russell Sage.

Tilly, C. 1985. War making and state making as organized crime. In

Bringing the State Back In, P. B. Evans, D. Rueschemeyer & T. Skocpol (eds.), 169–91. New York: Cambridge University Press.

Trimberger, E. K. 1978. *Revolution from above: military bureaucrats and development in Japan, Turkey, Egypt, and Peru.* New Brunswick, N.J.: Transaction Books.

Tsai, W. H. 1987. Taiwan's social development. In *Survey of recent developments in China (Mainland and Taiwan), 1985–1986,* H. Chiu (ed.), 125–38. Baltimore: School of Law, University of Maryland.

Tsai, W. H. 1988. State and modernization: a comparison of the role of the state in the modernization of China and Taiwan. *Journal of Developing Societies* 4, 238–54.

Tseng, O. 1990a. The burdens of wealth. *Free China Review* 40: 4, 64–6.

Tseng, O. 1990b. Plastic man stretches across the Straits. *Free China Review* 40:6, 58–61.

Tucker, N. B. 1983. *Patterns in the dust: Chinese American relations and the recognition controversy, 1949–1950.* New York: Columbia University Press.

United Nations 1983. *Statistical yearbook, 1981.* New York: United Nations.

United States Arms Control and Disarmament Agency various years. *World Military Expenditures and Arms Transfers.* Washington, D.C.: United States Arms Control and Disarmament Agency.

Vernon, R. 1966. International investment and international trade in the product cycle. *Quarterly Journal of Economics* 80, 190–207.

Vernon, R. 1971. *Sovereignty at bay: the multinational spread of U.S. enterprises.* New York: Basic Books.

Vernon, R. 1977. *Storm over the multinationals: the real issues.* Cambridge, Mass.: Harvard University Press.

Vincent, J. E. 1987a. Freedom and international conflict: another look. *International Studies Quarterly* 31, 103–12.

Vincent, J. E. 1987b. On Rummel's omnipresent theory. *International Studies Quarterly* 31, 119–25.

Vogel, E. F. 1979. *Japan as number one.* Cambridge, Mass.: Harvard University Press.

von Mises, L. 1983. *Nation, state, and economy: contributions to the politics and history of our times.* New York: New York University Press.

Wade, R. 1985. East Asian financial systems as a challenge to economics: lessons from Taiwan. *California Management Review* 27, 106–27.

Wade, R. 1988. State intervention in 'outward-looking' development: neoclassical theory and Taiwanese practice. In *Developmental states in East Asia,* G. White (ed.), 30–67. London: Macmillan.

Wade, R. 1990. *Governing the market: economic theory and the role of government in East Asian industrialization.* Princeton, N.J.: Princeton

University Press.

Wallace, M. D. 1979. Arms races and escalation: some new evidence. *Journal of Conflict Resolution* 23, 3–16.

Wallace, M. D. 1982. Armaments and escalation: two competing hypotheses. *International Studies Quarterly* 26, 37–56.

Walleri, R. D. 1978. Trade dependence and underdevelopment: a causal-chain analysis. *Comparative Political Studies* 11, 94–127.

Wallerstein, I. 1974. *The modern world system I: capitalist agriculture and the origins of the European world economy in the sixteenth century*. New York: Academic Press.

Wallerstein, I. 1979. *The capitalist world economy*. Cambridge: Cambridge University Press.

Wallerstein, I. 1980. *The modern world system II: mercantilism and the consolidation of the European world economy, 1600–1750*. New York: Academic Press.

Wang, C. S. Y. 1981. Social mobility in Taiwan. In *Contemporary Republic of China: the Taiwan experience, 1950–1980*, J. C. Hsiung (ed.), 246–57. New York: Praeger.

Wang, W. S. (ed.) 1990. *Foreign policy of the Republic of China on Taiwan: an unorthodox approach*. New York: Praeger.

Ward, M. D. & U. Widmaier 1982. The domestic–international conflict nexus: new evidence and old hypotheses. *International Interactions* 9, 75–101.

Weber, M. 1951. *The religion of China: Confucianism and Taoism*. Glencoe, Ill.: Free Press.

Weber, M. 1958. *The Protestant ethic and the spirit of capitalism*. New York: Scribner's.

Weede, E. 1980. Beyond misspecification in sociological analyses of income inequality. *American Sociological Review* 45, 497–501.

Weede, E. 1984. Democracy and war involvement. *Journal of Conflict Resolution* 28, 649–64.

Weede, E. 1986a. Rent seeking, military participation, and economic performance in LDCs. *Journal of Conflict Resolution* 30, 291–314.

Weede, E. 1986b. Catch-up, distributional coalitions and government as determinants of economic growth or decline in industrialized countries. *British Journal of Sociology* 37, 194–220.

Weede, E. 1987. Some new evidence on correlates of political violence: income inequality, regime repressiveness, and economic development. *European Sociological Review* 3, 97–108.

Weede, E. & H. Tiefenbach 1981. Some recent explanations of income inequality. *International Studies Quarterly* 25, 255–82.

Wei, Y. 1973. Taiwan: a modernizing Chinese society. In *Taiwan in Modern Times*, P. K. T. Sih (ed.), 435–505. New York: St. John's University Press.

Weng, B. S. J. 1984. Taiwan's international status today. *China Quarterly* 99, 462–80.

Weng, B. S. J. 1988. Taiwan and Hong Kong, 1987: a review. In *China Briefing, 1988*, A. J. Kane (ed.), 121–43. Boulder, Col.: Westview.

White, G. (ed.) 1988. *Developmental states in East Asia*. London: Macmillan.

Wickberg, E. 1981. Continuities in land tenure, 1900–1940. In *The anthropology of Taiwanese society*, E. M. Ahern & H. Gates (eds.), 212–38. Stanford, Calif.: Stanford University Press.

Wilkenfeld, J. 1968. Domestic and foreign conflict behavior of nations. *Journal of Peace Research* 1, 56–69.

Wilkenfeld, J. 1969. Some further findings regarding the domestic and foreign conflict behavior of nations. *Journal of Peace Research* 2, 147–56.

Winckler, E. A. 1981. Roles linking state and society. In *The anthropology of Taiwanese society*, E. M. Ahern & H. Gates (eds.), 50–86. Stanford, Calif.: Stanford University Press.

Winckler, E. A. 1984. Institutionalization and participation on Taiwan: from hard to soft authoritarianism? *China Quarterly* 99, 481–99.

Winckler, E. A. 1987. Statism and familism in Taiwan. In *Ideology and national competition: an analysis of nine countries*, G. C. Lodge & E. F. Vogel (eds.), 173–206. Boston: Harvard Business School Press.

Winckler, E.A. 1988. Elite Political Struggle, 1945–1985. In *Contending approaches to the political economy of Taiwan*, E. A. Winckler & S. Greenhalgh (eds.), 151–71. Armonk, N.Y.: Sharpe.

Winckler, E. A. & S. Greenhalgh (eds.) 1988. *Contending approaches to the political economy of Taiwan*. Armonk, N.Y.: Sharpe.

Wong, S. L. 1986. Modernization and Chinese culture in Hong Kong. *China Quarterly* 106, 306–25.

Wong, S. L. 1988a. The applicability of Asian family values to other sociocultural settings. In *In search of the East Asian development model*, P. L. Berger & H. H. M. Hsiao (eds.), 134–52. New Brunswick, N.J: Transaction Books.

Wong, S. L. 1988b. *Emigrant entrepreneurs: Shanghai industrialists in Hong Kong*. Hong Kong: Oxford University Press.

World Bank 1983. *World development report*. Washington, D.C.: World Bank.

World Bank 1987. *World development report, 1987*. Washington, D.C.: Oxford University Press.

World Bank 1988. *World development report, 1988*. Washington, D.C.: Oxford University Press.

Wu, A. C. 1989. Relations between the two sides of the Taiwan Strait: evaluation and prospects. *Issues and Studies* 25, 80–99.

Wu, R. I. 1987. Trade liberalization and economic development in Taiwan. *Journal of Chinese Studies* 4: 81–98.

Wu, W. C. 1990. Five-percent growth 'not bad.' *Free China Journal* 7 (Oct. 22), p. 5.

Wu, Y. L. 1985. *Becoming an industrialized nation: ROC's development on Taiwan*. New York: Praeger.

Yager, J. A. 1988. *Transforming agriculture in Taiwan: the experience of the Joint Commission on Rural Reconstruction*. Ithaca, N.Y.: Cornell

University Press.

Yang, M. M. C. 1970. *Socio-economic results of land reform in Taiwan.* Honolulu: East-West Center Press.

Yoffie, D. B. 1983. *Power and protectionism: strategies of the newly industrializing countries.* New York: Columbia University Press.

Yoon, Y. K. 1990. The political economy of transition: Japanese foreign direct investments in the 1980s. *World Politics* 43, 1–27.

Zeigler, H. 1988. *Pluralism, corporatism, and Confucianism: political association and conflict resolution in the United States, Europe, and Taiwan.* Philadelphia: Temple University Press.

Zimmerman, E. 1980. Macro-comparative research in political protest. In *Handbook of political conflict*, T. R. Gurr (ed.), 167–237. New York: Free Press.

Zysman, J. 1983. *Governments, markets, and growth: financial systems and the politics of industrial change.* Ithaca, N.Y.: Cornell University Press.

Subject Index

Author Index